# RIDLEY SCOTT

## INTERVIEWS

CONVERSATIONS WITH FILMMAKERS SERIES
PETER BRUNETTE, GENERAL EDITOR

Photo credit: Photofest

# RIDLEY
# SCOTT
# INTERVIEWS

EDITED BY LAURENCE F. KNAPP
AND ANDREA F. KULAS

UNIVERSITY PRESS OF MISSISSIPPI / JACKSON

www.upress.state.ms.us

The University Press of Mississippi is a member of
the Association of American University Presses.

Copyright © 2005 by University Press of Mississippi

Manufactured in the United States of America

12 11 10 09 08 07 06 05    4 3 2 1

∞

Library of Congress Cataloging-in-Publication Data

Scott, Ridley.
    Ridley Scott : interviews / edited by Laurence F. Knapp and Andrea F. Kulas.
        p. cm. — (Conversations with filmmakers series)
    Includes index.
    ISBN 1-57806-725-1 (alk. paper) — ISBN 1-57806-726-X (pbk. : alk. paper)
        1. Scott, Ridley—Interviews. 2. Motion picture producers and directors—
Great Britain—Interviews. I. Knapp, Laurence F., 1965– II. Kulas, Andrea F.
III. Title. IV. Series.

PN1998.3.S393A5    2005
791.4302′33′092—dc22                                        2004055496

British Library Cataloging-in-Publication Data available

# CONTENTS

# INTRODUCTION

Artisan, entrepreneur, impresario, master craftsman, and auteur, Ridley Scott is a true veteran of film and television production. Able to set up a film shot and maintain a balance sheet with equal proficiency, Scott has proven himself as an exceptional commercial artist. In an ever-evolving industry, Scott has outpaced many of his peers by acknowledging the compromises of feature filmmaking without sacrificing his imagination or integrity. Scott's class of filmmaker is one that accepts the profit motive as the only way to survive, and thrive, in an industry where there is little patience for grandiloquence or egocentricity. As Scott concedes to Paul M. Sammon in 1998, "Eventually, you come up against the marketplace. The reality is that filmmaking is an increasingly expensive proposition and, while I'm not saying you should trade what you feel are legitimate concerns for an increased box office, you do have to keep in mind that what you're involved in is a business, as well as a creative enterprise." While he may pay lip service to the free enterprise system, Scott is an unapologetic auteur, committed to using every element of film—from evocative lighting to digital composition—to overwhelm our senses and redefine how we perceive the future (*Alien, Blade Runner*), the past (*The Duellists*, 1492: *The Conquest of Paradise, White Squall, Gladiator, Kingdom of Heaven*), and the present (*Thelma & Louise, Black Hawk Down*).

Scott belongs to a small cadre of British filmmakers—Hugh Hudson (*Chariots of Fire, Greystoke: The Legend of Tarzan, Lord of the Apes*), Adrian Lyne (*Flashdance, 9½ Weeks, Fatal Attraction, Unfaithful*), Alan Parker

(*Midnight Express, Fame, Angel Heart, Mississippi Burning, Evita, The Life of David Gale*), Tony Scott (*Top Gun, True Romance, Crimson Tide, Enemy of the State, Spy Game, Man on Fire*), and Julien Temple (*Absolute Beginners, Earth Girls Are Easy, Bullet*)—who brought their innovations in the world of European advertising to Hollywood narrative. Scott describes himself to Sammon in 1998 as a visualist who uses mise-en-scene with the facility of a portrait painter: "When I start making a film, it's as if there's this little, invisible computer in the back of my head. That switches on and presets the overall look of the film at the very beginning of the process. It's not easy to articulate: I tend to think pictorially. Something just drops into place and rolls down a chute and I follow it." Scott considers each frame as a moving diorama: "It sounds pretentious, but I'm really an environmental Hoover (vacuum cleaner), sucking everything in. And I see beauty in everything. That sounds very 'California,' doesn't it? But that's how it is."[1] This penchant for mise-en-scene—a prerequisite for any auteur who wants to paint and sculpt with film—led to the critical complaint that Scott, and his British compatriots, had contributed to the fragmentation of narrative that characterized the high concept look and hard sell of American film in the 1980s.

Fresh from the experience of shooting his first feature *The Duellists*, Scott discloses to Donald Chase in 1978 that "I want to do my thing as a director in that way as much as, say, an actor wants to do his thing." In *Alien*, it was his fine arts background and love of comic book imagery that encouraged him to transform the cinematic frame into a kaleidoscopic spectacle of sound and vision. Inspired by the production design of Stanley Kubrick's *2001: A Space Odyssey* and George Lucas's *Star Wars*, Scott tried to invert Hollywood style by making mise-en-scene the primary source of narrative information and intrigue. While Scott hit the jackpot with *Alien*, he ran into financial and logistical difficulties with *Blade Runner* and *Legend*. Scott admits to Sammon in 1996 that "*Blade Runner* taught me that the American public tends to favor a high-fiber diet. Which infers that the American system is one containing a certain degree of optimism. I, on the other hand, tend to be a bit darker. To

---

1. Paul M. Sammon, *Ridley Scott: The Making of His Movies* (New York: Thunder's Mouth Press, 1999), p. 43.

look at the dark side. Not because I'm a manic-depressive, but because I find darkness interesting. Particularly in its more unusual aspects. I'm sure this has something to do with my own heritage. I am a Celt, after all. And the Celts are traditionally fascinated by melancholia." Scott, sensitive to the demands of dominant cinema, then shifted his attention to more contemporary genres, offering a continental perspective on the American experience in *Someone to Watch Over Me*, *Black Rain*, and *Thelma & Louise*: "There are a lot of things that Americans live with that they never really see, because they are such a part of their culture, because these things are so ingrained in their lives. As an 'outsider,' however, I can drive around the desert Southwest and get excited about miles and miles of telephone poles, telephone poles that the average American might just take for granted."[2] In the 1990s and 2000s, Scott has alternated from the present to the recent and distant past to satisfy his need for a variety of canvases and palettes.

Unlike many of his colleagues in the U.S. (Francis Ford Coppola, Brian De Palma, Martin Scorsese, and Steven Spielberg), Scott did not attend film school. Instead, he developed his visual sensibility at the West Hartlepool College of Art and the Royal College of Art (RCA): "I spent three fantastic years at the Royal College. I went in specifically as a graphic designer. But what was particularly good about the RCA was that it allowed you to move around and investigate different areas. I used to build a sculpture, do some photography, look in on the school of industrial design. Do a bit of this, and a bit of that. The RCA was an incredibly stimulating, well-rounded environment."[3] A product of Hollywood cinema (John Ford and the western) and the golden age of international art cinema in the late 1950s and the early 1960s, particularly the burgeoning British kitchen-sink school of working-class realism (Lindsay Anderson, Karel Reisz, and John Schlesinger), Scott felt equally at ease travelling to the U.S. in 1961 and observing the New York advertising and fashion industry and working as an editing assistant for Richard Leacock and D. A. Pennebaker, who helped introduce cinéma-vérite documentary cinema to American audiences.

---

2. Ibid, p. 101.
3. Ibid, p. 12.

Scott adapted easily to both worlds, and that of the BBC. By the mid 1960s, Scott formed his own production company, Ridley Scott Associates (RSA) to specialize in television commercials. RSA became an industry bellwether with its high-profile spots for Chanel No. 5 in the late 1970s and the "1984" Apple ad that aired exclusively during Super Bowl XVIII. RSA gave Scott the rare opportunity to master the texture and look of film, as well as the vagaries of on-location shooting and production design: "If you're a filmmaker and you're not filmmaking, that's a fallow period. It's like being an athlete. If you're not running around the track, you're losing your edge. It is like doing a pocket version of a feature film. The advantage with advertising is you don't have to live with something for months on end."[4] Scott admits to Danny Peary in 1984 that "My training in commercials was really my film school. It helped build my awareness of how to present suspense and— 'manipulate' is a bad word—fascinate the audience and hold it in a kind of dramatic suspension. I learned how to communicate immediately, to use every conceivable visual and aural device to work on the senses and grab the viewer's attention for a particular time-span."

Thirty years and counting, RSA still remains the heart of Scott's media empire/workshop, which now includes his feature film production company Scott Free Productions, Pinewood Studios, and Black Dog (a subsidiary of RSA that specializes in music videos, run by Scott's three children Jake, Luke, and Jordan Scott). Richard Natale's "Commercial Break" and Brendan Tapley's "Bond of Brothers" give us an inside view of how RSA balances creativity, commerce, and artistry. They also emphasize Scott's lifelong relationship with his brother Tony Scott, who starred in Scott's student film *Boy and Bicycle* and became the first associate to join RSA. Tony, who helped to revitalize American cinema with his aggressive use of style in *Top Gun* and postmodern chic in *True Romance*, today remains part of RSA despite his own feature film work. Ridley Scott continues to diversify into new forms of consumer entertainment, relying on his brother, children, and associates at RSA to stay relevant in a rapidly changing media universe. While many directors lose their technological edge by the time they reach their sixties,

---

4. Barbara Rosen, "How the Man Who Made *Alien* Invaded Madison Avenue," *Business Week* (March 24, 1986), p. 91.

Scott, approaching seventy, has used elliptical editing, variable shutter speeds, and color filters perfected by RSA in the 1980s and 1990s to give his recent work a kinetic charge (*G.I. Jane, Gladiator, Hannibal, Black Hawk Down, Matchstick Men*).

Scott's consistent ability to communicate his ideas through storyboards, nicknamed "Ridleygrams," gives him the self-confidence to take full responsibility for his work: "I spent three years training at art school as a painter and four years as a graphic designer. That background included photography and all sorts of other valuable things, which means I can talk to a costume or production designer at a fairly rarefied level. And, because I can draw to a pretty sophisticated degree, I prepare detailed storyboards for all my films. It's a way of maintaining visual control, so that there's no dispute over any point; everybody knows exactly what the end product should look like and is working towards it. I see the storyboards as a very useful inter-departmental instruction booklet."[5] Apart from complaining about the abortive distribution of *The Duellists*, Scott takes credit and assumes blame for the fate of his films. He tells Harlan Kennedy in 1982 that "I find the process of filming very difficult—maybe this is why I want to be a producer—because it's like trying to write a book with many hands or paint a picture with many hands. A film has to have a guiding mind, otherwise I think it flounders. Of course it is a team effort, but in the final analysis it should cohere round one person." He informs Sammon in 1998 that "A director's expected to be the expert on everything. You are expected to be the expert on sound, cameras, wristwatches, shoes, contact lenses, lighting, casting, you name it. When you're making a film, everyone asks you every conceivable question all the time, because you're the conduit through which everything goes. And you'd better be able to either enjoy or tolerate that. Otherwise, don't do the job. Because it can either stress the hell out of you and drive you crazy, or else you learn to deal with it, and take it in stride." For all of his independence, Scott spends a lot of time praising his many collaborators in James Delson's "*Alien* from the Inside Out," François Guérif and Alain Garel's "Ridley Scott," David E. Williams's "Stormy Weather," Paul M. Sammon's "Joining the Club: Ridley Scott on *G. I. Jane*," Douglas Bankston's "Veni,

5. Sheila Johnston, "The Visualist," *Films & Filming* (November 1985), p. 6.

Vidi, Vici," and Terry Gross's "Ridley Scott Discusses Making His Oscar-Nominated Movie *Black Hawk Down*." Donald Chase's "In *Black Rain*, East Meets West with a Bang! Bang!" and Jill Bernstein's "Eat Drink Man Woman" reflect Scott's ability to function alongside a gallery of personalities to bring a franchise or a star vehicle to market. With *Hannibal*, Scott gamely assumes responsibility for the visualization of the narrative without locking horns with Dino de Laurentiis, Thomas Harris, or Anthony Hopkins.

Scott sees narrative and performance as an organic part of his mise-en-scene. He explains to David E. Williams in 1996 that "If there are seven characters in a film, I treat the environment as the eighth character—or the first. After all, that's the proscenium within which everything will function. If the central character walks outside and you look at the city and think, 'Wait a minute, I don't believe this story could exist within this environment,' then the film becomes lightweight." All of Scott's films feature surroundings that give us crucial information about their characters and storylines: the corporate claustrophobia of *Alien*, the paranoia and urban decay of *Blade Runner*, the empty promise of freedom and movement in *Thelma & Louise*, the vainglory of empire as Christopher Columbus tries to civilize the natural world of *1492: The Conquest of Paradise*, the arid Armageddon of *Black Hawk Down*. While Tom Cruise couldn't compete with the vivid production design of *Legend*, Scott has been able to tailor his mise-en-scene to fit the needs of his performers, particularly in the late 1980s as stars became more essential to the packaging of his films. *Black Rain*, with its jarring use of Tokyo's neon architecture, accentuates Michael Douglas's xenophobia; *G. I. Jane* complements Demi Moore's preternatural dexterity and concentration; *Hannibal* brings out Anthony Hopkins's regal remastering of Hannibal Lecter with its neoclassical use of Florence and the Washington D.C. suburbs; *Matchstick Men*, with its singular focus on seclusion and sensitivity to gradations of light and sound, fuses completely with Nicolas Cage's neurotic mannerisms.

As a longstanding commercial artist, Scott avoids making overt statements about race or sexuality, but he has been willing to explore gender. By empowering Sigourney Weaver in *Alien* and the duo of Geena Davis and Susan Sarandon in *Thelma & Louise,* Scott contributed to the rise of action heroines in the 1990s and 2000s (Linda Hamilton in

*Terminator 2: Judgement Day*, Sharon Stone in *The Quick and the Dead*, Angela Bassett in *Strange Days*, Geena Davis in *The Long Kiss Goodnight*, Carrie-Anne Moss in *The Matrix*, and Uma Thurman in *Kill Bill*). And while *Thelma & Louise* has been canonized by film critics and cultural studies theorists as an epochal feminist text, Scott minimizes its politics, remarking to Maitland McDonagh in 1991 that "I think as a man watching the film you can't help but be amused, unless you have absolutely zero sense of humor and zero sense of self." *Thelma & Louise* represents a welcome moment of gender justice, but it is *G. I. Jane* that should be honored for its attempt to take gender parity to its logical conclusion. Those who focus on Scott's representation of women overlook Scott's equal interest in masculinity. Consider the themes of intercultural male fellowship in *Black Rain*, the elegiac call for civic pride and patriarchal duty and sacrifice in *Gladiator*, and the unconditional esprit de corps of *Black Hawk Down*. Perhaps Scott's signature "male" film is *White Squall*, a disarming boy's adventure tale that equates manhood with loss and suffering. Scott explains to Williams in 1996 that "The rite of passage has evaporated today, so I felt it was worth refreshing people's minds that this did once exist. I hate to sound cynical, but in most walks of life today, it really doesn't anymore." Scott, resolutely moderate in his politics, offers balanced views of masculinity and femininity that do not degenerate into caricatures or polemics. The remarkable *G. I. Jane*, with Demi Moore in full battle mode, determined to surpass the boundaries of biology and social convention, defies us to dismiss its protagonist as a mere feminist prop. The same could be said of Jeff Bridges's patriarchal stance in *White Squall* as he shepherds his adolescent charges into a biblical storm that challenges his call for masculine resolve and self-discipline. Bridges's gospel of teamwork and physical endurance turns his apprentices into men, but the price of Bridges's hubris is the loss of his wife and several of his students. In *Thelma & Louise*, *White Squall* and *G. I. Jane* gender is something to be challenged or resisted, but not without jeopardy or disaster.

Scott may acknowledge the demands and expectations of commercial filmmaking, offering us relatively closed and happy endings in *Alien*, *Legend*, *Someone to Watch Over Me*, *Black Rain*, *G. I. Jane*, and *Matchstick Men*, but an equal number of his films end with the death of the protagonist (*Thelma & Louise*, *Gladiator*), a lack of resolution (*The*

*Duellists, Blade Runner, Hannibal*), or a somber awareness of loss or defeat (*1492: The Conquest of Paradise, White Squall, Black Hawk Down*). Scott rationalizes his narratives by explaining to Michael Wilmington in 1996 that "Because I'm European, because I think I have one foot halfway into the truth behind documentaries and non-mainstream movies, I can't quite shake that mud off my feet. Some people call it perversity. It's not perversity. Life isn't a bed of roses. People die. People get cancer. And therefore one is always reminding the audience that there's a dark side to life. That attracts me. Because it's the truth." That darkness can be detected in the industrial anonymity of *Alien*, the retro-fitted architecture and oppressive materialism of *Blade Runner*, and the Gothic decadence and amoral one-upmanship of *Hannibal*. Scott's European education and demeanor accounts for what some perceive as a cool detachment. While Tony Scott used RSA's many innovations to bombard the audience with sound, color, and movement in *Top Gun* or *Enemy of the State*, Ridley's use of mise-en-scene encourages the audience to inhabit his many worlds. Despite the financial and cultural success of *Alien, Thelma & Louise, Gladiator, Hannibal*, and *Black Hawk Down*, Scott is continually asked to recall *Blade Runner* in most of his interviews. Referenced repeatedly, regardless of the context, *Blade Runner* has become a fetish object for both critics and cinephiles alike. Scott informs Sammon in 1996 that *"Blade Runner* works on a level which I haven't seen much—or ever—in a mainstream film. It works like a book. Like a very dark novel. Which I like. It's definitely a film that's designed *not* to have the usual *crush-wallop-bang!* impact." But, as he confides to McDonagh in 1991, "On first viewing, it may have been a lot to take in." Scott, in keeping with his reserve, minimizes the audacity of his vision but in the same interview with Sammon in 1996 he celebrates *Blade Runner* as a willful example of RSA's credo "Art first": "I think *Blade Runner* is a good lesson for all serious filmmakers to 'stand by your guns.' Don't listen to acclaim or criticism. Simply carry on." The twenty-year legacy of *Blade Runner*—its initial failure and subsequent cult status—did not handicap Scott as he shifted from visionary science fiction to historical epic as his primary mode of representation. The windfall success of *Gladiator*, a sleeper hit, has renewed Scott's appetite for creating worlds. Now that dystopic science fiction has become a standard template for the Blockbusters and comic book adaptations of the last fifteen years (*Batman, Judge Dredd, Tank Girl, The Matrix, Hellboy*), Scott treats the past as the next great undiscovered country, even as he admits to Anna Maria Bahiana in 1992 that the historical film can be a hard sell: "Historical films have always been difficult to mount because of the inherent resistance to the cost and by modern audiences who seem to be more concerned with escapism than realism today—understandably. But haven't they always preferred that? After all, movies are essentially a form of entertainment, not education." As with *Alien, Blade Runner*, and *Legend*, Scott forges ahead, keeping a jaundiced eye on his audience as he reinvents the technological boundaries of commercial cinema by resurrecting ancient empires and landscapes. Scott may tow the corporate line, but he is a visionary at heart: "Forget the box office. Just try to make a great movie. All you can do is try and create a good piece of work."[6]

In accordance with the policy of the University Press of Mississippi, these interviews are reprinted in chronological order in their original form to preserve their historical value. The reader may notice that certain topics or references recur in a number of interviews. Rather than eliminate what appears to be surplus or redundant, we preserved those repetitions to make the reader aware of how an auteur's public reputation and biographical legend fluctuate over time. One way to gauge that change is to note how an auteur handles the same inquiry. In Scott's case, his author-name is permanently associated with *Blade Runner* and its cult status. While some directors grow churlish when subjected to the same questions or allusions (Robert Altman and Spike Lee use that irritation as a form of promotion and name recognition), Scott maintains his decorum with the aplomb of a knighted English gentleman. Scott's patience with his interlocutors speaks volumes about the relationship between an auteur and the chaotic world of entertainment journalism. To maintain his author-name and marketability, Scott must accept what fascinates his interviewers or the public-at-large. He does so with an élan befitting an artist who doubles as a businessman.

This book would not have existed without the love and patience of my wife Moyenda and our two exceptional sons August and Christopher. I am also indebted to my parents John and Trilbie Knapp

---

6. Sammon, *Ridley Scott: The Making of His Movies*, p. 85.

and my father-in-law Peter Mutharika for their genuine interest and support. Ann Stascavage, my steadfast editor, kept me sane and on schedule. Andrea Kulas, my coeditor, provided invaluable insight and assistance. Thanks to all the contributors for their cooperation, especially Paul M. Sammon, who deserves to be regarded as the foremost expert on Ridley Scott and *Blade Runner*. Thanks also to Kathryn Bergeron and Marianne Dissard for their help with the French article. Lastly, I would be lost without the many students at Northwestern University who kept me energized and focused when the fatigue of fatherhood and dissertation writing tested my patience and spirit. You know who you are, and thanks.

In addition to Laurence's kind words, I, Andrea F. Kulas, would like to thank my grandparents Peter J. Kulas, Frances Kulas, Audrey Keene, as well as Edward Dombrowski & Dorothy Dombrowski and family for their sincere blessings in all my endeavors. I would also like to give thanks to my parents Ken and Kathy Kulas as well as my brother K. Peter Kulas for their patience and support with this project. A very special thanks to my coeditor Laurence F. Knapp, who has proved to be both a great mentor and friend. Thanks to all my colleagues, specifically Kathryn Bergeron and Chiara Ferrari, with their constant encouragement. Finally, I'd like to thank the steady enthusiasm of my small, but reliable, pillar of friends.

LFK
AFK

# CHRONOLOGY

1937      Born in South Shields, England, on November 30.

1943      Brother Tony Scott born on July 21 in Stockton-on-Tees, England.

1954–58      Attends West Hartlepool College of Art, specializes in still photography and graphic design.

1958–61      Earns degree in graphic design at the Royal College of Art (RCA) in London; in process becomes fascinated with film and television set design. Marries Felicity Haywood.

1961      Directs and produces *Boy and Bicycle* starring Tony Scott as lead. Accepts traveling scholarship in United States with advertising agency Bob Drew Associates; explores New York City fashion and advertising industry. Works for Richard Leacock and D. A. Pennebaker as an editing assistant at Time/Life Inc.

1962      Returns to U.K. and joins BBC as a television art director and set designer.

1963      Moonlights as television commercial art director. Takes BBC director's course and shoots test version of *Paths of Glory*; leads to work as television director. Directs first television program, "Softly Softly" a spin-off of "Z Cars."

1964      Directs "The Informer" for BBC. Directs first television commercial for Gerber Products Company. Leaves BBC to pursue career in independent television production.

1965    Establishes Ridley Scott Associates (RSA) in London; hires
        RCA graduate Tony Scott as his first associate. Directs and/or
        produces hundreds of commercials by early 1970s. British
        Film Institute (BFI) screens *Boy and Bicycle*. Son, Jake
        Scott, born.

1968    Son, Luke Scott, born.

1972    First attempt at a feature film, *Running in Place*, starring
        Michael York, falters in preproduction.

1974    French television company hires Scott to adapt Henry
        James's *The Author of Beltraffio* as part of the series
        "Nouvelles de Henry James"; Tony Scott directs the episode.

1977    *The Duellists* premieres in Europe on August 31. Wins
        Best First Work at Cannes Film Festival for *The Duellists*;
        develops *Tristan & Isolde* but abandons project after success
        of *Star Wars*.

1978    *The Duellists* opens in New York City on January 14.

1979    Marries Sandy Watson. *Alien* released on May 25. Shoots
        high-profile commercial "Share the Fantasy" for Chanel
        No. 5.

1980    Forms Percy Main Productions, a feature film development
        company. Drops out of filming *Dune* for Dino de Laurentiis.
        Daughter, Jordan Scott, born.

1982    *Blade Runner* released on June 25.

1984    Innovative "1984" commercial for Apple Macintosh com-
        puters airs during Super Bowl XVIII. Renames Percy Main
        Productions Scott Free Productions. *Legend* Pinewood sound-
        stage devastated by fire.

1985    *Legend* premieres in Europe on August 28.

1986    *Legend* released in United States on April 18. RSA opens
        offices in Los Angeles and New York City.

1987    *Someone to Watch Over Me* released on October 9.

1988    RSA moves headquarters to Los Angeles.

1989    *Black Rain* released on September 22. Divorces Sandy
        Watson.

1991    *Thelma & Louise* released on May 24.

| | |
|---|---|
| 1992 | Nominated for Best Director Oscar for *Thelma & Louise*. *1492: Conquest of Paradise* released on October 9. *Blade Runner: The Director's Cut* premieres in Europe. |
| 1993 | Develops *The Hot Zone* with Jodie Foster and Robert Redford; Twentieth Century Fox withdraws financing. |
| 1995 | Purchases Pinewood/Shepperton Studios in London. |
| 1996 | *White Squall* released on February 2. |
| 1997 | *G.I. Jane* released on August 22. |
| 1998 | Develops *I Am Legend* with Arnold Schwarzenegger; Warner Bros. withdraws financing. |
| 1999 | Son Jake Scott directs first feature *Plunkett and Maclaine*. Purchases the Mill, a British digital effects house, to support Shepperton studios. |
| 2000 | *Gladiator* released on May 5. |
| 2001 | Nominated for Best Director Oscar for *Gladiator*. *Hannibal* released on February 9. |
| 2002 | *Black Hawk Down* released on January 18. Nominated for Best Director Oscar for *Black Hawk Down*. Wins Outstanding Made-for-Television Movie Emmy for *The Gathering Storm*. Produces BMW Web shorts "Hire" directed by John Woo, Joe Carnahan, and Tony Scott. |
| 2003 | Knighted by Queen Elizabeth II. *Matchstick Men* released on September 12. *Alien: The Director's Cut* released on October 29. RSA opens Chicago office. |
| 2004 | RSA contracts with Atari to provide live-action short film "The Gauntlet" for video game Driv3r. |
| 2005 | *Kingdom of Heaven* released on May 6. |

# FILMOGRAPHY

## AS DIRECTOR

### *Student and Short Films*

1961/1965
BOY AND BICYCLE
British Film Institute
Producer: **Scott**
Director: **Scott**
Screenplay: **Scott**
Cinematography: **Scott**
Music: John Baker and John Barry
Cast: Tony Scott
B&W/16 mm
27 minutes

### *Feature Films*

1977
THE DUELLISTS
Enigma/NFFC/Scott Free Productions
Producer: David Putnam
Associate Producer: Ivor Powell
Director: **Scott**
Story: Joseph Conrad, "The Duel"
Screenplay: Gerald Vaughan-Hughes
Cinematography: Frank Tidy
Production Design: Peter J. Hampton

Editing: Pamela Power
Music: Howard Blake
Cast: Keith Carradine (Armand D'Hubert), Harvey Keitel (Garbriel Feraud), Albert Finney (Fouche), Edward Fox (Colonel), Cristina Raines (Adele), Robert Stephens (General Treillard), Tom Conti (Dr. Jacquin), John McEnery (Chevalier), Diana Quick (Laura)
Color/35 mm/Spherical (1.85:1)
95 minutes


1979
ALIEN
Twentieth Century Fox/Brandywine Productions Ltd.
Producers: Gordon Carroll, David Giler, and Walter Hill
Executive Producer: Ronald Shusett
Associate Producer: Ivor Powell
Director: **Scott**
Story: Dan O'Bannon and Ronald Shusett
Screenplay: Dan O'Bannon
Cinematography: Derek Vanlint
Production Design: Michael Seymour
Editing: Terry Rawlings and Peter Weatherley
Music: Jerry Goldsmith
Cast: Tom Skerritt (Captain Dallas), Sigourney Weaver (Ripley), Veronica Cartwright (Lambert), Harry Dean Stanton (Brett), John Hurt (Kane), Ian Holm (Ash), Yaphet Kotto (Parker), Bolaji Badejo ("Alien"), Helen Horton (Voice of Mother)
Color/35 mm/Panavision (2.35:1)
117 minutes (1979)/116 minutes (Director's cut, 2003)


1982
BLADE RUNNER
Blade Runner Partnership/The Ladd Company
Producer: Michael Deeley
Executive Producers: Hampton Fancher and Brian Kelly
Co-Executive Producers: Jerry Perenchio and Bud Yorkin
Associate Producers: Ivor Powell and Run Run Shaw

Co-Producer: **Scott**
Director: **Scott**
Story: Philip K. Dick, "Do Androids Dream of Electric Sheep?"
Screenplay: Hampton Fancher and David Webb Peoples
Cinematography: Jordan Cronenweth
Production Design: Lawrence G. Paull and Peter J. Hampton
Editing: Terry Rawlings
Music: Vangelis
Cast: Harrison Ford (Rick Deckard), Rutger Hauer (Roy Batty), Sean
Young (Rachel), Edward James Olmos (Gaff), M. Emmet Walsh (Bryant),
Daryl Hannah (Pris), William Sanderson (J. F. Sebastian), Brion James
(Leon), Joe Turkel (Tyrell), Joanna Cassidy (Zhora), James Hong
(Hannibal Chew), Morgan Paull (Holden)
Color/35 mm/Panavision (2.35:1)
117 minutes (1982)/112 minutes (Director's cut, 1992)

1985
LEGEND
Twentieth Century Fox/Embassy International Pictures/Legend
Production Company Ltd./Universal Pictures
Producer: Arnon Milchan
Co-Producer: Tim Hampton
Director: **Scott**
Screenplay: William Hjortsberg
Cinematography: Alex Thomson
Production Design: Leslie Dilley and Assheton Gorton
Editing: Terry Rawlings
Music: Jerry Goldsmith (1985 European release/2002 Director's cut) and
Tangerine Dream (1986 U.S. release)
Cast: Tom Cruise (Jack), Mia Sara (Princess Lily), Tim Curry (The Lord of
Darkness), David Bennent (Honeythorn Gump), Alice Playten (Blix),
Bill Barty (Screwball), Cork Hubbert (Brown Tom), Peter O'Farrell (Pox),
Kiran Shah (Blunder), Annabelle Lanyon (Oona), Robert Picardo (Meg
Mucklebones)
Color/35 mm/Panavision (2.35:1)
94 minutes (Europe, 1985)/89 minutes (U.S., 1986)/114 minutes
(Director's cut, 2002)

1987
SOMEONE TO WATCH OVER ME
Columbia Pictures Corporation
Producers: Thierry de Ganay and Harold Schneider
Executive Producer: **Scott**
Co-Producer: Mimi Polk
Director: **Scott**
Screenplay: Howard Franklin
Cinematography: Steven B. Poster
Production Design: James D. Bissell
Editing: Claire Simpson
Music: Michael Kamen
Cast: Tom Berenger (Mike Keegan), Mimi Rodgers (Claire Gregory),
Lorraine Bracco (Ellie Keegan), Jerry Orbach (Lt. Garber), John
Rubinstein (Neil Steinhart), Andreas Katsulas (Joey Venza), Tony
DiBenedetto (T. J.), James E. Moriarty (Koontz), Mark Moses (Win
Hockings)
Color/35 mm/Spherical (1.85:1)
106 minutes

1989
BLACK RAIN
Paramount Pictures/Pegasus Film Partners
Producers: Stanley R. Jaffe and Sherry Lansing
Executive Producers: Craig Bolotin and Julie Kirkham
Associate Producer: Alan Poul
Director: **Scott**
Screenplay: Craig Bolotin and Warren Lewis
Cinematography: Jan de Bont
Production Design: Norris Spencer
Editing: Tom Rolf
Music: Hans Zimmer
Cast: Michael Douglas (Nick Conklin), Andy Garcia (Charlie Vincent),
Ken Takakura (Mashahiro Matsumoto), Kate Capshaw (Joyce), Yusaku
Matsuda (Kogi Sato), Shigeru Koyama (Superintendent Ohashi), John
Spencer (Captain Oliver), Guts Ishimatsu (Katayama)
Color/35 mm/Super 35 (2.35:1)
125 minutes

1991
THELMA & LOUISE
Metro-Goldwyn-Mayer (MGM)/Pathe Entertainment
Producers: Mimi Polk and **Scott**
Co-Producers: Callie Khouri and Dean O'Brien
Director: **Scott**
Screenplay: Callie Khouri
Cinematography: Adrian Biddle
Production Design: Norris Spencer
Editing: Thom Noble
Music: Hans Zimmer
Cast: Susan Sarandon (Louise Sawyer), Geena Davis (Thelma
Dickinson), Harvey Keitel (Hal Slocumb), Michael Madsen (Jimmy),
Christopher McDonald (Darryl), Stephen Tobolowsky (Max), Brad Pitt
(J. D.), Timothy Carhart (Harlan), Jason Beghe (State Trooper)
Color/35 mm/Panavision (2.35:1)
129 minutes

1992
1492: CONQUEST OF PARADISE
Canal Droits Audiovisuels/Cyrk/Due West/French Ministry of Culture
and Communication/Gaunmont/Legende Enterprises/Paramount
Pictures/Spanish Ministry of Culture/Touchstone Pictures
Producers: Alain Goldman and **Scott**
Executive Producers: Mimi Polk and Iain Smith
Associate Producer: Garth Thomas
Co-Producers: Roselyne Bosch, Marc Boyman, and Pere Fages
Director: **Scott**
Screenplay: Roselyne Bosch
Cinematography: Adrian Biddle
Production Design: Norris Spencer
Editing: William M. Anderson, Francoise Bonnot, Leslie Healey, Armen
Minasian, Deborah Zeitman
Music: Vangelis
Cast: Gérard Depardieu (Christopher Columbus), Armand Assante
(Sanchez), Sigourney Weaver (Queen Isabel), Loren Dean (Older
Fernando), Angela Molina (Beatrix), Fernando Rey (Marchena), Michael
Wincott (Noxica), Tchéky Karyo (Pinzon), Kevin Dunn (Captain

Mendez), Frank Langella (Santangel), Mark Margolis (Bobadilla), Kario
Salem (Arojaz)
Color/35 mm/Panavision (2.35:1)
154 minutes

1996
WHITE SQUALL
Hollywood Pictures/Largo Entertainment/Scott Free Pictures
Producers: Rocky Lang and Mimi Polk
Executive Producer: **Scott**
Director: **Scott**
Story: Charles Gieg Jr. and Felix Sutton, *The Last Voyage of the Albatross*
Screenplay: Todd Robinson
Cinematography: Hugh Johnson
Production Design: Peter J. Hampton and Leslie Tomkins
Editing: Gerry Hambling
Music: Jeff Rona
Cast: Jeff Bridges (Captain Christopher "Skipper" Sheldon), Caroline
Goodall (Dr. Alice Sheldon), John Savage (McCrea), Scott Wolf (Charles
Gieg), Jeremy Sisto (Frank Beaumont), Ryan Phillippe (Gil Martin),
David Lascher (Robert March), Eric Michael Cole (Dean Preston), Jason
Marsden (Shay Jennings), David Selby (Francis Beaumont), Julio Oscar
Mechoso (Girard Pascal), Zeljko Ivanek (Captain Sanders), Balthazar
Getty (Tod Johnstone)
Color/35 mm/Panavision (2.35:1)
129 minutes

1997
G. I. JANE
Caravan Pictures/First Independent Films, Ltd./Hollywood
Pictures/Largo Entertainment/Moving Pictures/Scott Free
Productions/Trap-Two-Zero Productions, Inc.
Producers: Roger Birnbaum, Demi Moore, **Scott**, and Suzanne Todd
Executive Producers: Danielle Alexandra, Julie Bergman Sender,
and Chris Zarpas
Director: **Scott**
Story: Danielle Alexandra

Screenplay: David Twohy and Danielle Alexandra
Cinematography: Hugh Johnson
Production Design: Arthur Max
Editing: Pietro Scalia
Music: Trevor Jones
Cast: Demi Moore (Lieutenant Jordan O'Neil), Viggo Mortensen (Master
Chief John Urgayle), Anne Bancroft (Senator Lillian DeHaven), Jason
Beghe (Royce), Scott Wilson (C. O. Salem), Lucinda Jenney (Blondell),
Morris Chestnut (McCool), Daniel von Bargen (Theodore Hayes), John
Michael Higgins (Chief of Staff), Kevin Gage (Sergeant Max Pyro), David
Warshofsky (Sergeant Johns), David Vadim (Sergeant Cortez), Josh
Hopkins (Ensign F. Lee "Flea" Montgomery), James Caviezel (Slovnik),
Boyd Kestner (Wickwire), Angel David (Newberry), Stephen Ramsey
(Stamm), Gregg Bello (Miller)
Color/35 mm/Panavision (2.35:1)
124 minutes

2000
GLADIATOR
DreamWorks SKG/Scott Free Productions/Universal Pictures
Producers: David Franzoni, Branko Lustig, and Douglas Wick
Executive Producers: Laurie MacDonald, Walter F. Parkes, and **Scott**
Director: **Scott**
Story: David Franzoni
Screenplay: David Franzoni, John Logan, and William Nicholson
Cinematography: John Mathieson
Production Design: Arthur Max
Editing: Pietro Scalia
Music: Lisa Gerrard, Hans Zimmer
Cast: Russell Crowe (General Maximus Dacimus Meridus), Joaquin
Phoenix (Emperor Commodus), Connie Nielsen (Lucilla), Oliver Reed
(Antonius Proximo), Richard Harris (Emperor Marcus Aurelius), Derek
Jacobi (Senator Gracchus), Djimon Hounsou (Juba), David Schofield
(Senator Falco), John Shrapnel (Senator Gaius), Tomas Arana (Quintus),
David Hemmings (Cassius)
Color/35 mm/Super 35 (2.35:1)
155 minutes

2001
HANNIBAL
Dino De Laurentiis Productions/Metro-Goldwyn-Mayer (MGM)/Scott
Free Productions/Universal Pictures
Producers: Dino De Laurentiis, Martha Schumacher, and **Scott**
Executive Producer: Branko Lustig
Associate Producer: Terry Needham
Director: **Scott**
Story: Thomas Harris, *Hannibal*
Screenplay: David Mamet and Steven Zaillian
Cinematography: John Mathieson
Production Design: Norris Spencer
Editing: Pietro Scalia and Daniele Sordoni
Music: Hans Zimmer
Cast: Anthony Hopkins (Dr. Hannibal Lecter), Julianne Moore
(FBI Special Agent Clarice Starling), Giancarlo Giannini (Inspector
Rinaldo Pazzi), Gary Oldman (Mason Verger), Ray Liotta (Paul
Krendler), Frankie Fison (Barney Matthews), Francesca Neri (Allegra
Pazzi), Zeljko Ivanek (Dr. Cordell Doemling), Hazelle Goodman
(Evelda Drumgo)
Color/35 mm/Spherical (1.85:1)
131 minutes

2001
BLACK HAWK DOWN
Columbia Pictures Corporation/Jerry Bruckheimer Films/Revolution
Studios/Scott Free Productions
Producers: Jerry Bruckheimer and **Scott**
Executive Producers: Branko Lustig, Chad Oman, Mike Stenson, and
Simon West
Associate Producers: Harry Humphries, Terry Needham, and
Pat Sandston
Director: **Scott**
Story: Mark Bowden, *Black Hawk Down*
Screenplay: Ken Nolan
Cinematography: Slavomir Idziak
Production Design: Arthur Max

Editing: Pietro Scalia
Music: Hans Zimmer
Cast: Josh Hartnett (Ranger Staff Sgt. Matt Eversmann), Ewan McGregor (Ranger Spec. Danny Grimes), Jason Issacs (Ranger Capt. Mike Steele), Tom Sizemore (Ranger Lt. Col. Danny McKnight), William Fichtner (Delta Sgt. First Class Jeff Sanderson), Eric Bana (Sgt. First Class Norm "Hoot" Gibson), Sam Shepard (Maj. Gen. William F. Garrison), Ewen Bremner (Ranger Spec. Shawn Nelson), Charlie Hofheimer (Ranger Cpl. Jamie Smith), Tom Hardy (Ranger Spec. Lance Twombly), Tom Guiry (Ranger Staff Sgt. Ed Yurek), Ron Eldard (Chief Warrant Officer Mike Durant), Hugh Dancy (Ranger Sgt. First Class Kurt Schmid), Johnny Strong (Delta Sgt. First Class Randy Shughart), Gregory Sporleder (Ranger Sgt. Scott Galentine), Brian Von Holt (Staff Sgt. Jeff Struecker), Steven Ford (Lt. Col. Joe Cribbs), Zeljko Ivanek (Lt. Col. Gary Harrell), Matthew Marsden (Spec. Dale Sizemore), Nikolaj Coster-Waldan (Master Sgt. Gary Gordon), Orlando Bloom (Pfc. Todd Blackburn), Kim Coates (Master Sgt. Tim "Guiz" Martin), Glenn Morshower (Lt. Col. Tom Matthews), Enrique Murciano (Sgt. Lorenzo Ruiz), Jeremy Piven (C.W.O. Cliff "Elvis" Wolcott), George Harris (Orman Atto), Treva Etienne (Abdullah "Firimbi" Hassan)
Color/35 mm/Super 35 (2.35:1)
144 minutes

2003
MATCHSTICK MEN
Warner Bros./ImageMovers/HorsePower Entertainment/Live Planet/Rickshaw Productions/Scott Free Productions
Producers: Sean Bailey, Ted Griffin, Jack Rapke, **Scott,** and Steve Starkey
Executive Producer: Robert Zemeckis
Co-Producers: Gianina Facio and Charles J. D. Schlissel
Director: **Scott**
Story: Eric Garcia, *Matchstick Men*
Screenplay: Nicholas Griffin and Ted Griffin
Cinematography: John Mathieson
Production Design: Tom Foden
Editing: Dody Dorn

Music: Hans Zimmer
Cast: Nicolas Cage (Roy Waller), Sam Rockwell (Frank Mercer), Alison
Lohman (Angela), Bruce Altman (Dr. Klein), Bruce McGill (Chuck
Frechette), Jenny O'Hara (Mrs. Schaeffer), Steve Eastin (Mr. Schaeffer),
Beth Grant (Laundry Lady)
Color/35 mm/Panavision (2.35:1)
116 minutes

2005
KINGDOM OF HEAVEN
Twentieth Century Fox/Scott Free Productions
Producer: **Scott**
Executive Producers: Lisa Ellzey, Branko Lustig, and Terry Needham
Director: **Scott**
Screenplay: William Monahan
Cinematography: John Mathieson
Production Design: Arthur Max
Editing: Dody Dorn
Music: Hans Zimmer
Cast: Orlando Bloom (Balian of Ibelin), Jeremy Irons (Tiberias), Liam
Neeson (Godfrey of Ibelin), Eva Green (Sybilla), Jon Finch (Patricarch of
Jerusalem), Brendan Gleeson (Reynald), Edward Norton (King Baldwin IV),
Alexander Siddig (Imad), David Thewlis (Hospitaller), Marton Csokas
(Guy De Lesignan), Eriq Ebouaney (Firuz), Nasser Memarzia (Muslim
Grandee), Ulrich Thomsen (Templar Master), Velibor Topic (Almaric),
Shane Attwooll (Reynald's Templar Knight), Tim Barlow (Old Guard),
Samira Draa (Sybilla's Maidservant), Michael Fitzgerald (Humphrey),
Michael Shaeffer (Young Seargeant)
Color/35 mm

## AS PRODUCER ONLY

*Monkey Trouble* (1994) (executive)
*The Browning Version* (1994)
*Clay Pigeons* (1998)
*Where the Money Is* (2000)
*Hire: The Ticker* (2002) (executive)

*Hire: Beat the Devil* (2002) (executive)
*Hire: The Hostage* (2002) (executive)
*Six Bullets from Now* (2002)
*Tristan & Isolde* (2004) (executive)
*Emma's War* (2005)
*In Her Shoes* (2005)
*Diamond Dead* (2005)

RIDLEY SCOTT

**INTERVIEWS**

# Ridley Scott Directs *The Duellists*

## DONALD CHASE/1978

*The Duellists* is such an elegantly witty, visually breathtaking
evocation of the Napoleonic Era that I was somewhat taken aback when
its British director, Ridley Scott, arrived for an interview dressed in blue
jeans and wondering how badly the latest New York City blizzard would
hurt the film's box office and whether the Fine Arts Theatre was really
the most desirable showcase in the first place. It was only after speaking
to Scott for a while that I adjusted to the fact that the man is part risk-
taking dreamer and part pragmatist-pusher. I also realized that the
combination not only makes sense, but could serve as a prescription
for anybody—with talent—who yearns someday to direct a feature-
length film.

Thirty-nine-year-old Ridley Scott had his first experience as a filmmaker almost twenty years ago, when he was a student at the Royal
College of Art in London. "They happened to have a Bolex in a wardrobe closet, and a light meter, and I was one of six students (in the
College's just budding Department of Theatre and TV Design) who did
a film that year. Mine was made for 250 pounds—about $600—virtually
shooting 1:1, or certainly no more than 3:1. It was a fictional piece,
about half an hour long, about kids growing up against an industrial
yet somehow romantic landscape in a town on the Northeast coast of
England. The film really didn't do anything—it was shown at a few
festivals—but a gong went off in my head and I thought: That's what
I'm going to do."

What Scott actually did next was to accept an offer to work as a
designer—and only as a designer—for the BBC. "Those days in the early

---

From *Millimeter*, May 1978, pp. 142–47. Reprinted by permission of the author.

'60s were a terrific time for a TV designer. I was building elaborate double-decker sets with cameras on the second story, but I eventually discovered that there were only a few good directors, and I became very frustrated by what I considered mishandling of my constructions. If you design, I think it's natural to want to take the step into directing, so I was always pushing within the internal hierarchy at the BBC."

After many rejections, they finally allowed him to take a four-month "producer's course." Though intended merely to make designers more aware of the producer's problems, the course allowed each student studio facilities under airtime conditions to produce his own half-hour program. "I knew I had to do something fairly remarkable," Scott recalls. "Otherwise, it would be back to the design department."

He went beyond remarkable and did something outrageous, and it worked—temporarily. It was a compressed version of *Paths of Glory* (done as a feature by Stanley Kubrick in 1957), which utilized ten minutes of film shot on Wimbledon Common. "It was probably just mediocre," the director reflects. "TV, by encapsulating, often has the effect of making mediocre things seem really good. But it worked, it clicked, and as a result I was offered the direction of a couple of episodes of a popular police-action series called "Z Cars." After that, the hierarchy said I had to go back to the design department, so I resigned—a frightening decision, because during my three years at the BBC I'd married, become a father, gotten a new house. . . ."

The risk was well taken, for within a relatively short time came the opportunity to direct a few episodes of "The Informer," "a very intelligent semi-detective series starring Ian Hendry in the role of a disbarred lawyer and dealing with how he functions in life after his disbarment." Scott managed to incorporate about fifteen minutes of film into each hour-long episode, but was soon experiencing a new version of the frustration he'd known as a designer, "because you can't ever totally control what you're doing in episodic TV—you can never really get close to perfection in anything."

He'd art-directed many commercials and by this point had directed a half-dozen and "loved the idea of being able to play around with details and really present, even if it was for only thirty or sixty seconds, something that I could totally control. So, here I was again at a seesaw

point, doing all right in TV but with offers to go off into this new area."
What did he do? "I devoted myself to commercials almost full-time."

To say that made another wise, if seemingly risky, decision is an understatement. In the mid-to-late '6os England was the commercial-film
center for all of Western Europe, and, after proving himself with spots
for such local products as Benson & Hedges and a series of trend-setting
turn-of-the-century costume ads for Hovis Bread, Scott or the other
five directors he eventually contracted to work for his own production
company were constantly shipping out for assignments in Paris and
Berlin or Munich.

In addition, during a four-year period in the late '6os and early '7os,
Scott himself made as many as fifteen annual trips to New York or Los
Angeles to direct spots for such products as Diet Pepsi, Ford Motor Company, Schaeffer Beer, and Pit Stop. "There'd be a preliminary transatlantic phone conference, the storyboard would be air-freighted over,
followed by another call to discuss it, then I'd fly over on a Sunday
night, spend Monday in conference with the agency and looking at
locations or studio facilities, usually start shooting the next day, and be
back in England by Friday night. The change of pace was exciting, but
there were drawbacks, too.

"In England, I was used to controlling the project to completion
through my own company, and being in on the dub and the editing.
The agencies in the U.S. were perfectly happy about my disappearing as
soon as the shoot was over; they'd put it together their own way after I
left. Another thing: I did most of my work in the States when the real
heyday of TV commercials—in the sense of an excitement among filmmakers about working in the field—was starting to dissipate. Howard
Zieff had done his thing, Dick Richards was about to move on, and
things were getting a little tight moneywise."

But perhaps the real reason Scott called an end to his transoceanic
commutes and also began "gently de-escalating" his commercial production company was to devote more time and energy to his long-term
goal of directing feature films. He wrote one screenplay on his own—
"a very black, very violent comedy-heist somewhat influenced by *Performance*, which I greatly admire"—and developed another with writer
Gerald Vaughan-Hughes on the Guy Fawkes Gunpowder Plot.

The latter came very close to being made, may in fact be revived with Scott as producer and someone else directing; but, five years ago the bottom line seemed to be what the powers-that-were at the British major studios considered Scott's insufficient directorial experience. " 'You really ought to go back and do a little more filmed TV,' they kept telling me. Which I felt—I'd pushed through more celluloid in the previous ten years than say, Roman Polanski—was a bit like teaching your grandmother to suck eggs. I knew they were wrong—these blue-suited assholes—but I figured: If that's the name of the game, okay, I'll do some filmed TV."

The capitulation was only half-hearted, however, as Scott and his brother Tony who had been active in the commercial production company formed a new outfit with the intention of developing their own ideas for TV series. This was a bit of a miscalculation in that the British networks were extremely resistant to the idea of an independent production company supplying them with material, but it did lead indirectly to negotiations with a French TV company to produce a one-hour version of a Henry James story for a six-part series of classics.

That the Scott brothers had to come up with half the budget seemed less daunting after the show went over in a big way and the French company came back with an offer of more than $250,000 for a second project which Scott would direct. It caused him to resolve: "Somehow I'm going to make a feature out of this. It was the same thing as with my first TV exercise: you've got to make people aware of the fact that you're good and give yourself credibility."

Because of the money thus far committed, in searching for material Scott restricted himself to the literary past—the public domain—and after looking again to Henry James and at Jack London material, he came upon the Joseph Conrad story "The Duel."

"To be truthful, I'm not an admirer of Conrad. I find him heavy going, because I think that generally he has a low level of humor. But 'The Duel' is very tongue-in-cheek. I love the humor, the idiocy actually, of two men dueling over a period of twenty years. It's almost a Don Quixote insanity but also linked with fanaticism and obsession and, to the outsider, unreasonable violence. Yet to the insider, who's the exponent of the violence, it's perfectly reasonable. And that's a fairly contemporary theme."

In transforming "The Duel" into *The Duellists*, Scott worked with his old associate, screenwriter Gerald Vaughan-Hughes, to the extent that he contributed suggestions about the scenario, the characters, and the general tone of the material. The screenplay was so much better than anyone expected that the project started to escalate, exactly as hoped. "People said there's a film in this, not a TV film." But for all the interest shown in a post-production pickup, no one came forth with before-the-fact financing for *The Duellists* as a theatrical feature until Scott went to producer David Putnam and in desperation cried, "Help! Or at least read the script, and see what you think."

Puttnam thought well enough of it to pass it on to Paramount president David Picker, who initiated casting discussions. The two names that came up for the leads were Keith Carradine and Harvey Keitel. They share an agent in Harry Ufland, who felt the script was intriguing enough to give to them to read, and after a two-month visit to Los Angeles that encompassed many discussions with the actors, Scott had commitments from both. "They were the base line of my pyramid. The rest of the casting was simple: you simply began to stockpile talent. Albert Finney, who's tremendously constructive in the sense that he will help if he thinks a project is worthwhile, did a one-day cameo in exchange for a framed check for twenty-five pounds inscribed 'Break glass in case of dire need.' " Robert Stephens, Edward Fox, Alan Webb, and Jenny Runacre soon jumped on the bandwagon.

While thrust onto a new, more spacious plane of filmmaking with *The Duellists*, Scott suggests that the making of the movie included as many variations on old themes in his professional life as new experiences. For one thing, the film's budget was $1.5 million, almost unbelievably low for a period piece whose pictorial richness has invited comparisons to the many-times-more expensive *Barry Lyndon*. Scott didn't get a cash flow going until three-and-a-half weeks before shooting was to start, which meant that he had to open up his own coffers to meet some preliminary expenses. Once these were reimbursed and the picture started shooting, there was an additional personal financial pressure: Scott was completion guarantor on the project, which was "hair-raising in a way—I could have lost my shirt," but also helped him bring the film in on a fifty-day schedule, despite locations in France and in Scotland (doubling for Russia).

Also helpful in keeping on schedule was the fact that the entire script of *The Duellists* was storyboarded. The storyboarding, no doubt instrumental in holding down the shooting ratio at roughly 10:1, was "not so extensive that it was restrictive but rather served as a security for me, something from commercials."

As he did in commercials (but not in TV), Scott served as his own camera operator on *The Duellists*. (Frank Tidy was director of photography.) "In general," he admits, "I found there was far too much time wasted pontificating and politicizing with [camera] people who really didn't know what you wanted when you knew exactly what you wanted. It may sound egomaniacal, but because of my background as an art director I usually knew exactly how a room should be lit to get vastly more detail than one normally would. So after a time in commercials, when I had a lot of say because I was doing the employing through my own company, I took the bull by the horns and started working with new young lighting cameramen who were prepared to go along with the way I wanted to work.

We got into a method of lighting—the soft, bounced light which is the nearest thing to daylight—that probably originated with still photographers like Irving Penn and Bert Stern, but seemed tremendously unusual in English TV commercials at the time. Of course, it's become very standard since then and has greatly influenced the way feature films have looked over the last ten years. I've now come out of that and gone right over to the other side, to the classical methods practiced by people like Gregg Toland and James Wong Howe, using hard lights and Brutes. . . . The way a film looks is important. It's very gratifying to me that at least two American critics felt that the visual aspects of *The Duellists*, from the teacups to the way the sky looked, gave it an added dimension. I want to do my thing as a director in that way as much as, say, an actor wants to do his thing."

More than a year after shooting *The Duellists*, Ridley Scott still seems to entertain some self-doubt as to whether the combination of American leads Keith Carradine and Harvey Keitel and a British supporting cast works. Heartened by the opinion that the difference in accents between Carradine (whose relaxed California cadences are somehow suited to his aristocratic character) and Harvey Keitel (whose New York inflections seem appropriate to his role as Carradine's relatively low-born adversary), as well as the more obvious vocal dissimilarities between them and the Britishers, are a convention that one just accepts, the director goes on to discuss his working relationships with the performers in the film.

"Need I say, first of all, that the actor-director relationship is a two-way event based on mutual trust? Which is something that I tried to establish in advance of shooting by discussing the parts and getting to know the actors as people as extensively as I could before shooting. I had two-and-a-half-hour meetings with some of the actors who played the smaller parts instead of the fifteen-minute exchanges one can get by with. On the other hand, I had very little actual rehearsal; my idea was to throw them in and shoot as soon as possible in the hopes that the actor's own personality would give life and energy to the part.

"The English actors took to their roles more naturally than Keith and Harvey, but at the same time there was the pitfall of having them give the kind of full-scale performances that would have the effect of making you feel you were watching a piece of sludgy theater-on-film. So with them, the task was to get them to relax, to naturalize, if you will, their delivery so that it would be more in tune with Harvey and Keith. . . . Possibly because he was slightly intimidated by the material, Keith was more prepared than Harvey to approach it 'classically,' that is, play the script. Any improvisation that Keith and Harvey did had to do with physical action rather than dialogue."

In an interview in *Film Comment* magazine, Keitel complained that his role in *The Duellists* was materially altered in the editing of the film. Scott rebuts: "What was cut was preamble—physical things, like Harvey walking around the town square. He tended to milk things; at one point he touched a child on the cheek, apparently to make his character more sympathetic. But I don't feel that character was changed substantially and there were certainly no 'big' scenes of Harvey's that were cut."

The editing of *The Duellists* was a hectic process in that there were only ten weeks between the end of shooting and a locked-in date to show the film at the Cannes Film Festival (it won a Jury Prize). "Two editors worked on the film," Scott recalls, "splitting it roughly in half and working simultaneously. It's a great way to work, even without time pressures, because one doesn't always have to be waiting around for footage to look at. The editors gave me a perspective on pace and kept me from falling into a standard commercial director's trap, that is, from feeling that you have to have a payoff every thirty or sixty seconds."

Not that Scott is down on commercials. Even with two features lined up for the future—one a sci-fi piece called *Alien* and the other a somewhat, though not completely, modernized version of *Tristan and Isolde*—he realizes that the capriciousness of the film business may dictate a return to his former bailiwick. "Commercials have been my academy," he explains, "and as such have had a lot to do with hardening me up. I say 'harden' in the sense of making me more secure, though certainly not rigid about things, because the very nature of life argues against that."

In her largely favorable review of *The Duellists* in the *New Yorker*, Pauline Kael speculates on whether the scene in which Keith Carradine and Cristina Raines kiss after deciding to wed, while their horses, standing just behind them, nuzzle each other is "the luckiest shot a beginner movie director ever caught or the most entranced bit of planning a beginner ever dated." Scott clarifies the matter—sort of.

"The scene was designed to include the horses—I mean, God, here was another will-you-marry-me bit, and I wanted some kind of original touch. The mare was in season, so we knew the animals would be a handful, but both Keith and Cristina were Robert Altman veterans and I trusted their ability to get through it okay. We did three takes and all three times the horses nuzzled each other. So it was a combination of planning and fantastic good luck."

Which, considering Ridley Scott's career so far, is no surprise at all.

# *Alien* from the Inside Out: Part II

## JAMES DELSON/1979

FF:   *Carlo Rambaldi was brought in to create the mechanical effect of the alien's head. Was his employment a direct result of* Close Encounters?
SCOTT:   Absolutely. I thought that the alien in *Close Encounters* was great.

FF:   *Was it difficult getting him onto the project?*
SCOTT:   He was up to his eyes with work. But he came and saw the artwork. We virtually pleaded with him to do it, saying, "You're the only man who can make this thing work." And he said, "Yes, I am the only man who can make this thing work!" We persuaded him to do it, and he *made* it work.

FF:   *What was Rambaldi responsible for in operating the alien?*
SCOTT:   The head and the tail. You can go right into closeup and watch that face work.

FF:   *The head has two sets of teeth and a tongue that shoots out and goes right into the brain. Was it operated by a crew?*
SCOTT:   It's operated by two people. It's a lever system. Rambaldi discarded radio control as being too limited and went for a more sophisticated idea. He physically built steel ligaments into the alien head, like a doctor, using the mechanics of a real head. The operators of the head stand twenty-five feet away and use human pressure on levers that make the ligaments work through hidden cables.

From *Fantastic Films,* November 1979, pp. 21–31, 58–59. Reprinted by permission of the author.

FF:    *And the tail?*

SCOTT:    The same thing on the tail. When it was constructed, we screwed it to a table top for a demonstration. It looked like the tentacle of a massive octopus. It was screwed down onto a steel plate, because it was bloody heavy, but when it moved it could be controlled incredibly well. It was very strange.

FF:    *The full-sized alien is essentially a tall actor in a customized rubber suit. How was the design of the alien conceived?*

SCOTT:    We had gone through various sketches in the pre-production phase, and I'd seen drawings that other people had tried as well. They always seemed to be of scaly bodies with claws or huge blobs that would move across the floor. There was no elegance to them, no lethalness. What emerged was a H. R. Giger-designed humanoid with distinctly biomechanoid tendencies.

FF:    *In the alien's intermediate stage, when it kills Brett, how did you plan to show its growth since "birth"?*

SCOTT:    We wanted to show he was big, but we didn't want the audience to know *how* big. You're not quite sure whether he stands, hangs or what. At that point we wanted the whole interest of the audience to be focused on the head and the "umbilical cord." It's really just a long muscle with immense tensile strength but it looks like an umbilical.

FF:    *Had you ever considered using a Ray Harryhausen-type stop-motion animation that could be matted in with the actors, or did you want him there, physically, as a real menace?*

SCOTT:    I preferred to take the chance of putting the creature in with them even though I knew it would be a bloody hard thing to try and do.

FF:    *This goes back to your feeling that most special effects had failed to convince you of their reality?*

SCOTT:    Right. I mean, really, how many creatures in horror films have actually *worked* for you? People only accept them because that's what they're seeing.

FF:    *Having decided on the Giger-designed alien, how did you proceed?*

SCOTT:    Well, when we finally had something acceptable we stood back and looked at him. For better or for worse, we were committed to *that* thing as the beast. He was great on paper, and when Giger put the model together, he looked terrific. But then we had to fit a figure into it, and decide on all the other things to do with it. Our biggest problem, again, was time.

FF:    *How did the lack of time affect your effects work?*

SCOTT:    We were shooting one-for-one sometimes! We'd had a lot of *thought* put into each effect, so we knew how to do it, but if we'd had time to do things over a few times, we'd have been able to make what we did look two or three times better. By using different lighting, different camera angles or lenses, we could have improved the impact of some scenes.

It's like rehearsing actors. You're able to find things you didn't think of, or refine things you worked out beforehand but realized you could improve while the first take was being shot. We were forced to rely on instinct, but happily things worked out quite well.

FF:    *What construction problems were you faced with in the pre-production period?*

SCOTT:    The sets were difficult, because I wanted to create an oppressive, claustrophobic atmosphere of low ceilings. There was much argument and chat about how high the ship's ceilings should be. It's a bit difficult when you've got a producer who's six-foot-four and I'm five-foot-nine! So I'm insisting these ceilings are a perfectly normal height, and Gordon Carroll is standing there with his head pressed against the roof saying, "This is ludicrous! Yaphet is going to knock his brains out!" I argued that it would be good if Yaphet always had to duck, so that became one argument. I think the sense of claustrophobia worked out very well.

FF:    *Did that feeling of cramped-ness come out of a reaction to the Kubrick centrifuge in 2001?*

SCOTT:    I got a sense of very confined space from the wheel. That set was a masterpiece. I was desperately trying to think of something that would be as logical as the wheel. It was practical within the fact of men in space for a long time. There are two awake, and the rest are sleeping. I would think it's very NASA.

FF:    *There was also a definite feeling of claustrophobia in* Dark Star.
SCOTT:    I was really influenced by three films. Not so much in terms of sets from *Star Wars,* but definitely from *2001* and *Dark Star.* There was a great sense of reality, oddly enough, in *Dark Star,* especially of seedy living. It showed you can get grotty even in the Hilton Hotel if you don't clean it. Everything starts to get tacky, even in the most streamlined circumstances.

FF:    *In manufacturing props for* Alien *did you see what was available on the market or manufacture everything from scratch?*
SCOTT:    I'd love to have made everything from scratch like Kubrick did. He really designed everything for his ship. But we weren't doing that type of film. We would have needed double our budget. A lot of the logic of our designs came out of our very, very good art directors, Roger Christian and Les Dilley.

FF:    *What were their separate and collective contributions?*
SCOTT:    Roger is a brilliant set dresser. Though his department was not designing the corridors and sets, their "cladding" of the walls made everything look absolutely real. He would go out with his buyers and prop men and visit aircraft dumps or army surplus stores and drag masses of things in for me to see. They gradually concocted the look of the sets by combining various elements that looked as if they belonged together.

FF:    *Where did the concept of making the maintenance area into a "temple" come from?*
SCOTT:    As I was working with the art director, I decided to make it faintly glittery. I wanted to have sort of anodized gold everywhere. Not steel, gold. Did you know that space landing craft are covered with gold foil? Amazing! So I thought, "Why make this out of steel? Let's make it all warm and oppressive, massive, and gold."
    We got hold of marvelous, actual parts of actual huge jet engines and installed them, and they're like a coppery metal with some steel.

We used them as four main supports, like columns, and they give a lot of the feeling of a temple. We played the same music we used in the derelict alien craft and we had *two* temples. The idol I wanted was through these massive gold doors which were as big as a wall, with a gap in them through which the claw can be seen. When that set was dressed, it looked like Aladdin's cave.

The visual idea I had in mind was to fill this entire room with the "claw" so that it almost touches the walls and floor but is still apparently hanging free in the air. Just outside the claw room is a huge maintenance area, a garage, filled with the equipment that the crew would use in their work on and around the refinery, and when they land on various planets—land crawlers, helicopters, other flying machines.

FF:     *Like the "flying bedstead"?*
SCOTT:     Right. The one we were going to use in the sequence where they go outside to make repairs on the ship.

FF:     *You say you wanted everything to look real. And now, in 1979, it does. But even 2001 has dated, and it was futuristic state-of-the-art in 1968. Two decades from now you won't want people to think this is just another old movie. How did you approach this problem? How did you protect yourself from dating in areas like hairstyle, makeup and costume?*
SCOTT:     We held discussions on those topics, and tried to make everything fit in with the rest of the film. We went with the way most of them looked, but I wanted extreme crewcuts on a couple of them, so we went that way with Lambert and Ash.

I was very impressed with Lucas's *THX-1138* and the way he handled the future. The film was a bit slow, but the way it was conceived it was a very nice idea of the way to do *1984*. It was really good, but should have been opened up more. But I bought it. I was certainly influenced by it to a certain extent, because it was abstract. No, it wasn't abstract. It was nothing. It's very difficult to do nothing, you know. Kubrick managed to do nothing in *2001* with the spacesuits.

FF:     *By "nothing" do you mean a timeless future?*
SCOTT:     Yes. In two hundred years things won't change that much, you know. People will still be scruffy or clean. They'll still clean their

teeth three times a day. Kubrick was fantastic in the way he gave us that nothingness, especially with the costumes. He didn't have zippers all over the place, or satin fourteen-tone jerkins and all that crap. The suits they wore looked vaguely different, but not all that different from today. The last time I saw the film I was watching for those details. It's futuristic, whatever that means, but it's still hung on today's reality.

FF:    *How did you approach the costume design on* Alien?
SCOTT:    I wanted a more Eastern look, because I felt that the world would have been divided into three parts by the time the film takes place.

FF:    *Are there other indications of that in the film?*
SCOTT:    The owners of the Nostromo are Japanese. Look at their crew uniforms, and all the other things with the ship's name on it.

FF:    *The Japanese armor "look" of the spacesuits had come out of your work on* Tristan and Iseult. *Was there any sort of tie-in to the reality of the film intended?*
SCOTT:    John Mollo, who did *Barry Lyndon* and *Star Wars,* took all the Moebius costume sketches and adapted them to film. While the Moebius work was very good, it really wasn't cinematic, and Mollo was able to make it work on screen. Mollo took them to a model maker and an engineer who made them up. They worked very closely together on that. He also designed some lovely badges which the crew wore on their uniforms. He had them made up properly by a man who makes Army badges.

FF:    *Did the idea of the badges come out of* Silent Running?
SCOTT:    Yes. I quite liked that idea. When you're working for a large company everything is very sterile, very impersonal, so people find ways of making their surroundings a bit more their own.

FF:    *A great deal of the original effects footage was junked when you fin-ished shooting the live action. As a result you ended up reshooting the bulk of the effects shots yourself. Why?*
SCOTT:    It was a difficult situation. Brian Johnson was over there, working out of context away from the main unit. I could only look at

the rushes while I was working with the actors, and that's not a very satisfactory way of working. In the end, I think a director must be heavily involved with the miniatures, and that's why I shot them myself.

FF:    *Did you find the original footage wasn't real enough?*
SCOTT:    Partly, yes. It was a difficult thing to do since I wasn't there. I wanted a slightly grainy look, getting away from the hard-edged, crystal-clear look of *Star Wars*. The concept was to have the hull of the Nostromo covered with space barnacles or something. I was unable to communicate that idea, and I finally had to go down there and fiddle with the experts. We gradually arrived at a solution.

I was looking for something like *2001*, not the fantasy of *Star Wars*. I wanted a slow moving, massive piece of steel which was moving along in dead, deep silence. We had to end up adding sound, because the footage couldn't stand on its own. It's obvious. Everybody knows that sound is wrong in space, but we had little choice with the result we got.

FF:    *Sound in space seems to have become a standard element in contemporary science fiction films, even though it's wrong.*
SCOTT:    Everyone does it, right, but that doesn't mean I should have. I love Kubrick for actually having had the courage to hold on dead silence. If I had done it in *Alien* it would have become tedious; so the sound element was added to integrate the model shots with what's going on inside the Nostromo.

FF:    *What are your criteria for credibility in the design of alien spacecraft?*
SCOTT:    I have come to accept a wide variety of possibilities. And strangely enough, the more mundane something is, the more it can sometimes stagger people. Simplicity can be more powerful than you think. Take a UFO, for example. How do you design it so people believe it? One of the best UFO shots I've seen is the one from the thirties with the portholes. It looks like an inverted plate with a sort of cap on it.

And oddly enough, it's fairly archaic. And in a funny sort of way that appeals to me as a solution, rather than an incredibly refined, sleek spacecraft. I like the idea of a spaceship where you've got no idea what kind of energy drives it, and you've never seen anything quite like it before.

FF:    *Like Giger's instead of the Bob Foss conceptions?*
SCOTT:    Foss's ideas were interesting, but they all tended to look alike. Giger's craft was *definitely* not of this world.

FF:    *Nick Allder, one of your special effects directors, said something interesting. At one point you looked at the Nostromo model when it was being built and said it should be bigger. He just changed three bubbles on it and that made it look twice its previous size because of the change in scale.*
SCOTT:    Sometimes that's all you need to do. The camera does the rest.

FF:    *Did you have any qualms about doing a film with so many special effects? The chances of duplicating what someone else was doing must have been quite high.*
SCOTT:    We were very worried about doing our special effects, because there was such a big rush on them after *Star Wars*. So I went around to the *Battlestar Galactica* effects shop and looked at the setup before I set out to work on *Alien*. I was very impressed by the models, and everything I saw seemed to be set up quite simply. John Dykstra couldn't do *Alien*, mostly because he was so deeply involved in *Galactica*.

FF:    *The model work on* Alien *was not approached in the same way?*
SCOTT:    There's really no comparison. I'd have to say that what we've been doing here has been under very primitive circumstances, with very definite limitations on the model shots.

FF:    *But* Alien *is not a model-oriented film. They only play a part in the action.*
SCOTT:    But even so, we wanted to get the *reality* right. Otherwise no one's going to believe it's happening. We needed good model work to launch people into the reality of the Nostromo in space.

FF:    Alien *is fairly straightforward speculative science fiction. Things about the ship look real, not fanciful, as in* Star Wars.
SCOTT:    I'd wanted to go more fantastic, push the story farther into the future, but the limits had been set. We're beyond *2001* in terms of scientific advances. Our capabilities are more sophisticated. But our ship's still NASA-oriented, still Earth-manufactured.

FF:    *How did you go about casting?*

SCOTT:    I knew I wasn't going to get much from having actors come in and read, because *Alien* isn't the type of film where there were going to be prolonged speeches. Here the dialogue was so abbreviated and stacatto that it wouldn't be fair. So I researched the actors who were being considered by seeing their films. Once we had narrowed the list down, I had the actors come in for a meeting. I tend to cast my actors as a group, getting a physical balance between their types. The physical attributes are almost as important as their acting capabilities.

FF:    *Was there any feeling against having women in space?*

SCOTT:    There were a few challenges, sure. "If you have women up there, how come there's no love interest?" It's a pity that the one scene we did have in the screenplay that had sex in it had to be cut. It showed that you can't afford to have love affairs in deep space. If you do, you immediately have two groups aboard. The pair who are in love and the rest of the crew. That's the beginning of problems unless you are a space pioneer and settle down with your family.

FF:    *One draft of the script actually had two love scenes in it. Ripley makes it with two guys.*

SCOTT:    I liked that, and I think Sigourney Weaver liked the idea too. But the scenes came after Kane's death, and the sort of flippancy that they had just didn't fit in with the mood at that point.

FF:    *Had you ever debated using actors from other cultures?*

SCOTT:    Japan?

FF:    *Japan or Mars.*

SCOTT:    I would have loved it, but that's not what the story was about. I would have loved to take the opportunity to explore the realms of speculative fiction more, but it would have been a digression from the film we were making.

FF:    *What ideas did you consider?*

SCOTT:    Well, we could have had a Martian in the crew. He's not much different, perhaps just slightly waxy skin and two small holes in his head. Biological changes rather than mechanical ones. I was, to a certain extent, held down by my producers. They didn't know me from Adam, so they tried to keep things in balance. Alone I would have done more.

FF:    *I guess that also, by keeping the cast all human, the robot will come as a complete surprise. If you had a Martian they might have guessed something else was afoot.*
SCOTT:    Sure. That was another problem. If you have a Martian in there, the audience is going to be staring at him. Not only that, we could then have been directly compared to *Star Wars* or *Star Trek*.

FF:    *In working with the actors did you urge them to go beyond the script in creating their characters?*
SCOTT:    What I usually do, even if it's only for my own peace of mind, is draft a short bio of each character and give it to the actors before I go to work with them. I quietly sat down just for myself and wrote out seven bios. And it's funny. It's amazing. Suddenly you're writing a two page bio from birth through death. It starts to take on solidarity, three dimensions.

If you talk to an actor like this in the early days, it usually surprises the hell out of them. They start to argue about certain aspects of it, so you have contact. Any form of direction is a team effort. It's not, "You do that." "Yes, that wasn't quite right, do it this way."

That's crap. You have to do something to get a relationship with the actors so you can talk to them as friends rather than as employees. You want to get to the point where you *both* have this problem, which is the scene. And how are you *both* going to do this scene?

FF:    *What did you give to Ian Holm for Ash?*
SCOTT:    For Ash I created a ficticious background.

FF:    *Did he know he was a robot?*
SCOTT:    That was a consideration I had to deal with. There are a number of ways of approaching it, but the possibilities come down to either letting him know or programming him so he thinks he's human. All the space in between was open, but we went with letting him know. If we

had decided to keep it from him, there were all kinds of things we could have done, from programming him to know at a certain point, like an emergency, or even putting a complete memory tape in him that would give him a complete background—parents, schooling, brothers, the whole thing.

FF:    *What did Ash know about his "past"?*
SCOTT:    I told him which university he attended, what he read in, where he was born and so forth. I tried to keep off the years, because I didn't quite know what year *Alien* was set in. Maybe it was about 2075, when we'd have space colonies, but it was never pinned down. We should have colonies by then, and it'll escalate from there.

FF:    *But Ash definitely knows he's a robot.*
SCOTT:    He does in this instance.

FF:    *Did Ian Holm go along with your suggestions?*
SCOTT:    They all did, actually. I think they were slightly surprised. I found myself arguing about very abstract ideas a few times and had to point out, "I've written the bios for me, not you. It has no bearing on the plot, but I just figured this is where you came from. So let's forget it, all right?"
    But the bios did help, because they immediately started the actors thinking about their characters. In this instance I *had* to do them. In most scripts the main characters usually have an in-depth character-ization, background. In a normal story there's usually a reference to a father, a mother or something that's entwined in the plot. In *Alien* you have seven people about whom you know nothing. And therefore you have to create their attitudes.

FF:    *What was your rehearsal period like?*
SCOTT:    We had about five days of continuous discussion in my office with the seven actors of the original cast, which at that time included John Finch instead of John Hurt. In that time we pretty well managed to iron out and agree on the various characterizations, and managed to get some satisfactory reads out of the script.

FF:    *You went straight through the screenplay?*
SCOTT:    Yes, without stage directions, of course. Everyone's in their role, and you make whatever little changes are necessary, seeing if jokes work or not and so forth. Of course at that stage *anything* will pretty well work on paper. You can make it work. What you can't imagine is what effect a scene will have on the film.

FF:    *What was the intention of the chest-burster?*
SCOTT:    We wanted to do something so outrageous that no one would know it was coming. It's not a door being wrenched open with the monster behind it, or the monster coming roaring through some metal sheeting or grabbing somebody from behind. This is just the last thing you expect to happen. He could turn into green cheese and you'd be less surprised.

We had to make a living creature spring out of a man's chest and keep it from being hokey. Well, we did it, and that's why it's so staggering. From a technical point of view I think we were more worried about it than any other effect in the film. If we hadn't gotten it right, we might just as well have forgotten the whole thing.

FF:    *How did you approach the chest-burster sequence?*
SCOTT:    Well, Roger Dicken designed it, Nicky Allder and his crew made it work, and the actors made the audience believe it was real. We wanted it to hit the audience like a wave, to overwhelm them but still not be so strong that it would turn them off.

FF:    *In planning the shooting of the scene, did you manage to avoid telling the actors what was in store for them?*
SCOTT:    I never showed them. They'd read the script, but didn't know what it was going to look like.

FF:    *Was John Hurt included in your plan?*
SCOTT:    Of course. But it's a nasty thing for an actor to have to do. I was faintly embarrassed about going into great detail about it with him beforehand. It just erupts, so it was better not to tell anyone too much. I wanted to get the moment to work for the actors, to get their actual reactions when they saw it for the first time.

FF:   *What the audience sees in the wide shot is what really happened? It's honest shock, not just acting?*
SCOTT:   Those six actors all happened to be sensitive individuals. I think I am quite hardened to all that blood and gore. It doesn't bother me much. But that particular group were all a little bit queasy and therefore did react very naturally to what they saw.

FF:   *I've heard that Veronica Cartwright was knocked over by a blast of stage blood.*
SCOTT:   She was flung backwards over her seat, but we didn't keep that in the film. A bit too much for the women in the audience, I think.

FF:   *What was the initial shooting period like before the chest-burster?*
SCOTT:   A lot lighter than the period after it. It was so strong that the film suddenly took on a different weight. The chest-burster was an outrageous effect and by no means amusing. The reality it gave to the creature sort of stuns an audience rather than leaving them gasping and horror-struck.

You can feel a wave of repulsion when an audience sees it. And the weird thing is that they go silent. There's the odd scream, but it's more of a stunner. An eye-popper. You think, "What!?!" And then, when it's gone, the tension goes, and somebody laughs hysterically and somebody else says, "Wow!"

Well something similar happened to the actors after we shot the scene. The film took on a more serious identity. Suddenly there were certain jokes that couldn't be cracked any longer.

FF:   *Have you ever regretted not shooting the chest-burster sooner in the production?*
SCOTT:   In a way we should have done the chest-burster first. If we had done it, it would have made the actors see what the film was about.

FF:   *After that scene, did the cast take more of an interest in the effects?*
SCOTT:   They suddenly realized how important the effects were, how real they were. I remember two or three of the actors drifted in and sat watching Brett's death in what I call the claw room, the compartment that holds one of the Nostromo's landing legs like the chain locker in a ship.

FF:    *You've said that you wanted to individualize each of the crew member's deaths. Did they all want to go in a spectacular way?*
SCOTT:    Each one knew what his death was going to be like when he read the script, but yes, they each wanted to make their death scene work very well.

FF:    *Would you comment on the deaths of Kane and Brett?*
SCOTT:    Well, Kane was the worst, as far as the conditions under which the actor had to work was concerned. I always slightly feel for the actors when they're asked to do something particularly horrendous. John Hurt was an incredible sport about the whole thing, because it was a very nasty thing. I was very impressed with the way he dealt with it—not just giving the performance but having to do it over and over again.

FF:    *Brett was the next to go. . . .*
SCOTT:    That was a different case entirely. It's always difficult for an actor to relate to what is, essentially, a beast. They know what it is, and they know there's a man inside the suit, and they know the odds are they'll never have to experience anything like it in their real lives. So I had to try to inflict on Harry Dean Stanton a feeling he probably couldn't even imagine having.

In most instances like this, I think you'd probably die before the thing touched you anyway. I mean, you'd have a heart attack, right? You'd turn and see it and last about four seconds before you had a coronary, okay? So with Brett's death, and subsequent run-ins with the alien, it was always done to the ultimate feeling of a heart attack. The rush of a heart attack, even if the thing didn't ever touch them.

The thing I was always frustrated about was the absence of sense of smell with the beast. It's a real element with him, because his odor must have been incredibly powerful. I wanted a sense of a timeless, slightly decaying creature that, maybe, only has a limited life cycle of, maybe, four days like an insect. The alien life form lived to reproduce, and in reproducing took on the characteristics of its last inhabitant and its new host.

Thus the alien on board the Nostromo had the characteristics of the space jockey on the derelict and Kane. If the face hugger had hit the cat, it would have been a hybrid of the space jockey and the cat. When Ripley blasts off from the Nostromo with the alien aboard, it's dying, which is why it moves so slowly. She kills it, but it would have died soon anyway. It's like a butterfly.

FF:  *A great deal of curiousity builds in the beginning of the scene where Ripley confronts Ash in the infirmary. What was the reason for shooting that in one long take?*
SCOTT:  It's really for pace, for effect. It seemed to be a nice introduction to the scene in that it's a small red herring.

You come off Kane's body lying on the slab and start moving around the room and therefore, for that moment, you're working on people's unease until you find out there's a man sitting in the corner over there. For the moments it takes to get across the room you are uneasy. In some form or another I look for that in every scene, even quiet ones. I like to keep the buzz going.

FF:  *In one of the ealier scripts Ripley "kills" the onboard computer by a method similar to HAL's disconnection in 2001. Why was it dropped? Too close?*
SCOTT:  The killing of HAL was a marvelous sequence. And although our unused scene was very clever and funny, it turned out to be a bit too arch. Too humorous. I think it would have played well, but we cut it in a subsequent draft.

FF:  *The original ending was different. Can you explain it for us?*
SCOTT:  The alien was going to be blown out the door of the Narcissus, with Ripley trailing after it. It was an outrageous ending, but I thought it was wonderful. I thought it had to happen, but only if it could be so believably done that it would be real. It had to become so open-mouth outrageous that it would make you want to cheer or clap.

FF:  *In every good movie there is a dramatic turning point around which the film revolves. Did you regard the chest-burster sequence as this sort of heart-stopping moment when the film really starts?*
SCOTT:  It wasn't designed that way, but it seems to have worked out like that. The original concept was constructed 'round the notion of *Ten Little Indians.* In the planning and writing stages there were to be

seven major sequences, one of which was the chest-burster. As the script was re-worked, and as we shot the film, however, other sequences that were equally powerful, such as the air-lock depressurization, the flame-thrower death of Parker and Lambert, and the cocoon scene with Dallas were cut altogether or changed.

FF:    *Jim Shields was your sound editor on* Alien. *How long did he work on it?*
SCOTT:    Jim's been working on this for a year. I didn't want any sounds that were familiar, even the sound of a door opening or closing, so he gathered peculiar sounds that somehow matched the action but weren't what you'd expect to hear.

FF:    *One of the most interesting sounds is the opening and closing of the iris-type cutoffs in the airshaft sequence. They sounded like a sword being drawn from a scabbard.*
SCOTT:    The idea there was to make you uneasy. We tried to use something that reminded you of a guillotine, something that wasn't pleasant so maybe you'd start thinking, "Is the beast coming this way?"

FF:    *Do you feel that superior sound can help promote a film?*
SCOTT:    Absolutely. We found that the sound was sometimes overpowering for 2 percent of the *Alien* audience when it appeared around them, that they objected to it as overkill, but that it worked very well for the rest of the people who came to see it.
     For me sound is a critical factor, at least 50 percent of any movie I make. Sometimes more, but never much less.

FF:    *That will come as a surprise to a lot of people. You're generally regarded as a visual director.*
SCOTT:    Oh, no. I'm very attached to sound . . . very much. I get involved with sound as I do with lights and photography. Once I get into the editing room, I want to be armed with the maximum sort of "sound palate" possible. I want to be able to experiment when I go into the dubbing stage.

FF:    *How much do you think the film changed from the time it went into the first screening eight days after you were finished to where it is now?*

SCOTT:     I reckon probably 15 percent maximum. I think we were
pretty well right through. There were constant arguments: "You
don't need this." "You don't need this ending." "You don't need this
cat here." All that sort of thing. Always quite a lot of conflict about
whether one is finished with those particular scenes or not, but I
usually managed to somehow get it.

     With *Alien,* we had big arguments over the last three reels of the film.
Some people felt they were just too much. I knew it's *never* too much,
not when you get a proper balance. You've got to keep topping yourself. So if you start at a level that's already pretty heated, you've got to
keep going and keep going. That is the nature of this film.

     I was always slightly concerned about overkill. But I desperately
wanted this outrageous ending, you know. Not a ludicrous ending but
an *outrageous* ending. And I knew that it was very important to hold
that in after everything else had happened.

     In a way it's a bit like a release as well. Shooting him in the chest and
letting him fly away is not enough. But this is one of the big lessons
I've learned: you must stick to your own mental ground. If you're sure
about something, you've got to stick with it. It's very easy to get talked
out of things.

FF:     *When the film was finished, it was decided to screen it for heartland
American audiences to see what the average viewer's reactions would be.
Alien was first shown in St. Louis. Was that city picked because it was
typical middle America?*
SCOTT:     Yes. I liked the idea of doing it that way, because there they
are—there are the people you've made the film for.

FF:     *But didn't you screen it in England before it was shown in America?*
SCOTT:     Yes. We had a screening at Pinewood with an invited audience
of about thirty American families from an air force base and about forty
other people from the industry. Directors like Richard Donner, who was
doing *Superman;* staff drivers; Gary Kurtz, the producer of *The Empire
Strikes Back.* That screening was really valuable, because when you're
doing a film reel-by-reel, you never know how the pace is. I'd seen it
something like five or six times before in various cuts but was always
curious to get the final music and the final dubbing on.

FF:    *What did you learn from the Pinewood screening?*
SCOTT:    That it was too slow, yet it was totally absorbing. Perhaps too absorbing. We removed eleven minutes after it, and I still wonder whether we should have cut quite that much.

FF:    *Has there been any major difference between English and American audiences?*
SCOTT:    Well I think what's different about American audiences is that they've started to enjoy cinema again. I think it's something to do with the fact that these are children who grew up with TV, and therefore it doesn't mean a bloody thing anymore. TV is what radio was. And so they've got that out of their systems.

Before *Star Wars* I hadn't experienced audience participation in a film since I was a kid. I used to sit there with a bag of popcorn and sing with the rest of the kids. And everybody used to shout, "Look out behind you!" and all that. Then I saw *Star Wars* and it was amazing! I was knocked out. I thought, "God, this guy Lucas really knows what he's doing!" *Star Wars* changed my whole attitude about certain types of cinema that I'm interested in.

Finally, in Dallas, we started to get a bit of this, because it was obviously a young audience. There was a huge line outside. And Fox actually discussed opening the doors at twelve o'clock again so we could have a second performance, there were that many people there. Anyway, they quite rightly decided not to do that.

Well, the audience went in, and they were rustling and moving, which made me upset on *The Duellists,* but on this it didn't upset me any more. People get up and go in and out, in and out, in and out, throughout the entire bloody film.

They get their popcorn, their Coca-Cola, you know. And the great thing is they're real film freaks, because they know when to get up and go out as well! They know, "Okay, that's over, I'm going to have about a minute and a half to get that Coke." They scuttle out and come back and sit down again. And they get in just as the thing's starting up again. I've never seen anything like it. I eventually stood at the back, 'cause I couldn't bear to sit down any longer. I kept having to walk 'round the block, take a drink, then come back, and ask, "Where are we now?"

Well, right along the back of the auditorium there were high backs to the seats and a set of curtains. When I came back about half an hour before the end, I saw fifty people standing behind the curtains, peering through at the screen. They were standing in little bunches, in line with the gaps in the curtains! Some people were coming out and going, "Oh, Jesus," and then standing at the back and listening. They'd eventually move forward and lift the bloody curtain, watching from underneath it!

I couldn't believe it! The manager said, "The women's bathroom is like a battleground. There are forty women in there. There's vomit everywhere, and one of the women is stuffing a towel into the speakers to try and shut out the sound that was being pumped in there."

FF:    *What did you do?*

SCOTT:    I removed my jacket. I had on a dark blue jacket and a white shirt, and I thought I looked like an executive.

I left this bunch, and I walked out to the foyer again. You know, umpteenth bag of bloody popcorn—standing in the foyer munching away. And hearing the sound from the inside. And I started to go back in again, and there was this incredible crash! An usher came through the door head first and collapsed. He collapsed!

Just at that moment I had been talking to a Fox executive and he had said, "You know, I'm getting a bit worried, I think we're over-doing things. This is too strong." And I had said, "Nonsense. We're all right. We're in good shape." And then there was this huge thud, and the usher came face first through the doors and landed face down on the tiles! The manager rushed in and said, "Christ, this is too much, man!" They carried the usher outside and gave him fresh air and patted his face.

I went out and said, "You must have eaten something. Do you feel all right?" And he said, "No, no, I'm all right. That scene, you know, with the robot. He got his head knocked off." He'd seen the head knocked off and had passed out!

FF:    *Did the Fox executives react strongly at the next "board meeting"?*

SCOTT:    There was a slight panic followed by a prolonged discussion. The biggest reaction was to the fainting, and the restless movement of the audience. It was fear restlessness, and I think they were worried that we'd gone too strong.

We actually held position at that moment and said, "No. We don't think so. We think audiences hype themselves up, which is wonderful, terrific. That energy will carry itself forward to the next screening, so people will go in slightly more up." We convinced them to wait for the audience reactions.

FF:    *Was the reaction positive?*
SCOTT:    Very good, Very, very good.

FF:    *Did you make any cuts after that?*
SCOTT:    Nips. Nips. There was a big discussion at one stage to cut down the chest-burster scene, but I really held position. Can't touch that, because there's a rhythm to it, and cuts would upset that rhythm.

For instance, there's a heart beat throughout. Now, heartbeats are very corny things to use really, but I don't think one is ever aware of it during the whole film, right? But the sound of the engines is a synthesized heart beat rhythm. You're never aware of it, but it starts to work on you. One doesn't cross the line of corn. One stays on the side of the mechanics. But you think you're hearing something else.

FF:    *What else did you do that works subliminally?*
SCOTT:    My approach to the camerawork. If you ever analyze a shot, everything is always slightly on the move. I did that wherever I could. Even for a still setting, I tried to hand-hold it so that it would always be slightly moving. It's never still, which I think makes the audience slightly uneasy. The camera sort of just breathes, so you're always slightly aware of a presence. If that is the effect, it's part of my contribution.

FF:    *Do you think the ending that's on the film now will work for audiences?*
SCOTT:    Yes. Oh yes. I think there's a certain resolution, a relief I wanted to get in there for the audience. I wasn't doing an underground movie. If I was, Ripley would have gotten it. *Bang!* You would have thought she was going to get away, then *Wallop!* It gets her. Would've been marvelous.

FF:    *In shooting the end sequence aboard the Narcissus, were you allowed the time you needed to put it together?*

SCOTT:    Everything was done in a rush at that stage. When the alien is shot out the back door, we were allotted a day and a half's shooting. What's seen on screen is the test. We used the test. *That is madness.* I'd take four days to do the same thing properly in a television commercial! Madness!

If I'd gotten it totally wrong we'd have re-done it, but they said it was *good enough.* That was heard a lot on this film. "Don't go any further. That's good enough. Nobody's going to notice it." Well, *I* notice it.

FF:    *Because of all the changes made throughout the actual shooting, does it seem that you started out to make a different film from the one you eventually ended up with?*

SCOTT:    Yes, but what I missed most of all was the absence of a prognosis scene. There were no speculative scenes or discussions about what the alien was and all that sort of thing either. I believe that audiences love those, especially if they're well done. They give the threat much more weight.

If they make *Alien II,* and if I have anything to do with it, the film will certainly have all those elements in it. From a certain point of view, *Alien II* could be far more interesting than *Alien I.*

In fact, I'd like to do smaller science fiction features. Maybe a two-hour movie about a man in an outpost by himself on Neptune. His only companies are a dog and his digging machine. *That* could be a very low budget subject. Just shoot it in some incredibly marvelous environment in Alaska. Writers should consider subjects that are less elaborate. That Neptune idea for instance. You spend all your money on a land crawler that this man has to live in. The rest is just landscape.

FF:    *Does that mean you're still looking for a science fiction project?*

SCOTT:    I'm looking for another science fiction script right now. Something that has a little bit of speculation or prediction about it, rather than just a thriller. Purely, as an art director, I find the whole area of hardware and environment fascinating. One day I'll do a film just about people, hardware and environment. Actually, that's what science fiction is all about, isn't it?

# ...tury Nervous Breakdown

N KENNEDY / 1982

Do Androids dream of electric sheep?

Do Northumbrians dream of eclectic myths?

Every so often the British cinema hatches a mold-busting filmmaker, and the world stops, looks, and listens, aware that an accident has happened in the process of Nature.

Ridley Scott, Northumberland-born and forty-one, has made three feature films in six years: a measured pace à la that other British-based painstaker, Stanley Kubrick. There is brain-stretching contrast between Scott's Napoleonic France in *The Duellists* and his futuristic Space in *Alien*; now the future calls again in *Blade Runner*, but it's an earthlier, punkier clime.

Yet a closer gaze at Scott's work urges instant re-routing of thought. Scott was a scion of British TV advertising, honing his craft in the make-or-break thirty seconds of eulogies to sliced bread or tributes to chocolate bars. With his brother Tony (soon to make his own feature-film debut directing *The Hunger*), he founded Ridley Scott Associates and carved for the company a healthy slice of the commercials market in Britain. The shot-by-shot high polish and perfectionism that TV ads teach (at least in Britain, where they are a whole cine-subculture) impart a visual thrift and thrust learned on no other movie training ground.

Where Kubrick is an explorer and unraveler of special worlds—an accreter of mysticisms and resonances—Scott is a refiner, an intensifier, a compacter, and catalyzer of them. *Blade Runner* shares the same

From *Film Comment*, July/August 1982, pp. 64–68. Reprinted by permission of the author.

implosive, closed-world obsessiveness as *The Duellists* and *Alien*. All three films unfurl in fictive limbo-lands that have their special rules, parameters, and exoticisms.

Philip K. Dick's 1968 sci-fi novel *Do Androids Dream of Electric Sheep?*, on which *Blade Runner* is based, confronts us with a Future America where everyone who is anyone has left for Off-world (the planets), and the seething human detritus left behind copes with an increasingly inchoate globe. The streets are stalked by alien worker-robots, who've escaped to Earth from being *gastarbeiters* on other planets and must now be destroyed. The destroyers are bounty hunters like Rick Deckard (Harrison Ford); they pick up fat pay-checks for retiring "replicants" (androids) and look forward to a happy, less finite retirement themselves. But how does one tell a human from an android?

Los Angeles in 2020 is a maze of urban murk. Neon signs and neon-stemmed umbrellas ribbon the eternal night of steam, narrow-street grime, and growling garbage trucks. Above eye level, a pair of sparkling, pyramidal skyscrapers punch up their totemic tribute to Progress, threaded by the firefly traffic of airborne hovercars. Higher still, a floating blimp with loudspeakers and giant TV screen taunts: "Come to Off-world."

The movie's human-versus-humanoid chess game is instantly over-turned in a tingling confrontation that is the whole movie in blueprint miniature. A plump and sweaty greaseball chats across a desk to a sleek robotic suit-and-tie type. The suit-and-tie gives the greaseball the "Voigt-Kampff replicant-detection test." In mid-catechism the "rep" scents danger: "My mother, I'll tell you about my mother!" he ejaculates—and perforates his startled, sartorial, and human interrogator with two blasts from a laser gun. Pʜᴛᴛ! Pʜᴛᴛ! *Sic transit* Voight-Kampff.

The texture of the movie, as with all Scott's work, is a densely figured kinetic tapestry. There are antiphonal layers of color and shading. The burnished gold skyscrapers glint above the Stygian forlornness of the streets. Bulging Egyptian-style pillars stand amid the grime of sidewalks. The background is filled with throwaways of oddball action: an origami-obsessed policeman doodle-twists paper into animal shapes in the corner of a cop-headquarters scene, as Deckard receives his assignment. There are tangy mixtures of race, color, and lingo out in the streets, as Hispanics, Orientals, and WASPs jostle in an eternal *film noir* nighttown.

As in *The Road Warrior*, we're in a world welded from the waste-materials of past epochs: Scrap-Heap Futurism. But most of George Miller's film took place at bleached-bone high noon; Scott's is the midnight version: rain, steam, ethnic chaos. Bluish-smoky exteriors, whose miasma creeps into offices and corridors. Oriental street signs that spike and bewilder the Western eye. And in the *noir* landscape and the 2020 *omnium gatherum* of times and cultures, it's ever more difficult to peer through and discern the differences between humanoid and *homo sapiens*.

Gone are the B-pic days of sci-fi, when stony stares and speak-your-weight voices made pod-spotting something your aunt could do—when a valve on the back of the neck, or stray wires sticking out of an ear were dead give-aways. In *Blade Runner*, visual puns and mirror images suggest a *trompe-l'oeil* assault course through how-do-you-tell variations on human life. A gold glint in the eye is the only—and only occasional—hint of man-made humanity.

Take replicant-factory worker J. F. Sebastian (William J. Sanderson)—R. R. Isidore in the book, "chickenhead," a van-driver for an animal-repair firm. Sebastian lives in the "Bradbury," a giant moldering tenement awash with dolls, dummies, bits of dummies, and a-patter with articulated hand-crafted midget-humans who open the door to say "Hello" and then bump into walls.

With fitting and final irony, Sebastian's pad becomes the thronging-ground for the star replicants themselves: Deckard's bounty quarries Roy Batty (Rutger Hauer) and Pris (Daryl Hannah). Roy spouts battle poems, spews out rueful philosophy, and emits megahertz howls before charging at you. Pris comes at you with cartwheels and locks up your neck with her thighs.

The story's trajectory toward these Nietzschean spawns of man's own ingenuity—through a Dantesque Toytown where seething plurality aids sudden ambush—is the movie's main forward thrust. Its startling, tragic resolution is the death-rattle coda of companionship between Deckard and Batty. The replicant's hour comes—his man-made machismo seeping away—as he sits samurai-style, head bowed, through the night, waiting for death. At first the villain of the piece, he suddenly becomes its mythic, empathic center. Batty turns Frankenstein's monster to Biblical Adam; Deckard veers from hunter to homomorph. In a *film noir* future, an android Philip Marlowe puzzles over his own humanity, his own place between the animals and angels, men and machines.

It's no surprise that Scott's eclectic eye has since sought out a sci-fi project, *Dune*, and a film based on the Tristan and Isolde legend—worlds at once remote and masonic. And lurking within the esoterica of periods and settings in Scott's films, like a Minotaur in the maze, are apocalyptic appetites. Scott is interested in the point at which manners and mechanics yield to monomania in a society or a community.

In *Alien*, the space-capsule hypersleep in which the astronauts are first discovered is a movie metaphor for social-emotional auto-pilot. When they awake, it's to the ravenings of new emotions, new rules, penalties, and booby-traps in the game of survival. In *The Duellists*, the kid-glove protocol of the Age of Reason is seen to be mere social choreography camouflaging an inner dance of demonism; the demons dance out in Harvey Keitel's glittering aggression and in swordfights that are more like the collision of medieval broad-swords than the elegant knitting of Napoleonic rapiers. In Scott's new film, the streamlined conquests of the Space Age have left behind a litter-bin world ripe for anarchy and civil strife.

Myth and mist are time-honored bed-fellows, and Scott's flair for creating depth and dimension with smoke—it turns his sets into a round-the-clock incense bath—is synesthetic with his love for sequestered worlds where threatening urgencies stir through the opacity of time.

Scott is also one of the few movie-makers who meticulously storyboard their films. He was trained at art school and suckled on comic strips. *Alien* owes its slackless narrative to an action blue-print as purposive and pre-planned as Hitchcock's. Similarly, Scott's movies can't be re-cut by volatile producers or wildcat editors, using the usual spare parts of master-shots and close-ups.

In *Blade Runner*, the comic-strip concision is warped and sauced in Scott's supple gleam and swirling blends of tone and color. Blade-edge cutting meets sooty *film noir* fantasy and sci-fi fundamentalism in year 2020. Adjust your lenses for perfect vision.

HK:    *Where did the title* Blade Runner *come from? It's used to describe the bounty-hunter hero and his trade, but I notice it doesn't figure in the original novel by Philip K. Dick.*

RS:   I wanted a title for a hired killer or whatever a hunter is called when cast in that particular mold. And this man, Rick Deckard, is an efficient exterminator engaged in what is essentially bounty-hunting. He's paid to nail someone—some person, some thing—and it's legalized. What do we call him? Well, in about the fifth draft of the script, the phrase "blade runner" popped up. I thought, Christ, that's terrific! Well, the writer looked guilty and said, "As a matter of fact, it's not my phrase. I took it from a William Burroughs book." And the book, oddly enough, is called *Blade Runner: The Film*. So we got permission from Mr. Burroughs to use the name, and bought the title, and it just stuck, because it was fun.

We changed the character a bit from Dick's novel. In the book he's a bit of a renegade, a freelance, with a bonus for each job. But in the film he's part of a bureaucracy. We thought it would be nice to see this character gradually emerge as a very efficient exterminator who is almost Kafkaesque. A lot of elements in the plot are, in a funny kind of way, Kafkaesque.

HK:   *At first glance the story strikes one as being a reverse variation on* Alien. *Instead of six humans fighting a monster, we have one human fighting six replicants. It's also set in a menacing, industrialized, rather Gothic future. Did you think of* Blade Runner *as being theme-and-variation on your last film?*
RS:   No. My initial reaction on reading the script was that it seemed on the surface another futuristic script, and I figured I'd just done that, and I ought to change gear. But when I thought about it more, I thought it's not *really* futuristic. It's set forty-years on, but it could take place in any time slot. And so I started to back-date it in my head— as far as the look and feel are concerned—and what we're really doing is a forty-year-old film set forty years in the future. It's the Philip Marlowe world: *film noir*, ceiling fans. . . .

I came into the setting-up of the film quite late. The *Blade Runner* project had been developed by Michael Deeley and Hampton Fancher. They worked on it for probably a year before I came to it. I've been with it about a year and a half.

HK:   *The film's visual canvas is very crowded, eclectic, full of hybridized details. Especially in the architecture and streetscapes. Why?*

RS:    That's what's going to happen. I think the influence in L.A. will be very Spanish, with a big cross-influence of Oriental. But the film isn't "predictive," if that's the word; it's a kind of comic strip. I still relate very strongly to that kind of material, to comic strips and comic-strip characters.

HK:    *Any particular artist?*
RS:    Yes, Mobius, I think, is marvelous—probably the best comic-strip artist in the world. We had him working a little bit on *Alien*, and I tried to get him involved in *Blade Runner*. I'd love to do a complete film with him, but I always catch him on the wrong foot. My concept of *Blade Runner* linked up to a comic strip I'd seen him do a long time ago; it was called "The Long Tomorrow," and I think Dan O'Bannon [author of the original *Alien* script] wrote it. His work on that was marvelous, because he created a *tangible* future. If the future is one you can see and touch, it makes you a little uneasier, because you feel it's just round the corner. And you always get in his work a sense of overload, of cities on overload. We set the movie in L.A., but it could have been Chicago or New York.

HK:    *What about the characters who are at the center of the movie: the "new race," the replicants? Although there are some concrete details about them— their four-year lifespan, their vulnerability to the "empathy" test—their genesis and genetics are left mostly unexplored.*
RS:    We deliberately stopped, in screenplay development, going too far into the idea of genetic engineering, which we could have done. That would have been another, entirely different film. It would have been *2001*, in a way. In fact, to go into the study of genetics and its future is fascinating. But it was another can of beans.

So we drew a line: we wouldn't explore the laboratory details, the genetic explanations. Instead we'd ask: what if large combines in the next few decades became almost as powerful as the government? Which is possible. They'd move into all sorts of industries—arms, chemicals, aerospace—and eventually they'd go into genetics. And then you reach the point where genetics starts developing into the first "man-made" man. I think it could happen in the next twelve or fifteen years.

From there, as happens in *Blade Runner*, you can quite easily slip into breeding a second-class generation to do things which normally you or I wouldn't care to do or psychologically couldn't stand to do. For instance, going into space knowing you're not going to come back. You take a humanoid and dick around with his brain, bring him along certain psychological lines, and he's going to go quite happily.

HK:    *The movie is concerned with making us believe in the possibility of autonomous thought and emotion in the replicants. They're at the cutting edge—where programmed response turns into free-will consciousness. And they're looking for origins and parents.*

RS:    Parents and parent figures are important. There's a scene between Tyrell and Roy Batty, the replicant, when Tyrell says, "And what can the maker do for you?" And Roy Batty says, "I want more life, fucker." Well, he now has to say, "I want more life, father." Which, funnily enough, works better.

HK:    *Working with Harrison Ford, who's today's pop-adventure super-hero, did you want to bring echoes of Indiana Jones or Han Solo to his role?*

RS:    No, as it turns out, he's quite a different character in *Blade Runner*. You know, I hadn't seen *Raiders of the Lost Ark* when I first went to talk to Harrison about the role. I said, "I've got this great idea; we're going to do this Marlowe-ish character. Bogart and that sort of thing." And he said, "Just done it. Can't do it." And I said, "Hell." And then I next said, "What I want is this sort of unshaved individual. . . ." And he said, "Can't do that. I've just done it." So we suddenly changed gear completely and went through this rather frightening process of cutting all his hair off. It was a brave thing for him to do.

HK:    *The crop-headed style has also spread out to the rest of the movie. You've gone for a punk look in many of the characters and most of the extras.*

RS:    There's a reason for that. I think various groups are developing today—faction groups which are religious, social, whatever—and Punk, if you really trace it back, probably emerged from some louts, "bovver boys" as we used to call them, who developed their own little culture of protest. They probably stem from Manchester or Birmingham. And they decided out of sheer aggression to shave their heads. What could happen in the next forty years is that various of these groups will stick. And they will harden up, so that there will be religious, political, social, and just nut-case factions. And I think the police force will become a kind of paramilitary, which they nearly are now. We're just one step away.

We used a lot of real punks for the street scenes in *Blade Runner*. Because I had so much "crowd," it was better to save time and money by recruiting a huge number of extras: two hundred punks, one hundred Chinese, another one hundred Mexicans. And it was much easier then to have the two hundred punks turn up in the morning and dress them down a bit, dowdy them up, because they came in looking like bloody peacocks, which I didn't want. And by dressing them down, you immediately get the effect of the punk physical essentials: the oddball haircuts, that peculiar look of the face, because they either shave their eyebrows or their hair. And then the glimpses you get of them on the street are great, because they're desaturated—not full-blown punks, just odd people on the street. Because things will fade. That characterization will fade, and something else will take its place. But there may be vestiges or remnants of punk.

HK:    *The movie's set designs show a style of "additive" architecture: pipes and pillars and porches, etc., are superimposed on the outside of older buildings. Does this "exoskeletal" look have a secondary purpose or meaning in the film?*
RS:    Primarily a logical one. We're in a city which is in a state of overkill, of snarled-up energy, where you can no longer remove a building, because it costs far more than constructing one in its place. So the whole economic process is slowed down. Once a structure like the Empire State Building goes up, it's probably going to be there for . . . you name it. How the hell are they going to take it down? So it's a physical feeling you get about that society.

HK:    *Were many of the scenic effects and city vistas created by special effects?*
RS:    Yes, I was working with a guy called David Dryer, who did special effects on Doug Trumbull's film, *Brainstorm*. I was using Trumbull's studio-factory, so pretty well 90 percent of the special effects were done

with David Dryer and Trumbull's team. And although Doug initiated most of the effects and was there as a kind of mentor, generally speaking David was the special effects director. And a marvelous one, I think.

HK:    *On your two British-based movies,* The Duellists *and* Alien, *you operated your own camera. But there were problems in the U.S., I believe, because of the unions?*

RS:    When I first went to Michael Deeley—we were out in Hollywood then, piecing *Blade Runner* together—I knew I would have to face this, the practical problems of making the film because of the unions. I'm used to working very closely with the lighting cameraman and operating the camera myself; it's simply a faster process for me. The alternative is going through the whole communication hassle, and then you've got to be political and then diplomatic, and it's all bullshit when you're working against the clock all the time. Whether you're doing a big movie or a small movie, you're still working against the clock.

HK:    *How do you keep your stamina up—and your temper down?*

RS:    I find the process of filming very difficult—maybe this is why I want to be a producer—because it's like trying to write a book with many hands or paint a picture with many hands. A film has to have a guiding mind, otherwise I think it flounders. Of course it's a team effort, but in the final analysis it should cohere round one person. If or when I'm a producer and I hire a director, I'll want to know *why* if he's not pressing his points all the way down the line. Otherwise, I haven't hired the right individual.

HK:    *How's your determination on the set?*

RS:    Still right up there. It's difficult, and it becomes hard on other people and on me. But only temporarily. I find I may get depressed for half an hour, and that's it. If I get into a temper, I'm now trying to just walk away. There are several corridors in Pinewood Studios with holes in the walls!

HK:    *And what will your next film be?*

RS:    *Legend of Darkness.* It's written by William Hjortsberg, a Norwegian who lived, until a couple of months ago, in Montana and has now moved to Hawaii. It's literally a fairy story. I was going to do a film called *Knight*, about Tristan and Isolde, but we couldn't get the screenplay together, and I split from it. So I went right back to basics, and I looked at Cocteau's *Beauty and the Beast* and a little bit of *Siegfried*. This has all finally developed from the Tristan and Isolde idea. But I moved away from that story as such, because I thought it was too esoteric for the audience, and frankly too heavy. So I decided we must write an original, try to avoid all the normal clichés, but keep the dark and light sides of the story. There'll be no swords pulled out of stones, no dragons, no Celtic twilight. I figure we've got the first real medieval film.

# Directing *Alien* and *Blade Runner*: An Interview with Ridley Scott

## DANNY PEARY / 1984

DANNY PEARY:    *Prior to directing* Alien, *had you a strong interest in science fiction?*

RIDLEY SCOTT:    I had virtually *no* interest in science fiction until I saw *Star Wars* in 1977, other than having been tremendously impressed by *2001*. Fantasies don't work unless they quickly take on a reality of their own, and the sci-fi films I'd seen always contained silly, utopian ideas or tended to take the more extraordinary dilemmas of the day and assume they'd develop in nonlogical, unbelievable ways. The people who made sci-fi films didn't understand what they were doing.

After the completion of my first film, *The Duellists*, I prepared to do another period piece, *Tristan and Iseult*. While this was in progress, I was in the United States and saw the opening of *Star Wars*. It impressed me so much! It was innovative, sensitive, courageous—I saw it on three consecutive days, and it didn't diminish at all. I consider it to be a milestone film—one of the ten best I've ever seen. I was most struck by how Lucas took what is essentially a fairy tale and made it seem totally real. The combination of *2001*—a threshold film that presented science fiction as I thought it should—and *Star Wars* convinced me that there was a great future in science fiction films (which may sound naive in hindsight). So I decided to terminate my development of *Tristan and Iseult*; coincidentally, at that time I received the script of *Alien*.

From *Omni's Screen Flights/Screen Fantasies: The Future According to Science Fiction,* edited by Danny Peary (Garden City: Dolphin, 1984), pp. 293–302. Reprinted by permission of the author.

In my work on *Tristan and Iseult*, I had used *Heavy Metal* magazine as a reference. While I was absorbing the sorcery side of that magazine, I also looked with great interest at its visions of the future. So when I read the *Alien* script, not only was I fascinated by the marvelous, strong, simple narrative, but also I realized that because of my brief education reading *Heavy Metal*, I knew how to do the film. I accepted *Alien* almost immediately.

DP:    *Was it essential for those involved in* Alien *to have scientific knowledge or at least insight into how a believable futuristic film should be made?*
RS:    When I came onto the project, there were already people involved who did have scientific knowledge. My first in-depth meetings about how sci-fi should be and how it should look were with Dan O'Bannon, who'd written the original screenplay with Ron Shusett. O'Bannon introduced me to Ron Cobb, a brilliant visualizer of the genre, with whom he'd worked on *Dark Star*. Cobb seemed to have very realistic visions of both the far and near future, so I quickly decided that he would take a very important part in the making of the film. In fact I brought both him and O'Bannon to England during the making of *Alien*, and he became a very important member of the art department [as a conceptual artist]. We based a lot of our interiors of the Nostromo on Cobb's visuals.

DP:    *You were a designer yourself. . . .*
RS:    I was a painter and then a designer in art school, which totaled a period of seven years' training. I eventually ended up at the BBC as a set designer. I was a set designer for a number of years, so whatever film I do, I always have great input into the decision on how the sets and the atmosphere will be. This also means that my selection of a production designer is a painstaking process. I consider myself a good designer; therefore, I require an extremely good designer, because I push him all the time. It's fairly easy to find a production designer who can cope with contemporary environments or period pieces for which there are paintings or photographs to use as visual references, but production designers who are "into" visualizing future environments are few and far between. I believe I have a good take on the future, and it's vital for

the production designer I choose—be he Michael Seymour on *Alien* or Lawrence G. Paull on *Blade Runner*—to be in total sympathy with what I'm doing.

DP:    *In* Alien, *everything* looks *old, uninviting, bleak, disheveled. What was the look you wanted for your major set, the starship Nostromo?*

RS:    The look really was meant to reflect the crew members who, I felt, should be like truck drivers in space. Their jobs, which took them on several-year journeys through space, were to them a normal state of affairs. Therein lies the fantasy. The reality would not be like this for maybe a thousand years—but in our tongue-in-cheek fantasy we project a not-too-distant future in which there are many vehicles tramping around the universe on mining expeditions, erecting military installations, or whatever. At the culmination of many long voyages, each covering many years, these ships—no doubt part of armadas owned by private corporations—look used, beat-up, covered with graffiti, and uncomfortable. We certainly didn't design the Nostromo to look like a hotel.

DP:    *The characters in* Alien *seem more spirited than those in* Blade Runner. *But there is also a strong sense of melancholia, claustrophobia (which you've been quoted as saying frightens you most), and irritation. What personal views on space travel were you trying to get across? What about sex among crew members?—I know you cut out a sex scene involving Ripley [Sigourney Weaver] and Dallas [Tom Skerritt].*

RS:    I think the crew members of the Nostromo seem spirited only because of their argumentative nature, which is due to the fact they probably can no longer stand the sight of each other. It wouldn't matter how it was worked out in the prevoyage stage, when a computer probably determined the compatibility of the unit; like all crews in confined spaces, they'd get on one another's nerves and would be cutting each other's throats in six months' time. I tried to glean as much as I could from the problems that present-day astronauts go through preparing for prolonged periods in space. I then factored in ten years in space and tried to envision how a character would react to going off for that kind of period. Obviously it would raise all sorts of psychological problems, above and beyond claustrophobia and melancholia. The idea of spending *really* prolonged periods in space—say, of up to three years—is inconceivable and at the moment only exists in fantasies such as *Alien*.

We took out the scene where Dallas and Ripley discuss sexual "relief," because after the scene in which Kane [John Hurt] is killed when the alien bursts through him from the inside, it just seemed out of place. That scene proved much more powerful, *and* successful, than I expected, and for the sex to follow would have seemed totally gratuitous. The "relief" scene was to be our token attempt to answer the question about sex in space. If you think about it logically, the only way that mixed crews could work out on long missions is by neutralizing everyone and forbidding sex entirely, or by having free "open sex" for whoever wants it. Close relationships in tightly closed ships with small crews would certainly have to be discouraged. The problems that would result from some men and women pairing off and leaving other crew members on their own is obvious.

DP:    Alien *is the first space film, I believe, that features working-class characters rather than a crew of scientists, military men, or astronauts.*
RS:    That's absolutely accurate. At this point in time, I believe everyone in a crew can be a working-type. The Nostromo is driven by Mother, a computer, and, as far as running the ship goes, the crew is secondary. Once on the ship, their function is minimal. They need know only how to work the ship's basic equipment. That equipment can start itself, repair itself, think for itself, and act as its own monitoring system.

DP:    *At this point in time, has the value of humans diminished even further than today as far as the military-industrial complex is concerned? I am struck by the opening scene in which the ship's computers and machinery "come to life" before the humans are revived from their suspended-animation state.*
RS:    It's possible that the value of humans could have diminished. I'm now thinking on the level of the Big Brother idea of a lifeless megastructure and its attitude toward human employees, who are considered expendable. In this instance, the machinery, information data, and cargo are of more importance to corporations than the individuals on their ships. I certainly think this situation has parallels today. But the fact that computers can run the ship before the humans are revived is meant to be logical and not, as you suggest, antihuman—it really has

nothing to do with Big Brother and an unfeeling company. Ships will be run by computers specifically for efficiency reasons.

DP:    *I see the corporation, even more than the alien, as being the villain of the film. Its top priority becomes the alien, and it could care less about the danger that this causes its crew.*
RS:    The industrial-government complex is responsible for the attitude that allows such an alien to be brought on board the Nostromo. In fact, it is already responsible for the paranoia prevalent on all the ships because of its insistence on placing a company man on each vehicle. In this case, he takes the form of a robot, Ash [Ian Holm]. This would seem to be the normal development of a huge corporation trying to protect its interests. In this particular future, it would be very easy for "pirating" to exist. Corporations will have to find ways to assure that vehicles carrying minerals or vital information will not be hijacked.

DP:    *Was it the intention of the corporation that owns the Nostromo to bring back an alien, any alien? And for what reason?*
RS:    I think any corporation that sends probes into unknown territory is going to think of the possibility of finding something *new*. I'm sure that the crew members on all its ships would have been briefed to bring back anything of interest. It would be part of one's job to bring it back. An alien would, of course, be of top priority. This particular corporation didn't have a preconceived notion that an alien would be found on this mission, much less the particular alien that is brought onto the ship. The idea of bringing it back alive would not have been on the minds of the corporation executives when they first received the alien transmission. They just had high expectations when they ordered the Nostromo to investigate—it was purely out of curiosity.

DP:    *Yet the film seems to express a "topical" theme: For selfish reasons our leaders in government and business will side with "aliens" who have no regard for humanity at the expense of the people who trust them.*
RS:    Although I didn't set out to make such a statement, the parallels on both a political and company level are quite obvious.

DP:    *What is the nature of the alien? Is it vulnerable? Does it fear anything? Is it interested in the crew members for any reason other than food? Is it male or female?*

RS:    In relation to humans, the alien does seem to be indestructible. It does *not* fear anything. In fact it is a supreme being. The kind of creature we came up with emerged from the logic of how it could reproduce itself and, in fact, what its development or life cycle would be: Therefore, I guess, the alien is a hermaphrodite.

DP:    *In the film, Dallas seems to be killed instantly, but originally there was a shot of him trapped in the alien's cocoon. . . .*

RS:    That was simply a visualization of the alien's life cycle. What gave us the cocoon concept was that insects will utilize others' bodies to be the hosts of their eggs. That's how the alien would use Dallas and each of the crew members it kills. This explains why the alien doesn't kill everybody at once, but rather kills them off one by one: it wants to use each person as a separate host each time it has new eggs.

DP:    *Would the alien have killed Ash?*

RS:    Probably not. We theorized that the alien would feel or understand that Ash was a construction of robotics, however complex and strange. Because Ash wasn't human, he'd have been no use as a host for its eggs. The biological makeup of humans was useful, however, for the alien eggs to feed on—a revolting explanation!

DP:    *The alien is obviously intelligent and crafty. Does it sneak into the shuttle at the film's end, because it knows the main ship is about to blow up, because it expects Ripley to go there, or . . .*

RS:    . . . because we needed an end to the picture. . . .

DP:    *Sigourney Weaver told me that she believed the alien looked at Ripley in the final scene with curiosity and perhaps sexual interest.*

RS:    I never thought about it that way. I find that her comment is . . . certainly odd. Perhaps Sigourney has a touch of sympathy for the creature, because she looks at it from the viewpoint of her character. Ripley was part crew member and part scientist, someone who thought in logical terms. Maybe at that moment her scientist side emerged, and she began to study the creature like a scientist would and started to get a perspective on what it may have been thinking. Previous to this scene, remember, there had been absolutely no communication between the alien and the crew members, other than the violent experiences.

DP:    *Ripley is one of the bravest, smartest, toughest women in science fiction. Veronica Cartwright's Lambert character is also quite strong and capable. Are these two women such strong characters because today's audience demands such women in scripts or because that's how you expect women will be in the future?*
RS:    My film has strong women simply because I like strong women. It's a personal choice. I'm in no way a male chauvinist, nor do I understand female chauvinism—I just believe in the equality of men and women. It's as simple as that.

DP:    *Because the alien was not killed in* Alien, *but was merely blown into space, there may some day be a sequel. What should it be about?*
RS:    It certainly should explain what the alien is and where it comes from. That will be tough because it will require dealing with other planets, worlds, civilizations. Because obviously the alien did come from some sort of civilization. The alien was presented, really, as one of the last survivors of Mars—a planet named after the god of war. The alien may be one of the last descendants of some long-lost self-destructed group of beings.

DP:    *In* Alien, *you built suspense by having characters talking in hushed tones, smoking incessantly, drinking coffee, pacing nervously, sweating. . . . In* Blade Runner, *you emphasize characters' eyes to create tension, paranoia, mystery. Did you learn how to effectively manipulate an audience back when you made commercials?*
RS:    My training in commercials was really my film school. It helped build my awareness of how to present suspense and—"manipulate" is a bad word—*fascinate* the audience and hold it in a kind of dramatic suspension. I learned how to communicate immediately, to use every conceivable visual and aural device to work on the senses and grab the viewer's attention for a particular time-span.

The emphasis I placed on characters' eyes in *Blade Runner* was just my playing games with the audience. Obviously if every replicant in the film had glowing eyes, then there would have been no need for the Voight-Kampff machine to detect them. We went through a little tap-dance argument as to whether or not I should present something different about their eyes. I decided to take a middle line on this, to be deliberately intriguing and confusing rather than specific. So it varies throughout.

DP:    *In* Blade Runner, *the head of an enormous business conglomerate, Tyrell [Joe Turkel], is also the man responsible for the replicants' existence. Does he represent "science" to you? If so, do you believe this direction science is taking—its becoming part of private enterprise—is scary?*

RS:    Tyrell represents the ultimate in science and industry or scientific-industrial development. Here you see a large corporation that specializes in one area buying up another corporation that does something in an entirely different field. Obviously two separate sides of the conglomerate world—perhaps genetic engineering and biochemistry—will eventually merge, just as I think industries will develop their own independent space programs. It's bound to happen, and yes, it is scary.

DP:    *How does your vision of the future compare to what you present in* Blade Runner?

RS:    Much of what I envisage for the year 2019 is reflected in the look of the streets and the attitudes of the people in *Blade Runner.* The viewpoint speaks for itself. I thought about it very carefully. I presented a future world that I believe would come close to being a totalitarian society—if not quite 1984, then one step from it. It *is* 1984 in the sense that the world is controlled by perhaps only four major corporations, of which the Tyrell Corporation is one, and the people exist in what is almost a Kafkaesque or Orwellian environment. To cope with the anarchy in the streets there is a sort of a paramilitary-police group by which Deckard [Harrison Ford] is employed as a replicant exterminator. It's a world where the poor get poorer and the wealthy get wealthier and think it chic to protect themselves even more than they do in America today. Even Deckard lives in a condominium with electric gates. It looks rather like a fortress, and one only gets access to his floor by undergoing a voice-pattern check-out system in the elevator—otherwise it won't move. It's a time of self-protection and of paranoia.

DP:    *In the city of Philip K. Dick's novel* Do Androids Dream of Electric Sheep?, *on which* Blade Runner *is based, there are no murders, no abortions. . . .*
RS:    In the city of the film, I imagine everything would be done, from abortions to murders. In a city where only the wealthy can afford to protect themselves, and there is chaos on the streets, surely anything goes.

DP:    *The* look *of the city in* Blade Runner *is spectacular. Discuss your work with Syd Mead, the film's conceptual designer, specifically on the architecture.*
RS:    *Blade Runner* was a difficult project to conceive, because it is set only about thirty-five years from now, in a "tangible" future rather than in the obscure future of *Alien.* It was essential not to go wrong, or everyone would realize it. So it made sense to ask an industrial designer who is also a futurist, like Syd Mead, to design the film's hardware. We worked very closely on the vehicles, and he proved so prolific that I had him branch out and help us envision what would happen architecturally to existing cities.

I think that the mistake a lot of futuristic films make when they attempt short leaps forward in time is that they devastate whole cities and erect hokey-looking utopias. Things wouldn't work that way. Look at New York or Chicago. They have their business centers, middle-class areas, ghettoes, and central areas of development. One wouldn't possibly flatten it all. In today's cities there is already the practice of taking existing architecture and making applications to the outside of buildings—for example, because of cost factors, it's preferable to apply an air-conditioning or communication system to the outside than to rip the whole building apart to make it function. We took that line of thought further: As we move farther and farther into the future, the probability is that the construction of new buildings will diminish, except in certain areas of the city, and the constant repairing, shoring up, and modernization of older architecture will begin to take on a rather retrofitted look.

Our vision was really of a clogged world, where you get the sense of a city on overload, where things may stop at any time. Services may give out—in fact, they already have ceased in at least some parts of the city. Everything is old or badly serviced, and the bureaucratic system running the city is totally disorganized. One of the few things in fine order is advertising. I expect that by this time, billboards and electric signs will be everywhere. There will be an even bigger media explosion than there is today.

DP:    *One of the most intriguing features of your city is the constant rain and haze. I get the feeling that everything is contaminated, and everyone will soon die from radiation poisoning. Has World War III occurred? Judging by all the Orientals in the streets, could China have defeated America?*

RS:    I think the Cold War is still going on. If there had been a third world war, the world would not have been in the state we presented it—it wouldn't exist. Again, we were working in the context of a fantasy, so I don't necessarily believe there will be a future in which the air is so contaminated—at least I hope that at some point we'll actually do something about the way things have been going. The idea of a world filled with radiation is abhorrent. It was only presented that way as a dramatic device. The constant rain was "dramatic glue," if you like. It also amused me to think that it was taking place in Los Angeles, meaning the whole weather pattern would have changed by 2019. If L.A. gets all the rain, then maybe New York would get the sunshine.

DP:    *You switched the book's setting of San Francisco to Los Angeles.*

RS:    Originally we were going to begin the film with a title that read "San Angeles." Our idea was that San Francisco and Los Angeles would become one city and cover the entire western seaboard.

DP:    *What does your city smell like?*

RS:    New York City.

DP:    *Is there religion in this world?*

RS:    That's something I never really came to terms with. That is difficult to speculate about. But it may be stronger than it is today, when it seems to be on the wane in certain areas. Maybe the governments will have become the religions—then you've gone one step closer to 1984.

DP:    *In the novel Rachael and Pris look exactly alike—they are the same model of replicant. Why did you have two actresses—Sean Young, a brunette, and Daryl Hannah, a blond—play the two roles? And why was Rachael's last name changed from Rosen to Tyrell?*
RS:    It would have been confusing and not worked dramatically to have had Rachael and Pris played by the same actress. The name change was just a matter of us preferring Tyrell.

DP:    *Dick died before the release of the film. Did you have a chance to meet him?*
RS:    Only once. I showed him the special effects I'd just completed with Doug Trumbull's EEG [Entertainment Effects Group]. He was more than delighted—I think he was stunned by the look of our environment. He said it was exactly how he had envisioned the world with which we were dealing.

DP:    *Except for the fact that he tracks down renegade replicants rather than standard criminals, our hero Deckard is in many ways like the classic disillusioned, morally ambivalent detective—which is fitting considering the other* noir *elements found in the film, including his hard-edged narration.*
RS:    When we first meet Deckard, he is already thinking of giving up his job as professional exterminator. The job was in fact getting to him, as it did to, say, Philip Marlowe. His attitude toward his profession had already discolored his vision of the world and affected his attitude toward himself. As in classic detective stories, his background is not central to the film and is suggested by innuendo rather than fact; but what I wanted to do at the beginning was show a man who wanted to change his whole way of life and was in a way trying to find some kind of absolution or, maybe, a conscience.

DP:    *Deckard's romantic involvement with a replicant, Rachael, humanizes him to a certain degree—at least it causes him to release some of his pent-up "human" emotions and gives his personal life meaning. On the other hand, do you see his line of work, killing replicants, as being dehumanizing?*
RS:    I think Deckard is simply doing a job within his futuristic time slot. Therefore he should be unemotional about his work. I don't really believe that the nature of his job must necessarily dehumanize him.

What he does is act as a garbage disposal—it's rather like getting rid of industrial waste. Certainly because the replicants are highly sophisticated machines one starts to relate to them as human beings. But one must remember that they are *not* human beings.

DP:     *But when Deckard murders replicant Zhora [Joanna Cassidy], by shooting her in the back, you certainly intended viewers to not only find his brutal method devastating but also cowardly and upsetting.*
RS:     The audience reaction to Zhora's death is how you describe it. Of course, one was meant to feel sympathy and possible sadness for some of the replicants. But I must remind you that Deckard is just doing his job and following through on what he set out to do. Zhora could have come quietly, but she decided she had to have freedom, and she ran. So he did what he was there to do. The scene ends with Deckard looking down at this "woman" he has just killed, and we get one more facet of the reason he wants to quit his profession. For we're now dealing with a man who is guilt-ridden.

DP:     *How do you see the relationships between the replicants? I find them to be a bit schizophrenic. Sometimes they're loyal to one another. When Batty [Rutger Hauer] kisses the dead Pris, it indicates he loved her. Yet Rachael kills the replicant Leon [Brion James] in order to save Deckard, a human.*
RS:     To me, the way replicants relate to each other and to humans is one of the points of the story. Batty kisses Pris with affection and love. It demonstrates that even replicants can have those kinds of feelings. If you create a machine through genetic engineering, biochemistry, or whatever, the very fact that it has been created by a human being indicates to me that when it becomes truly sophisticated it will ultimately be free-thinking. I'm sure that in the near future, computers will start to think for themselves and develop at least a limited set of emotions, and make their own decisions. The same goes for the replicant that is so sophisticated that it's on par with the human being—in fact, in some ways it may even be superior. The replicants that Tyrell designed were the first of his "master race," which he planned to unleash to develop his interests on other planets, but within the context of this film, the replicants are more "human" than humans *or* "more equal" than humans. They are superior—they make their own choices.

DP:    *Aside from Rachael falling in love with Deckard, how do replicants feel toward human beings? With pity? With hatred?*
RS:    Certainly not with pity. The replicants would regard their human creators very much as a slave would a master he despises. Also I think they'd fear humans. And in some ways they'd empathize or want to identify with them.

DP:    *The female replicants, at least, are capable of having sex. Do you think they have the capabilities of enjoying sex and actually having orgasms?*
RS:    I never went into this in much detail, either. But I guess that if Tyrell went to the trouble of making *perfect* replicants, then he'd have taken into account their sexual capabilities. For obvious reasons. Maybe some female replicants like Pris were employed in military camps on space bases and were constructed for specific sexual purposes. . . . That's a very fascistic viewpoint, a very sick one, and I don't really like discussing it.

DP:    *Deckard finds himself sexually attracted to Rachael. Was it your intention to have male viewers find themselves attracted to the three female replicants in order to further diminish the distinction between humans and androids?*
RS:    No. I just happened to cast three actresses who are rather beautiful. Anyway, if you're going to make female replicants, why would you want them to be ugly?

DP:    *Comment on the climactic scene in which Batty saves Deckard. Batty's own death (with slow-motion employed) is quite stirring and dignified.*
RS:    Batty's death scene is in a way the final demonstration of his superiority over Deckard and the replicants' superiority over human beings. He could have taken Deckard's life—Deckard had just killed Pris—but decided as a gift to let him live. The white pigeon that he sets into the sky is, of course, a symbol of peace and life.

DP:    *In the novel, Deckard constantly worries he will mistakenly kill a human he thinks is a replicant. In fact, he constantly worries that he, himself, is a replicant.*
RS:    At one stage, we considered having Deckard turn out to be, ironically, a replicant. In fact, if you look at the film closely, especially the ending,

you may get some clues—some by slight innuendo—that Deckard is indeed a replicant. At the end there's a kind of confirmation that he is—at least that he believes it possible. Within the context of the overall story, whether it's true or not in the book, having Deckard be a replicant is the *only* reasonable solution.

DP:    *I see this film as possibly being about several endangered species, namely the human beings who roam the contaminated world, animals which, except for the pigeons, are no longer part of this world, and replicants, who have only a brief life span.*

RS:    I don't see the film as being this serious. I make films to entertain, and this was really meant to be a "heavy metal" comic strip about a future society and a character who just happens to be a replicant detective. I don't think the film is about several types of endangered species. It's a film about some goodies and some baddies. The baddies are presented as replicants who, we discover eventually, are like all good anti-heroes in that they have sympathetic streaks. At this point the balance of the drama changes—but this film does not have any deep messages.

DP:    *Yet wouldn't you consider* Blade Runner *to be cautionary?*

RS:    It doesn't say "watch out for this!" or "watch out for that!" It simply presents the kind of world I see in 2019. However, if you do take it seriously, then there are cautionary notes in regard to future environments and the way people relate to one another in them. Admittedly, the vision in *Blade Runner* isn't very promising, but unless we do something drastic to change the flow of things, I don't think the world will be a very pleasant place in the future.

# Ridley Scott

## FRANÇOIS GUÉRIF AND
## ALAIN GAREL / 1985

"Creating the environment excites me the most when making a movie," says Ridley Scott. "It's the most pleasing aspect about making a film. All the rest of it is work."

Of the four films that Scott has made, the only one not using an imaginary environment is *The Duellists*. In *The Duellists* Scott chose the countryside as a way of re-creating the Napoleonic era. His next film [*Someone to Watch Over Me*] will take place in a relatively contemporary setting, but it will still re-create another environment.

The way that Ridley Scott creates his films is that of a demiurge, a "maker of the universe," a term created by the science-fiction writer Philip José Farmer. Yet, when a real demiurge works, he starts from nothingness to create a world. Ridley Scott has always used a pre-existing universe, whether it is the countryside (*The Duellists*), H. R. Giger's books of paintings or *Necromancer* (*Alien*), or the films *Beauty and the Beast* and *Snow White and the Seven Dwarfs* (*Legend*). From that Scott has been able to create rich and very astounding variations that do not cease to be referential.

In other words, Ridley Scott comes from the set-dressing of commercials. His work shows that modern culture is a "melting pot," a means of diverse expression: classical literature, science-fiction, fairy tales, cartoons, painting, and architecture. What we witness is a blooming type of filmmaking that "recycles"—styles of happiness and success, cultures and media—from television commercials to modern painting of the

From *Revue du Cinema*, October 1985, pp. 55–60. Reprinted by permission of the authors. English translation by Kathryn Bergeron, Marianne Dissard, and Andrea Kulas.

most abstract language. In *Masculine Féminin*, Jean-Luc Godard said that the 1968 generation was "the children of Marx and Coca-Cola." Now, the generation of the 1980s is made up of the sons of Joseph Conrad and Gwendolyn, of the heirs of Vietnam and *The Twilight Zone*.

The art of Ridley Scott constantly reminds us that no matter what the beginning is, the only thing that matters is the art of creation. With him cartoons will stand head to head with paintings, fairy tales will become mythology, and the commercial aesthetic will feed from the pre-Raphaelites. He shakes up and pre-cognates references, proving culture's perpetual movement. *Legend* is a film for children, a horror film, a metaphysical melodrama, and, finally, a shining example of a culture becoming.

FRANÇOIS GUÉRIF AND ALAIN GAREL:     *After shooting* The Duellists *you planned on shooting* Tristan and Isolde. *Is* Legend *a substitution?*
RIDLEY SCOTT:     We had written a script for *Tristan*. My interest in *The Duellists* lay in the stylization of the landscape—my God, in *Tristan* it would have been the same countryside. I saw *Lancelot du Lac* by Robert Bresson which is totally pre-Raphaelite in a very bizarre, formidable way. It is the same story. I didn't do *Tristan*, because I didn't want to find myself on a narrow path. *The Duellists* did well in France but not in the United States, and I didn't want to retrace that path. You spend a year of your life making a movie, and at the end they make seven prints of it. Once the script for *Tristan* was finished, I put it aside; it didn't seem to be the right time to make it. But it stayed in my mind. *Tristan* is in the realm of the fairy tale and mythology. In January 1981 while I was preparing for *Blade Runner*, I had a work session with a writer to create a fairy tale. From both of us starting from the classics of that genre, we decided that we could get something out of it while using the archetypal structure. If I wanted to do a film like that, there was too much of a risk of it being too expensive, and I had to think of how it could touch the audience. We couldn't quite do a profoundly Celtic tale, an esoteric tale; we had to create a fairy tale that had a contemporary resonance. Looking at *Legend*, you can't really say it's a film from a historical point of view. There are all sorts of instances from Walt Disney to William Blake, a little bit of *Citizen Kane*, Sergei Eisenstein, and a lot of Jean Cocteau. *Beauty and the Beast*, one of Cocteau's great films, remains so because of how he creates

his own environment. It doesn't stay a prisoner of historical accuracy. In the house of the girl the costumes are all seventeenth century, but inside the castle there are a lot more influences.

FG AND AG:    *Like in* Beauty and the Beast, *the Beast is beautiful and powerful.*
RS:    Yes, he is sexy, eh? We wanted him like that, because the women love him. The beast in Cocteau is never horrible. When I was a kid, the beginning of the movie made me very afraid, but very soon you realize there is something else. I wanted that with Darkness. I didn't want to put a barrier between the audience and him. We could have created a monster that was horrible, disgusting, really horrible to look at, but we wanted something between beast and man. And we wanted to give the characters the most depth possible. I wanted Darkness to be healthy, not disgusting psychologically and physically, because I had the feeling that Evil treats itself better, more often than not, than Good.

FG AND AG:    *How did you choose Tim Curry?*
RS:    Originally, I had not thought of him. One of the scariest charac-ters in *The Exorcist* is that tremendous voice. The idea of giving this voice to the little girl was really powerful. That was my goal with Evil. First I thought of Peter O'Toole, but he was so skinny and so pale. I had never seen *The Rocky Horror Picture Show*, but I was looking for someone to be the sorceress of the swamps. One of the actresses from *The Rocky Horror Picture Show* seemed to fit that role. Then I saw Tim Curry and I thought, "Oh my God, this is Darkness." I like the control he has over himself. He is very physical and powerful, theatrically speaking. He knows when he needs to stop. It was great to work with him.

FG AND AG:    *What were the criteria that made you choose William Hjortsberg as a main writer?*
RS:    I read several of his books: *Symbiography, Angel Heart, Gray Matters,* and *Gates of the Poets.* He is an American cowboy from Montana, living on his own little ranch. I wanted to avoid a film that was profoundly European. With the exception of Gérard Brach who is not specifically French but universal (and universally optimistic), I couldn't see any European writer capable of escaping his roots. It was necessary for me

to find an American, not influenced by the European thoughts, but with sensitiveness. It was the ideal combination.

FG AND AG:   *Why did you decide to do a fairy tale?*

RS:   To escape once more. Seriously, my next film will take place in the contemporary world, but I like the way films try to obtain some level of escape. My first four films have no real relationship to each other on the surface; however, upon digging there are certainly some shared similarities. I simply felt I wanted to make this kind of film. Before making *The Duellists*, I worked on three scripts over a period of seven years. One was a contemporary film, a black comedy, the other historical. I had read a book, *The Once and Future King*, by T. H. White, which traces the history of Merlin the magician. We had already written a fairy tale–influenced script using *Beauty and the Beast*. We had even prepped the movie in Yugoslavia, but then the money disappeared. Yet, it still stayed in my mind. Then I wrote *Tristan* and finally *Legend*. Thus, quite obviously, I always have tried to make this kind of film. Fairy tales had a large impact on my childhood. In fairy tales there is always an element of the nightmare. That probably is the reason.

FG AND AG:   *In the end of* Blade Runner, *Rutger Hauer evokes the "incredible things" that he has seen. Maybe it is these "things" that you choose to show in* Legend?

RS:   I did not have the means of showing what he had seen. I had to be satisfied with him speaking about it.

FG AND AG:   *There are obvious commonalities among your films. All of them rest on a linear script built on the same scheme: an individual, or a group of individuals, who are under attack.*

RS:   Like in most stories, the films I like to see have stories presented in a very simple way. Most of history is. The films I like to see have histories presented simply. I try to do that: to simplify a script at the most direct point of possible communication. *Alien* is very simple. It is almost like good popular music, like rock 'n' roll. If you listen to rock lyrics, they are never sophisticated. The implications are that you if you desire, it will deepen. What I am trying to do, even if I start with a complicated story, is to bring it back to its primitive linearity. Then I try to modify it with all these things. In *Alien* some critics found that the characters were too thin. I do not agree: the spectator knows what is in relation to the story. Through the exchange of lines, you know enough of the character without slowing down the story. The essential dynamic is the story. For example, when you listen to the lyrics of Bruce Springsteen, you listen to them because they are excellent. In general, in rock 'n' roll or rhythm 'n' blues, you don't listen because it is a mass of sounds, as with the Rolling Stones, but if the lyrics are excellent, you listen to them, and you follow the story in spite of the music. I like films to function in this way.

FG AND AG:    *However, what seems to interest you the most is creating an environment.*
RS:    Absolutely. It's the most pleasant aspect about making a film. All the rest of it is work. In *The Duellists* I choose the landscape as a way of re-creating the time period. It was an attractive process. I am curious to see how that will shape my contemporary film; I cannot re-create the environment . . . well, actually, come to think of it, yes I can!

FG AND AG:    *What is the subject of your next project?*
RS:    I have two films in preparation; both are contemporary. One is about rock 'n' roll. The best rock film that I've seen is *Purple Rain*. The script is thin, but I like the dynamic. The interpretation of the music was incredible. The only person who made "musicals" from this point of view that I aspire to is Bob Fosse, who has not shot stories where, conventionally, everything stops and people just start singing. With *Cabaret* and especially *All That Jazz,* he tries to tell a story by mixing it with music. I'm going to try to take a step in that direction. As for the other film, it is *Love Story* situated in New York, with a police officer in the main role.

FG AND AG:    Blade Runner *is as much a* film noir *as a film of science fiction.*
RS:    At the beginning, there was the novel by Philip K. Dick. There was a misunderstanding because Dick was hurt when he heard people say that I had not read his book entirely. This, of course, was wrong. There was a script, a very good script, a linear story of a detective. I had started work on it with Syd Mead, my artistic director, who is an industrial designer

and speculator on the future. When you work on an adaptation, you take out the environment. I did not use the one referred to by Dick. On the contrary, I made sure that this near future would be according to my own imagination. Things will change in a drastic way. To see how the characters will live in it and behave in it will bring about changes to the storyline and thicken the storyline. When I started shooting, I had already shot a number of scenes with special effects of the urban environment. One day, I had a meeting with Philip Dick. I brought him to the studio and showed it to him, and he was astounded. "You have probably read another of my books," he said to me, "*The Man in the High Castle.*" I hadn't even heard of it. He was very happy because he saw that at least we were working in the same direction. He was also happy with the final script because it was falling back, one way or another, on what he was exploring in his source novel. This is where the exterior elements can change the entirety of the film or the original idea. Thus, this was the logic behind the Tyrell Corporation. I wanted something plastic. I saw Joe Turkel in *The Shining* who, in the best scene of the film, is fantastic as the bartender. I said, "This is *Blade Runner.*" He had a plastic aspect. He became the owner of the corporation! He also resembled Tutankhamen. That's why we had a pyramid. The idea was that in 2029 that cryogenisation was the norm. No doubt it will be different, but it is a good bet for the future. If you have an incurable disease, you will be put to sleep in a cold chamber, and you will be awakened only when we have found a way to cure you. When Batty kills Tyrell he does it by putting his fingers in his eyes and smashing his head. When he sees that there is no blood on his hands, he knows something is wrong, and he asks where the real Tyrell is, because this one is a replicant. He is brought into the chamber of the pyramid, which is the exact placement of the chamber in Egyptian tombs. The center of the pyramid has the body of the emperor in a sarcophagus. You go into the cryogenic chamber, and Tyrell is there, asleep, because everybody is diseased. That came logically by developing the environment, and the environment became part of the storyline. I like to work this way.

FG AND AG:   *How do you work with your collaborators to create that environment? Are you an artist yourself? Do you make sketches?*
RS:   Yes, I always draw my scripts. The first script of *Legend* was a succession of storyboards, drawings, and visual notes. At the moment, I

have an art director who listens immediately to my goals, and he takes over. I think my art director for *Legend* is the best I have ever worked with. He is brilliant.

FG AND AG:     *How long did it take you to create the forest for* Legend?
RS:     Day by day, everyday, for three months. Assheton Gorton, the set designer, was known for being very good at re-creating the period we tried to set. My first problem was convincing him that I didn't want a Celtic forest—initially it seemed like the way to go, but it became too narrow. I wanted it to be influenced by Disney, I wanted to make the forest lighter, like the rock 'n' roll version of a fairy tale. We looked at *Snow White, Pinocchio, Fantasia*—the backgrounds of *Pinocchio* work well, but the backgrounds of *Snow White* are too dark, too scary. We started from there, then we mixed it with Gustave Doré, pre-Raphaelite, etc.; it was a potpourri of images. I convinced Assheton that being historically accurate wasn't important, but that creating our own environment was important, as long as it seemed real, and it came from our inner creativity.

FG AND AG:     *You didn't mention* Bambi, *in which the forest plays an essential role.*
RS:     I never saw it, but I've heard it's great. In fact, I love Disney today, now that I'm an adult. In making reference to it, I wanted to interest a young audience. Trying the other way, doing a fairy tale that is seriously Celtic, where the characters would have been scary, almost like animals, also would have been interesting.

FG AND AG:     *There's also a reference to Disney with the characters Jack and Una, which seems to recall* Peter Pan.
RS:     Yes, exactly. Una was originally invented because Jack and Mia are not together during the film; they are in fact only together in the beginning and the very end. So I had to find a way to remind the audience of Mia.

FG AND AG:     *What is surprising is that you put in the air itself into the film; it is always suspended.*
RS:     Yes. Insects, pollen, flowers, etc.—it's very dynamic. It was to keep the forest in movement. The forest was very artificial, and I had to

make it come alive. I had to work constantly with the whirring of fans which drove me crazy. Paradoxical as it seems, the original concept behind the film was to make it a celebration of nature. We wanted more animals—in one of the first versions of the script, there was a prologue, which would have been nice to do, but it was quasi-impossible to try to film it. It would have started in the dark corner of the forest with the goblins, and it would have followed a mysterious light that comes from something that is on the other side of the hills. Every time they would get to the top of a hill, the light would have been behind another one. They would have been led by animals, birds, antelopes, foxes, etc. They would all go to that light. The goblins would have followed in disguise until they came to a ravine, where they would have been witness to some sort of nativity. What they would see would fascinate them. The fox would be next to the rabbit in the grass, a wolf would have birds on his head, and a deer would have a snake in his antlers. They would all be together without any conflict. Then a goblin would make a false move, and an animal would find out who they were, and the light would disappear and escape again, and they would say, "We'll never get there. We have to find the innocence; the innocence will lead us to what we're looking for." I had to give up that idea because it would have taken six months to shoot it.

# In *Black Rain*, East Meets West with a Bang! Bang!

## DONALD CHASE / 1989

After four grueling months that included location work in Japan
and New York, the director Ridley Scott is completing *Black Rain* at
Paramount Studios, on a hi-tech-with-Deco-accents hostess-bar set that
is supposed to be in Osaka. Two scenes, filmed on successive days, seem
to underscore the theme of the conflict-of-two-cultures thriller, which
opens Friday at Loews Astor Plaza and 34th Street Showplace and casts
Michael Douglas and Andy Garcia as New York cops pursuing a capo in
the yakuza—or Japanese Mafia—in an uneasy collaboration with the
Japanese police.

In one scene, Mr. Douglas, frustrated and angry, tries to extract information from Kate Capshaw, ultra-blond and sequinned to play the
American expatriate manager of the club. "Look," she tells him in a
tough-shady-lady-adrift manner that recalls Jean Harlow and Rita Hayworth. "I've been here seven years, and I still can't read the headlines.
Yes means no and maybe means never. . . . No one's going to help a
gaijin." Mr. Douglas is unfamiliar with the Japanese word, which
Ms. Capshaw then defines: "A foreigner. Stranger. Barbarian. Me.
You. . . . More you."

But in the other scene, also set in the club, Andy Garcia coaxes the
formerly hostile, now alcohol-soaked Japanese police detective played
by Ken Takakura onto the bandstand for a duet of Ray Charles's
"What'd I Say?" This moment of musical communion soon signals an
about-face in Mr. Takakura's character. When Mr. Garcia falls prey to a

---

From *The New York Times*, September 17, 1989. Reprinted by permission of the author.

vicious yakuza attack, Mr. Takakura risks his job and his life to join Mr. Douglas in pursuing the responsible parties.

It was the opportunity to explore the question raised by these scenes—Is it East, East and West, West, or are we all part of the Family of Man?—that attracted Mr. Scott, producers Stanley Jaffe and Sherry Lansing and Mr. Douglas to Craig Bolotin and Warren Lewis's original screenplay.

"I read a lot of newspapers," Mr. Douglas says during a break in filming, "and the movies I'm drawn to both as an actor and as an actor-producer tend to have a current-events mode. I'm thinking about *The China Syndrome* and *Wall Street.*" The former, which he produced and acted in, was about a nuclear-plant accident that, in fact, prefigured the Three Mile Island crisis of spring 1979. The latter, for which he won the 1987 Academy Award for best actor, but did not produce, focused on the still-controversial mergers-and-acquisitions fever and its effect on the financial community's ethics.

"I felt," he continues, "that there was something between us and Japan that was unresolved, that was a mixture of hostility and admiration on both sides—really confused. It involves Japan's cultural imitation of the United States, followed by its economic supremacy over the United States, all of which is colored by lingering memories of World War II." More specifically, by the bombing of Hiroshima and Nagasaki: "You turned the rain black," one Japanese character reproaches Mr. Douglas, referring to the combination of ash and precipitation that fell on the devastated cities.

"I thought," adds Mr. Douglas who is also involved in *Black Rain* in a production capacity, "that this particular picture, as a cop-action picture, could explore some of the differences in customs and behavior—explore some of the hostilities that our two cultures and societies have for each other."

"The way in," Mr. Scott says, "is the conflict between police methods. Michael—as Conklin—is a New York homicide detective with a certain disgruntlement, a certain dissatisfaction with the system and a certain renegade quality. It's even suggested that he's on the take in a minor way. Ken, on the other hand, is a thorough, by-the-book, hardline bureaucrat who is part of what seems to be this wonderful machine in Japan.

"Michael, I think, re-establishes some lost values in himself—traditional values, which somewhere along the line have been lost in the West but which I think still exist in Japan, such as a sense of honor and a sense of family—through his experience with this Japanese character. And Ken—who plays a kind of Japanese Everyman, the salaried man, the bourgeois, what we think of as the automaton—loses his rigidity and opens up through his contract with Michael and Andy Garcia. For Ken Takakura—both as that character and as an actor—to stand up and sing is an incredibly alien and even painful thing."

Mr. Scott—whose extraordinary eye was evident in *The Duellists, Alien* and, rather ironically, in the Japanized Los Angeles of 2019 that he presented in *Blade Runner*—admits that at first he was stumped as to how to visualize Japan in *Black Rain*.

"Japan is difficult visually, awkward visually," the English director says. Looking first at Tokyo and Kyoto as possible filming sites, he concluded that "it's all this squeaky-clean New Town. Everything is well-kept, with gigantic freeways and a gigantic scale of architecture. . . . But the architecture is really not definitively Japanese, except in pockets and pieces and bits."

Then the director was taken to Osaka by Alan Poul, the film's resident Japanologist and associate producer, who served Paul Schrader's *Mishima* in the same capacities when it was filmed in Tokyo. Mr. Scott found Osaka, whose population of three million makes it Japan's third-largest city, suitably "big, but provincial, [with a] European feel because of a lot of parks and also a gentility." It is also, on the screen, an industrial center whose streets are dense with pedestrian and motorized traffic and whose skies are dense with pollution.

Though Michael Douglas usually involves himself deeply in the preparation of the films he produces, he did not in this case accompany Mr. Scott, Mr. Poul and Mr. Jaffe on their location-scouting expeditions. "I wanted to see Japan with fresh eyes, as the character does," he explains, "so I held off going there until the casting sessions for the Japanese actors."

The casting sessions were the first of a series of life-imitates-art cultural clashes between the film makers and the Japanese.

"As far as we were concerned," Mr. Poul says, "the casting sessions were conducted very civilly, along the lines that you cast a film in

America. Which is, you ask a lot of top actors, top talent to come in at twenty-minute intervals; you talk to them for a while; they read for you; you get them on videotape, and they go.

"In Japan, though, actors do not audition"—especially actors of the stature of Mr. Takakura, who enjoys a status comparable to that of Clint Eastwood. "The idea of putting yourself in a position that's potentially humiliating is very disagreeable—and very alien to the Japanese experience. They spend their lives making each other's lives easy—often that's a priority over honesty, over frugality. . . . But here, we had within the space of a few days many of the nation's top actors coming in and out of the Imperial Hotel, which is the most prominently situated hotel in Tokyo."

"Each actor would arrive with his manager," Ridley Scott recalls with a chuckle. "The manager being fairly angry at having to be there at all. But because we were so well promoted, they were torn between not coming at all and coming to see what was going on."

Differences in customs and mentalities were also evident during the six weeks of actual shooting on *Black Rain* in Japan.

"If you look at most Japanese movies, contemporary Japanese movies," Stanley Jaffe says, "you will see that they take place mostly on [studio-built] sets, and that what on-street scenes as there are were clearly shot with a hidden camera. You don't see real scenes staged in populated areas, as we would expect them to be staged here in the States."

This lack of familiarity with shooting in real locations—plus what Alan Poul calls a "literal-minded and image-conscious" strain in the Japanese psyche—led to problems in securing shooting sites. "People," Mr. Poul recalls, "thought that having their store or their house used as a place frequented by yakuza would reflect badly on them. And when we wanted to play a row of shops in a fish market as someone's apartment, we were told, 'But people don't really live here. . . .' "

Lack of familiarity with street shooting also meant that the Japanese police were totally unacquainted with the notion of controlling crowds to accommodate a film unit. When Mr. Scott and Mr. Jaffe wanted to film scenes in the Dotonburi night-club district of Osaka with police co-operation, they had to agree to do so over a number of days, in the quiet hours between three and six in the morning, instead of in one dusk-to-dawn sweep.

"It was a bit troublesome," admits Mr. Jaffe, "[but] it meant that we could, during those hours, shoot anything we wanted, and shoot it with complete control."

Mr. Jaffe is perhaps a bit disingenuous, because in fact the control was achieved by a fifty-strong private security force hired by the production, while, Alan Poul says, "the cops stood around and watched. . . . And then the police would come out and say, 'Look, look at the disturbance you're creating.' I don't have a lot of kind things to say about the Japanese police, except that ultimately they let us do it, ultimately we got the shot. . . . And the fact is that, though the Dotonburi is one of the single most famous urban landscapes in Japan, it's never—before this—been adequately captured on film."

In fact, no matter the difficulties, the principal Westerners involved in *Black Rain* returned to the United States feeling that the Japanese experience was a positive one. And just as in the film, it was individuals who broke down cultural or institutional barriers.

Of the 120 Japanese who joined forty-five Westerners on the crew, Mr. Scott says: "We communicated through interpreters, but I found there's an international language in film making. Once they know how you're functioning, they all move very quickly, like an army—they were great." And despite being required to work, on the average, two hours more per day than is normal for them, "they had endless stamina. . . . Once they were for you, they would die—absolutely die—for you."

Mr. Scott directed the Japanese actors through an interpreter, and in the scenes in which Japanese characters speak Japanese among themselves, he had to rely on the interpreter to evaluate the niceties of their line readings. "But it's funny," he notes, "when you're dealing with a good actor, you know what's going on. I found the Japanese actors were brilliant. I thought I was going to get Kabuki Theater, and I didn't get that at all. I got very good, very balanced, very contemporary, very real performances."

Mr. Scott cites especially the performance of Ken Takakura, and, like Alan Poul, points to the "courage" of the Japanese actor in diverging from his customary strong-silent antihero screen persona to play an establishment figure in his first American film.

"Actually, there's a Japanese banquet of actors in the movie," says Andy Garcia, referring, in addition to Mr. Takakura, to Yusaku Matsuda,

Tomisaburo Wakayama, Shigeru Koyama, Yuya Uchida, who play yakuza or police types, and Miyuki Ono, who plays a Dotonburi hostess.

"It's been a real joy, because you learn that acting is really an international language," he adds, echoing Mr. Scott. "It doesn't matter to me how or where they trained—it hasn't even occurred to me to ask them what their process was. . . . I'm just looking in their eyes. The graciousness and honor these people bestow on themselves, and the people they work with is enlightening. If other cultures patterned themselves after the Japanese as represented by these actors, we'd be a lot better off—certainly a lot of movies would be better off. There's not a lot of ego that I find."

Asked for his opinion on the making of *Black Rain,* Ken Takakura, whose conversational English is limited, replies: "It is an experience I will never forget."

# *Thelma & Louise* Hit the Road for Ridley Scott

## MAITLAND McDONAGH/1991

Dark, dark, dark . . . that's the world of Ridley Scott by way of *Alien, Blade Runner, Someone to Watch Over Me* and *Black Rain*; even the sunlit fantasy *Legend* pivoted on a character named "Darkness." Born and raised in England, Scott has simultaneously pursued careers in advertising (his company, RSA, has offices in New York, London and Los Angeles) and feature filmmaking and has succeeded at both, perhaps to his own detriment. The "Ridley Scott Look" is so distinctive any fool can identify it: equal parts intricate art direction and glossy technique, his films are about dangerous, seductive cities, iconic characters and frustrated, erotically charged relationships. They bristle with cynical despair and high-voltage violence. Like Michael Mann (*Thief, Manhunter*), Scott's the prisoner of his own success: his movies look so good that the surface becomes all anybody ever sees. *Someone to Watch Over Me*, not a great movie, *looks* as fabulous as *Blade Runner*, a movie that gets better with each passing year, so they're lumped together as "all style and no substance." Of course, to make the argument airtight you have to forget about his first film, *The Duellists*, a period piece about honor and obsession ("I always thought of it as a western, actually," says Scott); though handsomely mounted, it has few of the stylistic flourishes that later became Scott's calling cards. And you'd have to ignore completely his new film, MGM-Pathe's *Thelma & Louise*.

*Thelma & Louise* is all light, bright Southwestern sunlight streaming down onto two pretty, ordinary women: a housewife and a coffee shop

From *Film Journal*, June 1991, pp. 6, 38. Reprinted by permission of the author.

waitress out for a weekend of fun. A would-be rapist spoils their idyll before it's had a chance to get properly started, and Thelma (Geena Davis) and Louise (Susan Sarandon) find themselves on a desperate run across John Ford country that ends in the Grand Canyon. It's a shaggy kind of story, a distaff road movie that mixes humor with violence and, just when it looks as though it's going too far in the direction of simple-minded wish fulfillment (after our two heroines punish a repellently lewd trucker by blowing his rig to kingdom come), comes to an uncompromising end: rather than return to their unsatisfying lives, Thelma and Louise floor the accelerator one last time, which is why the film ends *in* the Grand Canyon, not *at* the Grand Canyon.

*Thelma & Louise* is almost all location exteriors, where the rest of Scott's films have been studio-bound. It's about rural rather than urban landscapes, two ordinary women rather than aliens or neo-*noir* cops. The atmosphere is sunny rather than awash in symbolic stormy weather. It's as though Scott deliberately chose to do exactly what you wouldn't expect of him, daring critics and audiences to say, "Oh, Ridley Scott's up to his old tricks again."

FJ:    *Your previous films have relied heavily on special effects and art direction;* Thelma & Louise *is totally character-driven. That's a conspicuous change for you.*

RS:    I feel all the films I've done have been character-based. But the events in my films have been a little larger than life, and those events, and certain exotic elements, have been the engine behind the movie. Visual elements are a strength for me . . . . They ought to be; I spent seven years in art school. In *Alien* you don't want to depart from the action for twelve minutes to find out who Harry Dean Stanton's mother was, you know? But I think *Alien*'s ensemble cast was pretty damned good, considering it was pretty much a genre film—*The Old Dark House* with science-fiction elements. The same with *Blade Runner*, which has had a very strong life since its initial release. I think that's mostly because people got used to the proscenium, the tapestry, so the story was allowed to come through. On first viewing, it may have been a lot to take in.

So, no, I don't think I was looking to explore characterization for the first time. But looking for material that was less exotic, and more based in reality, yes. *Thelma & Louise* isn't so much a departure as a choice to foreground an element that's maybe been more in the background.

FJ:    *How did this project develop?*

RS:    Scripts that are written on spec fly around Hollywood like confetti, and most of them aren't that good. But we [Scott and producer Mimi Polk, executive VP of his production company, Percy Main Productions] came across this piece of material from a first-time writer, read it, thought it was interesting, and that's where it started.

At first, I wasn't going to direct at all. I was in the very beginning stages of another project, so I thought I'd produce. I had to go through the rather strange process of interviewing directors; I mean, I meet lots of directors, but this was on different ground, you know? I was getting marginally alarmed by the fact that they all wanted to fix it up, and I didn't think any of it needed fixing. And they all wanted to know why I wasn't doing it myself. So I did it.

FJ:    *It's a road movie like* Easy Rider *but with the twist that the guys on the road are now two women.*

RS:    Thirty years ago, a road movie was about two hippies who were looking for liberation. But times have changed, fortunately, and the fact that you can now make a film about two women who have, if you like, liberated themselves, is a sign of that. Obviously, the casting was very important. With the average Hollywood movie costing about $24 million, we came in well under—at about $17 million—but that's still a lot of money. You can understand that they want to shore up their investment a bit with stars. And you name the actress, we talked to them. Jodie Foster, Meryl Streep, Goldie Hawn . . . we talked to *everybody*. Ultimately a lot of it came to down to scheduling and availability, as well as chemistry. Because of the nature of the material, the two actresses not only had to be great, they had to be great together. We had Geena first—she'd gotten hold of the script and called up to say she wanted to talk to us—and the chemistry she and Susan had together was extraordinary.

FJ:    *Major studios often shy away from so-called "women's pictures," because they don't make as much money as films aimed at young men.*

RS:   I don't think there's any difficulty in Hollywood looking at female-driven scripts. I think it's just that there aren't any. People haven't sat down and dealt with it.

I also don't really think of *Thelma & Louise* as a women's film: it's a men's film as well. I think there's something for everybody. We males can sit in the audience and be amused at what we see coming back at us, and I think it's pretty accurate—and funny—in that respect.

FJ:   *Weren't you put off by the fact that Callie Khouri's script takes a pretty dim view of men? The best male characters in the film are ineffectual, and the worst are pigs.*

RS:   We're not all like these characters in this movie, you know. This is a comedy, and the characters are rather broad generalizations, but that's not to say there isn't truth in them. The truck driver is clearly just a symbol of the guys who flash themselves on the freeway, and he could be anybody, a guy in a limo just as easily as a guy in a truck. Jimmy, the guy who cannot commit, is always moving in the other direction until Louise moves away from him; then he wants to get her. There's Thelma's husband, who's casually selfish; I think there's a lot of him in every man, if not so broad. J. D., the hitchhiker, represents what you get when two males sitting in a car see what they'd call a great piece of ass walking across the road in front of them. They say, "My God, Christ, look at that. . . ." and all kinds of other things. I think as a man watching the film you can't help but be amused, unless you have absolutely zero sense of humor and zero sense of self.

FJ:   *You're known as a studio-bound director, yet this picture is all location and very American locations at that.*

RS:   Route 66, that piece of heartland, is a little bit of what we Europeans like to think of as the American dream. We've all seen it in movies. Early on, we drove from Arkansas to the Grand Canyon, which all seems to be developing into mall towns joined together by concrete strips; Route 66 seems to be vanishing fast, and there's no one out there protecting it. What I originally wanted to do was to have one of the subtexts of the movie be the changing face of America; I wanted to shoot in and around mall stopovers, modern ghastly hotels and these freeways that go straight across the country and look exactly the same every mile of the way. But that became so depressing I decided that if I wanted to hit this note of *Thelma & Louise* being about an almost mythical "last journey," then it had to be more like the *idea* of Route 66. So we consciously set out to show that landscape at its most beautiful and expansive.

FJ:    *We always hear that everybody in Hollywood wants a happy ending, but you didn't supply one here.*

RS:    We were never pressured for an "up" ending; I think the ending was just extending the journey. It's an emotional choice, and you either fly with it or you don't. The alternatives are impossible: Thelma and Louise could have taken out that gun and started to fire, in which case they would have been shot at by this army of very hostile men. Or they could have got up and negotiated, and they would have ended up doing ten to fifteen, maybe got out after seven if they were good girls. What they do at the end is decide to continue the journey. In a way, I think it *is* an "up" ending.

FJ:    *What do you have coming up next?*

RS:    The next film will be *Christopher Columbus* with Gérard Depardieu. The writer is a French journalist, who writes for *Le Point,* and what's interesting is that it's an examination of history from a contemporary point of view and from a journalist's point of view.

# Ridley Scott's Road Work

## AMY TAUBIN / 1991

Its high spirits and dazzling good looks notwithstanding, *Thelma and Louise* suggests that the situation of American women is dire indeed. When Louise (Susan Sarandon) comes to the rescue of Thelma (Geena Davis) and kills the man who's attempting to rape her, few in the audience feel that murder is unjustified. And when Louise rejects Thelma's suggestion that they go to the police with a despairing, "A hundred people saw you dancing cheek to cheek. Who's going to believe us? What kind of world do you live in?," we know she's probably right about that too.

Opening in the U.S. on 24 May, one day after the Supreme Court handed down a decision barring employees of federally financed planning clinics from any discussion of abortion with their patients (thus drastically curtailing access for poor women to abortion), *Thelma and Louise* has turned out to be amazingly prescient. In a society which punishes women for their sexuality, women's reproductive freedom is as tenuous as their legal redress against crimes of rape and physical assault. David Souter, the recently appointed Supreme Court judge who cast the deciding vote in the family planning clinic case, wrote an opinion a few years ago against the complainant in a rape case characterising her behaviour as "provocative." Why should Thelma and Louise expect to be justly treated in his blame-the-victim court? What choice for them then except to become outlaws—and movie legends.

From *Sight and Sound*, July 1991, pp. 18–19. Copyright 1991 Amy Taubin. Reprinted by permission of the author.

Ridley Scott, director and co-producer of *Thelma and Louise*, knows how important a test case it is for "women-driven" material. The film has everything that's needed for a traditional box office success. Everything, that is, except a male protagonist.

The following is excerpted from a ninety minute interview with Scott just prior to *Thelma and Louise's* U.S. opening. At that point, the film was already showing signs of critical success. (It opened to enthusiastic reviews in both the local and national press.) Its commercial prospects were, however, far from settled. And Scott, while pleased to be regarded as something of an auteur (on the basis of *Blade Runner* and *Alien*), is careful to present himself as responsible Hollywood businessman, making movies for mainstream audiences.

Scott began his career at the BBC, first as an art director and then as director of *Z Cars*. He left after three years to form his own TV commercial production company. Twelve years later, he started directing feature films. He says that one result of having made thousands of commercials is that he doesn't have to think about visuals—it just happens.

"I have a development group in Los Angeles. We have our net cast out for ideas. They can come from newspaper articles, from conversations, from books. Also, there's a snow storm of scripts, most interestingly from new writers. We met Callie Khouri and she presented this script [*Thelma and Louise*], and I loved it. At that moment I was involved in another large-scale project—only two or three weeks in, thank God. So I went through this odd process—which I'm going to have to go through sooner or later anyway, because I'm curious about producing—of interviewing other directors for *Thelma and Louise*. The more I talked to them, the more possessive I became. Directing is partly a job to change things if they're wrong. But I felt the overall balance of the script shouldn't be tampered with—we did a bit of work with it, but basically it was all there. I felt so protective that I decided that I should direct it myself."

In that *Thelma and Louise* is driven by characters rather than events, it's a departure for Scott. Like his best films, however, it situates an allegorical narrative within a realistically detailed visual world. When one walks out of *Thelma and Louise*, one feels, as after *Blade Runner* and *Alien*, that one's been in a place one won't forget.

"It's a far less exotic world than *Alien*, although I tried to make the heartland look as exotic as possible. To us Europeans it is. The scale of things is so vast. We can eulogise about roads with telegraph poles, and Americans think we're crazy. I looked for days to find one. They don't actually exist very much any more, but they are very much part of what I believe is the American landscape. Oddly enough, I found it in Bakersfield (Southern California).

"When I started off on this project, I decided to take the actual journey that they take in the script, because your educational process begins there. When I location hunt, I'm not just looking at locations: I'm meeting people, I'm hearing voices and accents. So the production designer and the location hunter and I drove the route. We started in Arkansas and drove to the Grand Canyon. I couldn't haul 149 people around for three minutes in Texas and four in Arkansas, but I had a brief education on what everything looked like. I felt I had to find definitive examples of the landscape they passed through because it's allegorical and I felt that their journey, the last journey, should be part of the allegory. I felt it was better to lean to the vanishing face of America, which is Route 66, rather than the new face of America, which is malls and concrete strips."

Although *Thelma and Louise* is obviously a Ridley Scott film, the clarity and wit of the script and sense of the irrepressible in Davis's and Sarandon's performances suggest a high degree of collaboration between director, actors and writer. It's clear from Scott's description of working with the actors that he realises just how crucial to the film their performances are.

"I spend a long time casting. Finally the casting process comes down to a gut decision. There are a lot of actors out there who will give you a good cold read, and I used to be impressed by that, but then that's all you'd get, no surprises. I'm always hoping the actors I've cast are going to surprise me about where this character is going to go through the envelope—whether at that moment it's going to be maniacal or funny or subdued.

"There's always an element of taste involved in that, even if it's bad taste, and it's my job to adjust that—to be the barometer. But I want it to come out of them. Therefore, we talk a lot. We sit around the table with a script. I want to discuss their character and how they will function. The best sign is when the actor starts to get possessive about the role and says. 'Well I wouldn't do that,' even if it's about how they dress. 'I wouldn't wear shoes like that,' Once that happens I know they are starting to key into who they are. Then we start reading. I never ask them to read with, to use a corny term, feeling. It's usually a flat read. Then they say, 'I can't say this, what I'd like to say is this,' and I agree, unless it affects the drama or the humour. It becomes a partnership, so by the time we start doing the lines, we're very close to shooting.

"When we walk on the floor, we've usually already negotiated how the scene is going to go, and I've already done a kind of down and dirty lighting job. Then we do an immediate rehearsal, but with them saving it—I don't want to see it [meaning the performance]. We walk around and make some chalk marks and fix the focus. Then I say, 'Do you feel comfortable?' It's not like everything's cast in stone. If it's wrong, it's wrong, and we do it again. Then they go off and get made up, and they come back and we shoot.

"So there's this adrenalin, which I've found is really important. There's a spontaneity, and what I discovered is that both girls prefer it this way. Susan always used to laugh, and say, 'I'm the money actress. You don't see it until you say action and then you pay me.' I think there's nothing worse than when you rehearse: rehearse until every ounce of adrenalin is gone. That's when you end up with forty takes trying to make it look spontaneous. If we did five or six takes, it was a lot. Invariably if you've got the right people involved, you're going to start seeing it on the first or second take."

Not unlike Clint Eastwood, Scott has been dragged by his interest in strong women characters into some unpredictable political places. While *Thelma and Louise* is definitely a feminist film, Scott is no theoretician. And his conversation reveals a couple of contradictions that he hasn't thought through, much less resolved. He seems surprised, for example, when I object to his including the Sean Young character in *Blade Runner*, a robot whose sexuality is programmed by the Harrison Ford character, in his pantheon of strong women. He's similarly taken aback, although more than willing to hear me out, when I tell him that I, like many of the strong women I know, feel betrayed by the ending of *Thelma and Louise*.

Given that a handful of open-ended outlaw films already exist, why should Thelma and Louise not have been allowed to live out their days in Mexico drinking margueritas? Or conversely—given that the temper of the times makes it not unlikely that women who defend themselves against rapists or otherwise defy the patriarchy are risking death—shouldn't we be forced to look at Thelma and Louise's bloody bodies at the bottom of the Grand Canyon and thus to realise our complicity in their death?

Such a depressing ending, however, might have alienated precisely the audience that Scott claims he's trying to reach and probably would have destroyed the film's chances at the box office. Instead, we get tragedy with an upbeat ending. Via the freeze frame, Thelma and Louise become legends without having to go through all the grisly stuff of dying. Scott disagrees.

"There's a price for everything", he counters, adding that this applies to men as well as women. "From the first moment of reading the script, I never had a second thought about the ending. It just seemed appropriate that they carry on the journey. It's a metaphorical continuation. The film's not about rape. It's about choices and freedom. The only solution is to take your choice which is to take your life."

Perhaps it's a measure of how radical the film is that no ending feels satisfactory. Along with rapists, condescending husbands, irresponsible boyfriends, thieving lovers, lecherous truckers, sadistic cops and paternalistic detectives, *Thelma and Louise* leaves narrative closure by the wayside.

Scott is currently in production on *Christopher Columbus* with Gérard Depardieu as the explorer. Scott's description of Columbus as "the first astronaut" might suggest a Hollywood pitch, though the film is in fact very much a European production.

"I find America terribly stimulating, but my home is in England. I cut and mixed *Thelma and Louise* in Pinewood. That's been my pattern with [post-producing] all my films. The journalist community in the U.K. criticises us for opting out. I haven't opted out, but there's no film industry in the U.K. I simply go where I can make films—and not at such a mini-budget that it impedes what I want to do.

"The first film that really gonged me was David Lean's *Great Expectations*. But there's no point in making a movie if you don't have a market for it. Film is too expensive for that. It shouldn't be insular.

"I'm hoping that at some point in the near future Europe may open up. I'm hoping that will happen with *Columbus*. We've financed it by selling it territory by territory, like the independents have been doing; for years—like Dino De Laurentiis. And then we came to the U.S. for distribution.

"*Columbus* is going to be very unpopular. We're going to have every Indian society after us for racism. But his vision was very extreme— even more extreme than NASA's and more daunting. His crew believed he was going to sail to the edge of the world. The NASA people, at least, have their co-ordinates when they send up a mission."

# 1492: Conquest of Paradise

## ANA MARIA BAHIANA/1992

It may seem rather odd that Hollywood didn't realize what a cinematic opportunity the five hundredth anniversary of Columbus's arrival in America was until two independent productions virtually grabbed at each other's throats for the privilege of doing it. But that is exactly what happened back in early 1991, when the father-and-son producing duo of Ilya and Alexander Salkind (of *Superman* fame) and director Ridley Scott announced different visions of the man and his already controversial deeds.

Some flame-throwing at the 1991 Cannes Film Festival, a lawsuit (moved by the Salkinds against Scott, who they claimed was their initial directorial choice) and some stirring in the Spanish press (divided between the two projects) followed in quick succession. The Salkinds' project, titled *Columbus: The Discovery* and financed in part by the Spanish government's Fifth Centennial Commission, went on to be a much-troubled (and financially bankrupt) pop version of Columbus's travels, treated very much like an aggrandized television movie.

Scott's film, named *1492: Conquest of Paradise* to avoid further lawsuits, and supported by the Spanish Ministry of Culture, is something else. Its springboard is a carefully-researched script by French journalist Roslyne Bosch. While preparing a story on Spain's plan for the five hundredth anniversary, Bosch (at that point a staff writer for the newsweekly *Le Point*) stumbled upon a wealth of material about the visionary Genovese mariner. It wasn't what she discovered that fascinated her;

From *Cinema Papers*, October 1992, pp. 30–35. Reprinted by permission of the author.

rather, it was the vastness of Columbus's mystery that did. "People think, 'Ah, Columbus, a legend'," Bosch said to the *Los Angeles Times*. "They didn't think of him as a person. But he was obviously an extraordinary person, a complex person like all of us."

Bosch went on to write a précis of what would be the 1492 script: Columbus's many journeys, the existential as well as maritime ones, as narrated by one of his illegitimate sons. Through a literary agent, the draft reached Alain Goldman, the thirty-year-old president of the French film company MK2, who paid her to develop it into a full screenplay.

With Bosch's script and Ridley Scott's commitment to direct, Goldman proceeded to knock on Hollywood's doors, initially with no luck. A $45 million period piece seemed utterly unpalatable to the major studios, even with the five hundredth anniversary looming on the horizon. The fact that Gérard Depardieu had already attached himself to the project to play Columbus, and that the film boasted a first-class cast (Armand Assante, Tcheky Karyo, Angela Molina, Frank Langella and, at the eleventh hour, Sigourney Weaver as Queen Isabella of Spain) apparently didn't help.

Goldman finally financed the project by pre-selling its foreign rights, a strategy that's becoming common practice in these recession-plagued, cash-tied times, and principal photography began in late 1991 in Seville and Granada, Spain. Thanks to the endorsement from the Ministry of Culture, Scott and his crew were able to film on such centuries-old locations as the Alcazar in Seville and the Convent of San Esteban in Salamanca.

From there the production moved to Costa Rica, chosen after months of exhaustive scouting to portray the pristine New World that Columbus encountered at the end of his journey. In Costa Rica, the cast was joined by one hundred and seventy Indians from four Costa Rican tribes, and six Waunana Indians from Colombia, assigned to play their ancestors. As Scott describes, it wasn't the tense, accusation-ridden encounter one might imagine, but a rich, exciting experience. Says Alejandrino Moya, the Waunana Indian who plays Chief Guarionex, one of the tribesmen that Columbus brought with him back to Spain, "I feel that the people we are portraying are both noble and dignified. I would have been proud to have been part of his tribe."

*1492* stays clear of the recent revisionist wave that has all but reversed Christopher Columbus's status as a hero of humankind. As Scott discusses in this interview,[1] his Columbus is a man of his time, who should not and cannot be analyzed and judged by today's historical standards. His wasn't a glorious, idealized world—Bosch's script deals with slavery, religious persecution and the bloody expulsion of the Moors from Spain—but an era struggling to break free from ignorance, sickness and misery, in which a man like Columbus, not born into the landowning aristocracy, could, for the first time in aeons, afford to have dreams of wealth and greatness. "Columbus wasn't sure where he was going to land or whether he would even land," Scott says. "What he found was an earthly paradise which became his hell."

AB:   *What attracted you to this project, especially considering it represents such a thematic and stylistic departure from your last film* Thelma & Louise?
RS:   I was looking for a period film. In a way, I was returning to my first film, *The Duellists,* which had given me tremendous satisfaction—reconstructing the period and exploring period behaviour and attitudes.

My last three movies—*Someone to Watch Over Me, Black Rain* and *Thelma & Louise*—have all had extreme contemporary points of view. I needed new ground to break; what better than this larger-than-life character whose efforts changed the world forever.

AB:   *It has often been said—even by you and 1492's writer, Roslyne Bosch—that Columbus, the man, is still a mystery. Was that a concern of yours while preparing for and shooting this picture? Was it necessary for you to fill in the blanks, so to speak, or did you work with the mystery itself?*
RS:   Very little still exists of first-hand information—personal or otherwise—of Columbus's true nature. The script was a carefully drawn assessment between the known facts and the "exaggerated truth." It

---

1. The interview was conducted by Bahiana in Los Angeles with Scott in London by submitting written questions, to which Scott later responded. Naturally, this method (all that could be arranged at short notice) meant Bahiana was unable to follow up answers with a new question. In some cases, the questions have been edited to encourage flow.

was a matter of trying to fill in between the lines: we did not work with the mystery.

AB:    *How much impact did you have in the final shaping of the script?*
RS:    I usually have a fair degree of input at the earliest stages of a script—formulating the direction of the story and then, at the final stages, when a lot of work is done going through the screenplay, beat by beat, line by line. I'm the one who finally has to make it. By definition of that, I am obliged to become the "devil's advocate": I need to convince myself before I can make anything.

AB:    *What areas of Columbus's personality and of the socio-political background of his travels did you feel were paramount to your vision of his story?*
RS:    Columbus's personality was formed clearly by the times he was born into, and by his travels and experiences of the following years, through his childhood and early manhood. Clearly the socio-political background plays an enormous part in forming his character and his views, like it does to all of us today. In that respect, people don't change much: they are the product of their own environments.

AB:    *How do you see "his times" and their uniqueness? Was Columbus, in your opinion, not only a product of his era but also a catalyst of the immense changes that were soon to come?*
RS:    Columbus was one of those fortunates (or unfortunates) who are ahead of their time. Historically, they have had to pay a price for their "forward thinking." His contemporaries were Leonardo da Vinci, Michelangelo, Thomas More . . . all men emerging out of darkness into light, all creators of this movement toward a renaissance.

AB:    *You have been quoted as not being very patient with the recent revisionist upsurge that tries to blame Columbus for every single evil that befell America. Could you elaborate on your point of view regarding his historical role as displayed in your film, and your opinion on this blame-assignment campaign?*
RS:    Taking into account all I have said before, it is a pointless exercise to criticize him for his methods and results in the fifteenth century.

He was a product of his times: what was considered "normal" behaviour then, "socio-political" or otherwise, cannot be judged by today's standards. He had not had the benefit of the following five hundred years of "colonization," with all its brutality, to be the humanist he may have been by today's standards. Besides, we do not see much evidence of us having learned anything by our present performance, either last century or this one. If anything, it seems to be getting worse—except the world does now seem to have a humanitarian overview, so that we all hope and believe something will be done and there will be control. . . . Will there?

AB:    *Was it especially difficult finding locations for this film, considering the widespread development in Europe and the Caribbean?*
RS:    It was extremely difficult to find appropriate locations which would afford me all the elements I required for Columbus's experiences in the Indies. We location-hunted in Mexico, the Dominican Republic, Cuba and Colombia before finally settling for Costa Rica. I was told that Costa Rica could be compared as the "Switzerland of the Middle Americas," a stable political society, ecologically unspoiled, with a Hispanic community and, most important, with a fairly large population of the original inhabitants, who proved invaluable in the making of the film.

AB:    *You are an extremely visual director. What were your stylistic choices for the look of* 1492?
RS:    Reality.

AB:    *Would you comment on the casting? What qualities does Gérard Depardieu bring to your Columbus? Was he always your first choice?*
RS:    Gérard Depardieu was my first and only choice for Columbus. His natural character seems to dovetail into my perception of who Columbus may have been: a strong, physical man, driven by his emotions and instinct, a strong orator with the personality to persuade men to follow him.

AB:    *How was the experience of working with Indians as extras and supporting actors? Was there any special training or preparation required?*

RS:    Working with the Indians from Costa Rica and Colombia who were playing individual parts was, at first, as nerve-racking for me as it was for them—communication being our biggest problem, not to mention the task of coaxing performances from them, both as a mass group and as individuals. But what happened was thrilling. With the help of Claudia Gomez from Colombia, they became marvellously uninhibited actors who never held back—ever—and portrayed some of the most authentic Indians I have seen on screen.

AB:    *Were there any hard feelings considering the recent Indian protests against the five hundredth anniversary?*
RS:    We never, ever, experienced any difficulties from Indian society, only support. They were fascinated with what they were doing and seemed satisfied that they were being portrayed accurately.

AB:    *Apparently, this project was a rather difficult one to finance—not only because it was necessarily costly, but also because most studios resist the idea of "period" films. Why do you think this is so?*
RS:    Historical films have always been difficult to mount because of the inherent resistance to the cost and by modern audiences who seem to be more concerned with escapism than realism today—understandably. But haven't they always preferred that? After all, movies are essentially a form of entertainment, not education. But it'd be good if they can occasionally do both: *Dances with Wolves, Amadeus, Dangerous Liaisons.*

The financing of this project really did not seem to take any more time than the process that one would probably go through on a large historical project. The only difference, apart from having absolute creative control, is that, as an independent, you have no one to "watch over you" financially. So you have to be right in all "cases" throughout the production and you *must* "deliver" on time.

AB:    *Has the five hundredth anniversary of Columbus's voyages helped the project in any way?*
RS:    The five hundredth anniversary, of course, helped through building "awareness" for this project, although last year the studios surprisingly

had not really taken the celebration into account as a useful promotion factor.

AB:   *This film has the endorsement of the Spanish Ministry of Culture. What is the extent of this endorsement? Did it facilitate the production in any way? Was it a concern of yours in terms of maintaining creative autonomy on the project?*
RS:   Certainly in Spain we had enormous financial aid from the Ministry of Culture, which was planning the celebration three years ago. There was no real problem with the Ministry in terms of accuracy of the story other than minor requests. I guess we were well-rehearsed.

AB:   *It was reported last year that you would work on a definitive director's cut of* Blade Runner *for release sometime in* 1992. *Is this really going to happen? And, if so, what will we see?*
RS:   Yes, we are re-releasing *Blade Runner* in early September in America with my version of the story. I felt the released cut was over-explanatory. The Deckard (Harrison Ford) voice-over became a disturbing factor. The happily ever-after ending was always silly and really worked against the nature of the "beast." *Blade Runner* is a *film noir*, where the happiest ending one can hope for is at least philosophical and may even leave you wondering as to the fate of the two characters—certainly a bitter-sweet ending.

AB:   *What are your feelings and ideas regarding what happened to the film in the early* 1980s *and the re-emergence of a "director's cut" in* 1991?
RS:   The film in the '80s was received with mixed feelings. Mostly, audiences were devastated by the near future that we presented (accurate or otherwise). Video and laserdisc sales proved that there was an over-riding curiosity for the film, so that people were able to re-examine the film. When a director's cut was shown in L.A. in '91, the attendance was terrific. The rest followed.

AB:   *What will be your next project? It has been reported that you were interested in doing a film about the Brazilian Indian leader, Payakan. Is that still in the works? Have the recent allegations against Payakan[2] hindered the project or changed your mind about it?*

RS:    I have not decided yet. However, I am still interested in making a film about Payakan, and his friendship and accomplishments with Dr. Darrell Possy. The recent allegations against Payakan have not hindered my enthusiasm for the story. It is still a story that holds a great deal of importance for me and should be told.

---

2. Payakan has been accused of the assault, rape and battery of a young white woman in Brazil. He is scheduled to go to trial in October.

# Interview with Ridley Scott

## PAUL M. SAMMON / 1996

Ridley Scott was born November 30, 1937. His feature film credits (as of 1995, and as a director) are: *The Duellists* (1977), *Alien* (1979), *Blade Runner* (1982), *Legend* (1985), *Someone to Watch Over Me* (1987), *Black Rain* (1989), *Thelma & Louise* (1991), *1492: Conquest of Paradise* (1992), and *White Squall* (1996). He has also functioned as a producer, a capacity which actually began with *Blade Runner* (the end credits list the motion picture as "A Michael Deeley–Ridley Scott Production"). Scott also produced *Thelma & Louise* and *1492: Conquest of Paradise*. Other directors for whom Scott and his company Scott Free have produced films include 1994's *The Browning Version* (produced by Ridley Scott) and *Monkey Trouble* (1994, executive producer, Ridley Scott).

In 1993, Scott was set to direct an adaptation of the best-selling nonfiction work *Crisis in the Hot Zone* (based on a true story concerning a near-outbreak of the deadly Ebola virus in Washington, D.C.), but that deal blew apart. At the time of this writing, Ridley is preparing to direct *G.I. Jane,* the story of the first female Navy SEAL, which is to star Demi Moore.

The following interview is an edited composite of a series of formal conversations concerning *Blade Runner* which took place between Ridley Scott and this author on the following dates: September 10, 1980; May 15, 1981; June 12, 1982; February 17, 1994; September 22; 1994; September 13, 1995; and December 4, 1995.

From *Future Noir: The Making of* Blade Runner by Paul M. Sammon (New York: HarperCollins, 1996), pp. 375–93. Copyright 1996 Paul M. Sammon. Reprinted by permission of the author.

PAUL M. SAMMON:    *I'd like to begin with a query regarding one of* Blade Runner's *biggest question marks: the "Unicorn Scene" in the Director's Cut, that moment in the film when Harrison Ford is slumped at his piano and daydreaming about this mythical beast. Before we get into that shot's thematic meanings, I'd like to ask about its origins. Was it in any way influenced by* Legend, *the film you did after* Blade Runner, *which also featured unicorns?*

RIDLEY SCOTT:    No. That unicorn was actually filmed prior to any thought of making *Legend*. In fact, it was specifically shot for *Blade Runner* during the post-production process. At that point in time I was editing the picture in England, at Pinewood Studios, and we were heading towards a mix. Yet I still, creatively speaking, had this blank space in my head in regards to what Deckard's dream at the piano was going to be all about.

That was distressing, because this was an important moment for me. I'd predetermined that that unicorn scene would be the strongest clue that Deckard, this hunter of replicants, might actually be an artificial human himself. I did feel that this dream had to be vague, indirect. I didn't mind if it remained a bit mysterious, either, so that you had to think about it. Because there is a clear thread throughout the film that would later explain it.

Anyway, I eventually realized I had to think of an image that was so personal it could only belong to an individual's inner thoughts. And eventually I hit on a unicorn.

PS:    *You mentioned the word "dream," which is interesting. Because the way you staged that scene in* Blade Runner, *it's almost as if Ford's drifting off into a reverie.*

RS:    Yeah. Well, actually, he's pissed. He's drunk. On a rather strange bottle of twenty-first-century Johnny Walker Red. Which he took with him, you may remember, when he went to get his hard copy from the Esper.

Unfortunately, I don't think I really played Deckard drunk enough in that scene. What I mean by that is the Deckard character was supposed to be somewhat Marlowesque, after the Raymond Chandler antihero, you know? And Marlowe was always a little tiddly. So I thought that that scene would be a good opportunity to see our own hero a bit drunk while he was trying to work, as he was puzzling over these old photographs.

PS:    *Ah,* Blade Runner*'s infamous photographs. Why did you choose that particular device to associate with the film's replicants?*
RS:    Because photographs are essentially history. Which is what these replicants don't have.

PS:    *One final question regarding the replicants' fascination with photographs—couldn't these snapshots also be interpreted as hard-copy analogs of the artificial memories implanted in the androids?*
RS:    Definitely. Don't forget that just prior to the unicorn scene, Deckard has told Rachael that her memories are not hers. Then he gives her a couple of examples of these implants, like the spider giving birth outside her window. At which point Rachael basically breaks down and leaves Deckard's apartment. And he feels, I guess, guilty about that process.

We next find Deckard poring over the photographs and doodling at his piano. And of course what we then do is reveal an extremely private and innermost thought of his, which is triggered by the music Deckard is playing. Now, music, in my mind at least, is a very visual medium. It can provoke intense imagery. So when Deckard kind of drifts off at that moment, I thought that the image which came into his mind ought to be something which we would otherwise never see in the movie.

PS:    *I must confess that when I first saw the completed film at the San Diego preview, I felt the exclusion of the unicorn scene seriously disrupted the connections you were trying to make. I picked up on the other clues that Deckard might be a replicant—his collection of photographs, the scene where Ford's eyes glow—but without that specific shot of the unicorn in the woods, I felt more inclined to accept Olmos's act of leaving behind the tinfoil unicorn as merely an indication that Gaff had come to Deckard's apartment and decided to let Sean Young live. But then, when I saw the Director's Cut, the inclusion of the live unicorn made a more emotional impact. Now I could see that that tinfoil origami was a sign Gaff knew Deckard's thoughts.*

*So it's almost as if there are two different movies there. In the original theatrical release, Deckard might be a replicant; in the Director's Cut, he is one.*

RS:    They *are* two different movies. But the Director's Cut is closer to what I was originally after.

What I find interesting about that unicorn scene is that while so much has been made by the critics of the unicorn, they've actually missed the wider issue. It is not the unicorn itself which is important. It's the land-scape around it—the green landscape—they should be noticing.

PS:    *I understand what you're saying. But, to be fair, I can also understand the confusion. The original prints of* Blade Runner *did, in fact, conclude with green landscapes. Even if they were tacked-on ones.*
RS:    Tacked-on, as you say. By some of the producers, and by the studio. Which I'm sure we'll talk about later.

But before that happened, my original thought had been to never show a green landscape during *Blade Runner.* We would only see an urban world. But I subsequently figured, since this moment of Deckard nood-ling at the piano offered the pictorial opportunity of a dream, why not show a unicorn? In a forest? It's an image that's so out of place with the rest of the picture that even if I only run it for three seconds, the audi-ence will clearly understand that they're witnessing some sort of reverie.

PS:    *Given the confusion that that unicorn has raised in some circles, I'm not sure your faith in the audience was justified.*
RS:    I know what you mean. Maybe I should amend that to say, I was sure that the part of the audience which was paying attention would understand it! [laughs]

PS:    *Besides creative differences, I understand another reason the unicorn shot was deleted from the original theatrical prints had something to do with the fact that you'd filmed it relatively late in the game.*
RS:    True. Besides the tacked-on ending, the unicorn scene was more or less the last thing I shot for the picture. By that time, the pressure had grown quite intense to just get the bloody film into theaters.

PS:    *That raises another question. Over the years, you've been quoted as say-ing that you very much wanted that unicorn footage back in the film. Yet my own research indicates that when certain producers originally requested that you delete that shot, you didn't necessarily object. What's the real story here?*

*Had the* Blade Runner *pressures grown so great, the problems so numerous, that you finally just threw in the towel?*
RS:    No. You see, by then I'd been through the whole process of going to war. Which was making the movie, with all its attendant budgetary problems and "clashes with certain producers" and so on. Still, I really thought I'd got it with *Blade Runner,* you know? I genuinely felt I'd made an interesting movie.

Then came the confusion that followed the previews in Texas and Colorado. Which created—I guess the word is insecurity. A certain insecurity was going around at the time between myself and the Ladd Company and Michael Deeley and Bud Yorkin and Jerry Perenchio, the film's other producers. It was that insecurity which led to the original deletion of the unicorn sequence.

PS:    *Frankly, I'm not surprised.* Blade Runner *is quite an unusual, stylized and, if I may say so, artistic product. Especially for the studios. That must have been difficult, particularly since you and I are both well aware of the fact that—at least in terms of the Hollywood commercial mindset—anything smacking of "art" automatically breeds insecurity.*
RS:    I never thought about it that way. My way of thinking was, hey, I just made the movie.

PS:    *Moving on, why did you decide to primarily film* Blade Runner *on the Warner Brothers back lot? That seems an unusual choice for you, given the penchant for location shooting I've noticed in your other pictures.*
RS:    Actually, Michael Deeley and I did quite a bit of location scouting on *Blade Runner*—Boston, Atlanta, New York, even London. Funnily enough, today I could probably shoot *Blade Runner* in the city of London because of the way it's being developed. It's as spectacular as New York.

In any event, we had done all this location hunting before I finally realized I'd never be able to control the two or three real city blocks we'd need to dress as a set for the length and space of time I'd need them. Which would have been months. We never could have done that in a genuine city and kept a lid on the situation. Therefore, it became very apparent that my only alternative was a studio back lot. Which I was really scared to death of, because back lots always look like back lots.

PS:    *You managed to make it not look like a back lot.*
RS:    Well, the fact that we were shooting at night was certainly a helpful factor. But Warner's back lot isn't that big. So if we hadn't filmed *Blade Runner* at night, you would have been able to see beyond the margins of our sets to all those small hills which surround the Warner Brothers' studio. That's also the reason it's raining all the time in *Blade Runner,* you know. To disguise the fact that we were shooting on a back lot.

PS:    *Were the constant rain and night-time exteriors purely pragmatic decisions? I mean, that ubiquitous damp and darkness certainly adds to* Blade Runner's *atmosphere.*
RS:    It does help lend a realistic quality to the story, yes. But really, a lot of the reason we finally settled on all that rain and night shooting was to hide the sets. I was really paranoid that audiences would notice we were shooting on a back lot.

PS:    *This is a basic question, but how did you latch onto the actual title for this film? I do know you bought the rights to the words "Blade Runner" from William Burroughs and Norton, but who initially discovered those words? And why did you choose them?*
RS:    That's a good question, but a long answer.

We actually spent months, in early 1980, when I first came out here to Los Angeles—Hampton Fancher and I, and sometimes Michael Deeley—spending every day slogging through the *Dangerous Days* script. Now, Hampton had composed a clever screenplay about a man who falls in love with his quarry. But for budgetary reasons, he'd kept it very internal. So I said to him, "You know, Hampton, as soon as this Deckard character walks out a door, whatever he looks at must endorse the fact that his world has reached the point where it can create replicants. Otherwise this picture will not fly. It'll become an intellectual sci-fi."

This was the point where we began to create the architecture of the film. Not long after, we'd arrived at a screenplay which I think nicely integrated Hampton's original storyline, characterizations, and dialogue with what we'd managed to logically decide what *Blade Runner's* outside world had to be like.

But then I finally said to Hampton, "You know, we can't keep calling Deckard a goddamn detective." And he said, "Why not?" I replied, "Because we're telling a story in 2019, for Christ's sake. The word 'detective' will probably still be around then, but this job Deckard does, killing androids, that requires something new. We've got to come up with a bloody name for his profession."

That was on a Friday. Hampton slunk in the next Monday. We had our meeting, and he said, "By the way, I've come up with a name." And I asked, "What is it?" But instead of telling me, he wrote it down. And as he handed the slip of paper Hampton said, "It's better that you read it than hear it."

Of course, it read "Blade Runner." I said, "That's great! It's wonderful!" But the more I enthused about it, the more Hampton looked guiltier and guiltier. So I asked, "Where'd it come from? Is it yours?" [laughs] Finally, he said, "Well . . . no, not really. Actually, it's William Burroughs's. From a slim book he wrote in 1979 called *Blade Runner: A Movie.*" And I said, "Well, we gotta buy it, we gotta buy it!"

Burroughs, who turned out to be a fan of Philip Dick's, then said "Sure!" when we approached him, and gave it to us for a nominal fee. So that's how the title was acquired. I thought the words "Blade Runner" very well-suited our needs. It was a nice, threatening name that neatly described a violent action.

PS:    *It also neatly describes Deckard's character, which runs on the knife's edge between humanity and inhumanity.*
RS:    Yes, it does. What's more, there are a lot of delivery services in Hollywood that now have exactly the same style of typeface. [laughs]

PS:    *How did you get along with Hampton?*
RS:    It used to vary a bit day by day, but basically I thought we got along extremely well. Incidentally, I think Hampton's definitely got a touch of genius. He'll be amused to hear me say that.

PS:    *One thing I've always found amusing about the response to this picture is how it's perceived as being such a deadly serious work. Now, don't misunderstand me—I think you created a motion picture which is both thought-provoking and mature—but I also remember you telling me you were trying to create a live-action version of* Heavy Metal. *A comic book, in other words. And* Blade Runner *is a comic book.*

RS:    It is indeed. I really made a film which is a comic book, and you've got to remember that. But people always misinterpret this aspect of the production.

They also underestimate the huge problem of taking a comic strip and adapting it to the screen. That's a difficult process, because comic strips work on a two-dimensional level. You're looking at one line here, one line there, some terrific artwork and dynamic layout, and your brain supplies the rest. But to duplicate that experience in a film requires enormous discipline and preplanning. This is one reason that I won't even touch a futuristic picture until I get its script into reasonable shape. Because everything else springs from that, including the picture's visual aspects. Which in turn creates the concrete environment of that future.

Therefore, if I do a science fiction, it's got to somehow not be wasted, if you know what I mean. Sci-fi presents a wonderful opportunity, because if you get it right, anything goes. But you'd better have drawn up your rule book for the world you've created first. Then you'd better stick to it.

PS:    *What about the ethical problems regarding the replicants in* Blade Runner? *More than once, they're compared to slaves.*
RS:    I always felt I'd been a bit fanciful with the underlying concept of the replicants, really. Because if a society decided to produce a second-class species, that society would also probably develop it with subhuman capabilities. You wouldn't want your twin objecting to your going to its cupboard to remove its kidney. The fact that the replicants in *Blade Runner* are indeed intelligent complicates the situation. You immediately have a huge morality problem. But I must say that I'm not comfortable with these issues. If I'd gone into them in *Blade Runner,* I would have had a totally different picture. So I didn't.

PS:    *Why not?*
RS:    Two absolutely essential considerations are critical to the success of any so-called Hollywood picture. The first is that the end result of any film is communication with its audience. And the second is, the larger the film,

the larger your budget—which also means the larger the audience you have to consider. I think a lot of people actually don't realize that.

So what you've got to set in your mind, right up front, is what kind of audience you're hoping your subject will reach. Therefore, unless you're a fool, you construct your story and budget and the scope of your film accordingly. In other words, if you're going to end up in an art cinema, you should stay within the confines of a small budget movie, which will allow you to explore most any esoteric idea you wish. But if you're going to attempt to follow along the path of a Spielberg, then your choice of subject matter and the way you're going to explain and communicate your story to that larger audience is, of necessity, going to be on a slightly more simplified level. I wouldn't say on an any less intelligent level, just less esoteric.

PS:    *Choosing to present your subject matter in this manner sounds like a delicate balancing act.*
RS:    Well, it all gets down to instinct. If you apply pure logic to your choice of subject, that's dangerous. Potentially sterile. So to a certain extent you're drawn into a film by your own instincts. And I think that my instincts happen to be fairly commercial ones.

PS:    *Moving on to a plot point, one that's constantly discussed, is the matter of how many replicants Deckard's supposed to be hunting. Specifically, I think you know what I mean—the confusion from Bryant saying that out of the six original escaped androids, one was already dead, leaving five. But Deckard only retires four. I already know the answer to this question, but could you officially put it on the record?*
RS:    I assume you're speaking of Mary, the sixth replicant we had to drop. I'd actually cast that part. Given the role to an interesting young lady about the same age as Daryl Hannah, whose name I can't recall—

PS:    *Stacey Nelkin?*
RS:    That's it. Actually, we removed Mary's scenes, because we couldn't afford to do them. We suddenly realized, about the third week into filming, that with the kind of detail I work with, we were going to have to build in a hedge against going over budget. In other words, we'd have to remove some scenes, remove some action. Mary's action, as it turned out.

PS:    *So all this confusion resulted from a money issue.*

RS:    Yep. Stacey was devastated, poor thing. I still feel a bit badly about that. I'm also sorry the character itself had to be written out; Mary was going to be the only replicant that the audience would have gotten to see naturally fade away. What we'd come up with was a situation that took place early on in the film. In a dark room, with the other replicants watching Mary die. That's how we were going to introduce the replicants.

PS:    *That's interesting, because in the last draft of the script I have mentioning Mary, she survives up until the end of the film. At which point we see her hiding in a closet in Sebastian's apartment. Until Deckard shoots through the closet door, killing her.*

RS:    We'd rewritten that. Mary's primary scene was now going to take place very early on. You'd witness all these replicants hovering over her deathbed before you even met Roy Batty. So it gave these replicants an instant sort of sympathy. I was sorry to see that go—it was rather a sad scene, actually.

PS:    *Let's discuss an interesting visual motif that runs throughout* Blade Runner. *It begins with that giant eye at the start of the film, the close-up of the blue iris which is intercut with the wide shots of the industrial landscape. Was that meant to be a symbolic or literal eye?*

RS:    I think it was intuitively going along with the root of an Orwellian idea. That the world is more of a controlled place now. It's really the eye of Big Brother.

PS:    *Or Eldon Tyrell?*

RS:    Or Tyrell. Tyrell, in fact, had he lived, would certainly have been Big Brother.

PS:    *I ask this, because* Blade Runner's *special effects storyboards suggested that the eye belonged to Holden, the Blade Runner shot by Leon in the interrogation room.*

RS:    That was the early intent, yes. But I later realized that linking that eye with any specific character was far too literal a maneuver and removed the particular emotion I was trying to induce.

PS:    *Inserting that gigantic, staring orb up front set up an interesting para-noid vibe, I thought. Because instead of the audience watching the film, the film is watching the audience. . . .*
RS:    You hit it. *Blade Runner*, in a sense, actually is about paranoia. And that eye underscores Deckard's dilemma, because by the end of the film, he believes he may be a replicant himself.

PS:    *Continuing with* Blade Runner's *use of vision, there seems to also be a definite "eye motif" in the film. I mean, besides the giant eye in the first act, you have the Voight-Kampff machine that looks into eyes. Chew works at an eye lab, Batty holds up artificial eyes in front of his own, Tyrell's eyes are gouged out, the replicant's eyes glow. . . . This sort of thing persists through-out the picture. Was this insistent repetition intentional on your part?*
RS:    Well, who was it that said that the eyes are the window to the soul? I believe that. Just as I believe that they are the windows in your head.

But the basic reason I started out the film on an eye and then contin-ued to emphasize eyes through action or dialogue was because of the Voight-Kampff machine. It just sat there and focused on the windows in your head. Therefore, it was logical that I begin the film on this window and attempt to develop and sustain that imagery throughout the film.

Also, you know, when you think about it, the eye is the single most vulnerable aperture in your body. Without your eyes, man, you've got nothing. And sticking something through someone's eye is a very sim-ple way of killing somebody. That feeds right back into the atmosphere of paranoia I was attempting to create.

So it all comes back to the Voigt-Kampff machine. Which was a stroke of collective genius. First came Philip K. Dick, who invented this totally believable instrumentality and term—"Voigt-Kampff" sounds like a real piece of equipment, like an Arriflex. Then Hampton Fancher brilliantly expanded and deepened Dick's concept. Finally, Syd Mead came up with a marvelous design for a working model of this imaginary thing. All of these accomplishments were quite extraordinary.

PS:    *The use of the Voigt-Kampff instrument raises a basic question, though. If Blade Runners have photographs and videotapes of what replicants look like—and you establish both of these facts early in the film—why do they have to give them a Voigt-Kampff test to determine if they are indeed replicants?*

RS:    If replicants have been replicated from human beings, then I guess a law would have to be passed as a "fail-safe." One demanding that all replicants had to be tested in case you found the real thing. Either way, they would deny being replicants.

PS:    *Obviously, the glowing eyes of the replicants were meant to be a dramatic and not a literal device, correct?*

RS:    Yes. Because if you could walk into a room and see someone's eyes shining away at you, why take the trouble of testing them? You'd just blow them away where they stood. So that retinal kickback was primarily a cinematic technique, mainly used as a tip-off for the audience.

However, I'd also intended a couple of other, more subtle things with the replicants' glowing eyes. One was semihumorous and slightly ironic—the fact that, despite all their technology, the genetic designers of *Blade Runner*'s world still hadn't quite perfected their product's eyeballs. So that kickback you saw from the replicants' retinas was a bit of a design flaw. I was also trying to say that the eye is really the most important organ in the human body. It's like a two-way mirror; the eye doesn't only see a lot, the eye gives away a lot. A glowing human retina seemed one way of stating that.

PS:    *Your casting of Sean Young was an interesting choice—she's almost too beautiful to be true.*

RS:    But that was the point, you see. If this patriarchal technology could create artificial women, then they'd surely design them to be young and sexually attractive. *Blade Runner* even obliquely comments on this, through Pris's designation as a "pleasure unit." That's a totally fascistic concept, by the way, and I don't agree with it. I don't even want to discuss it. But that would be the reality of this civilization.

Also [laughs], when Sean was made up in her forties outfit, she somewhat reminded me of Rita Hayworth. She had that look. And Hayworth had been my ideal of the sphinxlike femme fatale ever since I saw her in *Gilda* [1946, and an important *film noir*]. So I suppose you could say Rachael was my homage to *Gilda*, in a way.

PS:    *I'm sure this has been brought up to you before, but the only people Deckard kills in the film are women. And the first one he kills, Zhora, he shoots in the back. Now, the film noir hero was always cynical, but Deckard's actions seem to carry things beyond that. What this further deconstruction of the film noir protagonist intentional on your part?*
RS:    Yeah, but you know, I was going down this avenue of exploring Hollywood. The first real Hollywood movie I'd done was *Alien,* and *Alien* was pretty dark. So I decided to make *Blade Runner* a further inversion of Hollywood values.

What I was really dealing with in *BR* was an antihero, an almost soulless man who really didn't give a shit whether he shot these artificial humans in the front or shot them in the back. He's simply there to do the job. But what we learn at the beginning of the film through the voice-over, which is now gone, thank God, is that he's also begun to act with a certain amount of remorse. Deckard starts the picture realizing he's getting touched by his work. Which of course sets up ensuing situations that turn his world upside-down.

PS:    *The fact that Deckard eliminates only women in the film perversely feminizes him, then.*
RS:    Yes.

PS:    *Personally, I found those moments when Deckard kills Pris and Zhora to be a fairly savage commentary on male chauvinism.*
RS:    Exactly. I would totally agree with that.

PS:    *I also noticed there's a similarity between Harrison Ford finding a snake scale in a tub in* Blade Runner *and Michael Douglas finding a sequin in a tub in* Black Rain. . . .
RS:    That's very well spotted. But I have to tell you, I didn't like that. We needed a clue in *Black Rain*, and somebody on the crew who'd seen *Blade Runner* suggested the sequin. And I said, "No, we can't. I've already done this once." But we couldn't think of another goddamn clue! So in fact, it's absolutely a repeat. I hated doing it.

PS:    *One touch which has caused endless speculation among hard-core fans of the film is the chess game that's played between Sebastian and Tyrell, the one which Batty uses as a ploy to finally meet his maker. The theory has been raised that the moves and pieces on the boards seen in* Blade Runner *are an homage to an actual, classic chess match played in 1851, called "The Immortal Game." Is that correct?*

RS:   I've seen that speculation somewhere myself. The answer is no. What's that line you see at the end of film credits? "Any resemblance between this photoplay and actual events is purely coincidental?" [laughs] I'm afraid that's the case with *Blade Runner*'s chess game—it's purely coincidental.

PS:   *Could you talk a bit about the final night's shooting? I understand it was fairly brutal.*

RS:   You could say that. Most of the final evening was taken up filming Ford and Hauer on this twenty-foot-high set we'd constructed on the back lot to stand in for the roof Deckard's hanging from at the end of the picture. And I had the completion bond people breathing down my neck—they were going to rip me off that roof. Yet we still managed to squeeze Rutger's "tears in rain" speech in.

Then I needed a shot of the dove Rutger releases flying away into the sky. We'd tried to grab that earlier, but the bird had become rather wet under the sprinklers we had going, and when it was time for it to fly off, it merely hopped out of Rutger's hand and walked away. So I later shot another bird during the day, as an insert, in London, next to the incinerator at Elstree Studios. Which of course didn't quite look right.

PS:   *Tandem was pushing you that hard to wrap things up?*

RS:   Yes. I did manage to grab another shot or two the last day by moving that rooftop set into a soundstage. But basically, the completion bond people were just saying "screw that" to anything else I wanted, so we closed down. In fact, you can notice in the last scene after Rutger has died that the sky behind him is going blue. That was dawn. A real dawn. That was literally it—it's a wrap, babe.

PS:   *If all the other animals of* Blade Runner*'s world are artificial, why is that dove real? Were you sacrificing internal accuracy for symbolism? Using that bird to represent Hauer's departing soul or as a "dove of peace"?*

RS:   I think the dove came from Rutger. Hauer was good to work with and very much a contributor. He used to come in with lots of ideas.

Rutger said, "Can I use the dove?" And I said, "It's a bit on the nose, don't you think?" But he was so intense about it I eventually said, "Go for it." I think he pulled it off. But it was a last-second idea—I mean, we photographed it that morning, so we had to run off and get some pigeons very quickly.

Of course, technically, in that particular world of 2019, there would be no live pigeons there. Everything would be dead.

PS:    *Speaking of Hauer improvising, did he actually improvise that evocative final line, "Tears in rain?"*

RS:    Yes. "Tears in rain" was Rutger. I was never going to get to shoot all those wonderful sights Rutger described, "c-beams glittering in the Tanhauser Gate," and so on, because we couldn't afford it. Yet somehow it worked better just staying on his face as he described what he had seen, and how we would never see that in our lifetimes.

PS:    *Hauer's death is a moving moment.*

RS:    Very. You know, I was up on the rooftop set about to shoot that, and I told an A.D. to go get Rutger. But the assistant director told me Hauer wanted to speak with me first. So I had to climb down a bloody ladder and walk across the lot to Rutger's trailer. And there he was, smiling, saying, "I've written some of this scene." Which was his "Tears in rain" line. I thought it was wonderful. As was Rutger's performance as Roy.

PS:    *You ran up against the studio hierarchy for the first time on* Blade Runner, *resulting in a reputation for being difficult and for going over budget. What's your side of this story? I'm sure your troubles with Tandem enter into this at some point.*

RS:    They do. But let me answer your budget question first.

By the time of *The Duellists*, I was a pretty successful commercial director, who ran his own company with other directors under its roof and made sure that their budgets didn't get out of hand. Now, I'd been able to function on *The Duellists* and in fact get it going by taking no fee and doing a completion bond. In other words, I could afford to do that. I'd also paid for the screenplay, chosen the writer, etc. Then *Alien* came to me as sort of an invitation to dance. With Hollywood. And the entire time I was filming that, I had my own line producer in there keeping a close watch on the budget, as well as a completion bond guarantor who always let me know where we were, spending-wise. I say all of this to illustrate the fact that I've always run my own stage.

Anyway, we were pretty well on budget on *Alien*. I do remember that I came to a point where they felt that we were going to go over a little. But the film was budgeted at $8.9 million and we went to $9.2, or $9.4. So I went about $500,000 over budget. Today if you did that, you'd be a fucking hero. I mean, today there are guys who go $20 million over budget and move on to the next movie! Anyway, I went $500,000 over, by commission, mostly because of one scene. Because certain people didn't want to do the end capsule, "sleeping beauty" scene of *Alien*. I said, "Are you kidding? We must shoot this! That is the real last act!" And it was, when Sigourney Weaver gets into that capsule.

So I walked into *Blade Runner* from *Alien,* believe it or not, with a tiny reputation for being excessive. And I thought, "Well jeez, if that's all it takes to get this reputation, guys, I'll be excessive."

Anyway, it was some time before I decided to saddle up back onto science fiction. It took me almost two years to kick off with *Blade Runner,* and that was after a lot of hemming and hawing and trudging around looking at various locations. At which point I decided that the only way for me to do *BR* was to somehow fake it up on a studio back lot. So we budgeted it out, and I think it came out at somewhere near $15 or $20 million.

Now, this figure was already well above what had been projected for the original *Dangerous Days* script. But Hampton had written a certain type of film, of a certain scale, and then *Blade Runner* grew. Really, I think, in terms of what I wanted to add to it.

Finding that initial $15 or $20 million, though, wasn't easy. First we had Filmways drop out, although they were actually quite nice about the way they handled that. Then we couldn't find the start funds we needed, because at this point in time it was about two years after *1941* [Steven Spielberg's costly WWII comedy], and about one year after *Heaven's Gate*. Both of which had cost considerably more money than our estimated budget, and both of which had flopped. So there was some fiscal hesitation going on in the industry. Yet $15 or $20 million certainly wasn't inordinate, it was about medium high.

So Michael Deeley said to Filmways, "Okay, okay," and quickly bailed out and went and saw a few people, and then brought back in the Ladd

Company and Tandem. Tandem basically came in with expenses money, which is the money that you are short of. With a view to also picking up any money we went overbudget on as well. Right?

PS:   *Yes?*

RS:   So I think that by the time Tandem signed on, we'd finally budgeted the film out—and I'll get to the point in a moment—to about $22.5 million.

PS:   *Which ultimately ended up costing a little over $28 million.*

RS:   Yes. So I think Jerry Perenchio and Bud Yorkin were originally obliged to put in somewhere between $3 or $4 million for *Blade Runner*, which then rose by another $3 million or so. Which in those days was a lot of money. But for those guys, I think it was a drop in the ocean.

Anyway, eventually I was rightly beaten up because of our involvement with Tandem. And that was the crossover point for me. Because when I looked around—and this is not being superior in any form and mustn't come out as being superior—I realized I was essentially with, for the most part, the wrong kind of people to make this movie. We'd started the process with people who, on the surface, felt pretty supportive. On reflection, however, and I discovered this fairly quickly, I found out that Tandem and I just didn't think on the same wavelength. They were people who were basically—well, let's call them sophisticated television people. People who weren't capable of visualizing the type of accurate film budget I required for a film. Tandem, I think, always felt that my asking for additional funds while we were shooting *Blade Runner* was, to some degree, some kind of indulgence. It wasn't. It was me, as the director of that film, having a certain vision. And I was sticking to that fucking vision!

PS:   *You were simply being true to your project.*

RS:   That's right. Something else Tandem didn't understand.

PS:   *I know you also had problems with your crew while you were filming* Blade Runner. *To what do you ascribe that?*

RS:   Well, I didn't have problems with everyone on the crew. But you know what? I think it might have been something as simple as certain people on the crew not understanding what I was trying to get.

I mean, Jim Cameron, when he makes a film, nobody asks a fuckin' question. Because now the world is educated as to special effects and such. But in those days, they didn't know what the fuck I was doing! I was the only one saying, "We do this, we do that, we paint it gold, we paint it black. . . ." And people around me were giving me blank stares and saying, "Gold? Black? Why?" Eventually, I would get really angry and say, "Just do it!" Which was frustrating, believe me.

PS:    *In* Future Noir, *I mention the tension that grew up between you and Harrison Ford while you were shooting the film. It's certainly not my main focus in the book, but I'm curious—what do you think caused this rift?*
RS:    I think it's honest to say that doing *Blade Runner* wasn't tremendously smooth in terms of a working relationship with Harrison. There's no point in pussyfooting around that.

Harrison's a very charming man. But during the filmmaking process I think we grew apart, mainly because of the logistics of the film I was trying to make. In concentrating on getting *Blade Runner*'s environment exactly the way I wanted it, I probably short-changed him.

PS:    *By not giving him as much attention as the environment?*
RS:    Yes. That was a failure on my part, I suppose.

But when a film is being made, nobody ever thinks about the director, you know. In fact, there were times when I could tell Harrison was displeased with me, and I'd think, "What about me?! I've got nineteen thousand other things to think about and deal with."

I actually said something like that to him once. I said, "Listen, this is my movie, I have my performance as well as you have yours. And, you know, both will be brought together. That's all I can promise." Because if I hadn't, a lot would have gone out the window. To put that kind of thing on screen requires enormous attention to detail. And it can finally only be accomplished through one pair of eyes.

PS:    *You still sound conflicted about the experience.*
RS:    Well, our rift was very draining. At the same time, our collaboration was an exciting one, because Harrison is so smart. He's a very intelligent, incisive, and articulate man. At the end of the day, though, as I say, I think I probably short-changed him.

Funny enough, we got along much better after the production was over and during the process when we were doing our *Blade Runner* press junkets. Even though those junkets varied between the film getting thrashed and people kind of eulogizing it. That was very confusing— when you get that sort of response, you don't believe anybody.

In any event, Harrison and I did get on better later. So it's not as if we parted mortal enemies. I was never really able to talk to him in depth to find out whether Harrison liked the film or not, however. Or liked what we had done.

PS:   *Another controversial aspect of* Blade Runner *was Ford's voice-over. Now, in almost all of the scripts I read, Deckard does narrate the story in one form or another. Which I always assumed was a nod toward the old Marlowesque,* film noir *convention of the hard-boiled private-eye narrating his story in a world-weary voice. But I understand you were never really comfortable with Deckard's voice-over.*

RS:   No. Nor was Harrison. *Apocalypse Now* was made—when?

PS:   *It was released in 1979. Why?*

RS:   Because I always felt that one of the main backbones of *Apocalypse* was its voice-over. Which actually gave another dimension to Martin Sheen's character, by letting you inside his head. That voice-over worked very well; it was somehow well written and somehow well delivered. But voice-over is extremely difficult to pull off, because in a way it has to be totally internal and reflective. If the tone of what you're saying is just a bit off, it's never working. And then you start to struggle with the performance—is it not functioning because it's tonally incorrect, or what?

The bottom line of Deckard's narration was that we just couldn't get it. We wrestled with it and wrestled with it. Which frustrated Harrison to no end, because he's clearly a talented and formidable actor. So neither he nor I were comfortable with it. The trouble is, the more you do it, the more you start to convince yourself that, well, it's going to be okay. You don't become pragmatic. That's unfortunate. It's only when you really view and hear these things years later that you think, "Oh my God! It's awful!" Because, A) *Blade Runner*'s voice-over was overexplanation, and B) the narration, although admittedly influenced by Raymond Chandler, wasn't Chandleresque enough.

Do you see what I mean? I felt Deckard's narration could have been more lyrical. Because Marlowe, I always felt, was a little bit of a street poet. *Blade Runner*'s narration wasn't really written that way. We struggled to have it written that way, but nobody could put that spin on it.

PS:    *Were the weaker elements of the narration also influenced by the Denver/Dallas sneaks?*
RS:    Actually, we dropped most of the voice-over at first, and then previewed that version without it in Denver and Dallas. But the studio felt there were certain areas of confusion within the storyline. People didn't know this and didn't know that. To which my initial response was, "Well, that's the whole point of watching the goddamn movie. To find out what *Blade Runner*'s all about!"

But frankly, I then became puzzled myself by the preview audience's reactions. Because I'd felt that *Blade Runner* might have been subtle, yes, but also comprehensible. So I think I let myself be swayed by my own confusion.

Anyway, I was losing wicket at that point. So we ended up struggling to put the voice-over onto *Blade Runner* not for street poetry, which was our original intention, but to clarify things. Which I think became ridiculous. So did Harrison.

PS:    *How did the idea for tacking on* Blade Runner*'s happy ending with helicopter footage from* The Shining *come about?*
RS:    By the time I agreed to add the happy ending, I was so beaten up, so on the ropes, that I was spittin' in the bucket. I was punchy, really. Because prior to this I'd been insisting that we had to end *Blade Runner* when Rachael and Deckard go into the elevator.

But Tandem said, "No, that's too depressing. And this is already the most depressing film we've ever seen. [laughs] We've got to end this on an up note! Something heroic, with them driving off together in the countryside." At first I fought that. I said, "But there is no countryside! It's all either industrial wasteland or factory farms!" And they replied, "Well, shit. There you go again!" *[laughs]*

So I eventually capitulated and said, "Look, I'll tell you what. I've got an idea. Since I don't want to go off reccy-ing *[looking for another location]* for another four weeks to try to find this perfect landscape—and we'd already tried to shoot some landscape footage in Monument Valley and failed—let me talk to Stanley Kubrick. I know Stanley a little bit, and I'm going to have him help me solve this." And they said, "What?!?" I just replied, "Leave it to me."

So with the help of Ivor Powell, who'd worked with Stanley on *2001*, I got Kubrick's number and called him up. Because I figured, if anybody's going to know where the best mountain scenery is, it's got to be Stanley!

Now, this was the first time I'd ever called Kubrick, but he was quite cordial. I explained the problem I was having getting hold of the proper landscape footage for this new ending on *Blade Runner*—which he'd heard about—and then said, "You know your opening footage of *The Shining*? I'm sure you must have shot hours of that. . . . Have you got anything I could use from that?" Stanley said, "Sure. I'll send you something. Go ahead and take a look, and cut what you want. As long as you don't use anything that I used."

Within two hours I had seventeen two thousand-foot rolls of helicopter footage. And that's how it happened.

PS:    *By this point you had a new happy ending and a new voice-over on the film. So now you're at the San Diego sneak preview—and you cut a few scenes after that sneak as well, including a shot of Deckard reloading his firearm and a couple of other shots. Were these moments edited out after that preview, because they were deemed unnecessary padding?*

RS:    I think people felt generally that the film was a little slow after the San Diego preview, so I trimmed a bit here and there. *Blade Runner is* a bit slow, in a sense, since it has its own pace.

PS:    *The overall critical reaction to* Blade Runner *wasn't very kind during the film's initial release.*

RS:    God, no. You would have thought we were boiling babies or something.

PS:    *Pauline Kael's review of the picture was particularly scathing.*

RS:    You know, there are cases when I think that the taking up of valuable media space by critics, for destruction, seems pointless. Not to mention the fact that Ms. Kael wouldn't have had a job if we didn't have a film industry.

PS:    *Why do you think the general public initially rejected the picture?*
RS:    I think people were confused, because they expected another experience from the one they got. *Star Wars* had already happened twice by then, Harrison was an established star because of *Raiders of the Lost Ark—*

PS:    *—A very particularized star, of a very particular type.*
RS:    As you say. An action hero. And I had done a film without action, with visual density substituting action, with essentially an unsympathetic character. *Blade Runner* taught me that the American public tends to favor a high-fiber diet. Which infers that the American system is one containing a certain degree of optimism.

I, on the other hand, tend to be a bit darker. To look to the dark side. Not because I'm a manic-depressive, but because I find darkness interesting. Particularly in its more unusual aspects. I'm sure this has something to do with my own heritage. I am a Celt, after all. And the Celts are traditionally fascinated by melancholia.

Anyway, so what circa–1982 American audiences got from *Blade Runner* was not what they expected. It's funny. I remember going to the very first *BR* preview, and since Harrison was now a known face, he had to be snuck into the back of the theater. He came with his wife Melissa Mathison, a very sweet lady who's a good writer.

After the preview was over, Harrison and I were sitting in this little office in the cinema. And I was depressed. Because there had been a kind of a silence emanating off the people who were watching our movie. Harrison was a little confused and a little worried as well. But then Melissa came over—and I'll never forget this—and she said, "I just wanted to tell you how much I loved your movie." She said it very quietly, and she really meant it. That was great. It helped a lot.

PS:    *Professionally speaking, how did you react to the initial failure of* Blade Runner?
RS:    Relatively philosophically. Remember, not long before *Blade Runner* I had done *The Duellists,* to very good critical acclaim and virtually no box office. Then came *Alien,* which in one sense was almost the reverse situation. So I had already experienced both extremes in my professional life.

PS:    *How did you take the film's failure on the personal level?*

RS:    I think it's safe to say I was quite disappointed, because I did think *Blade Runner* was quite unique.


PS:    *We began this discussion with an examination of one of* Blade Runner*'s most controversial elements: the unicorn. I'd like to wind our talk up with its other most high-profile ingredient: the question of whether Deckard is or isn't a replicant.*

RS:    Well, in preparing the storyline, it always seemed logical to me that in the full turn of events, which pertained to a film of paranoia, that Deckard should find out he was a replicant. It seemed proper that a replicant detective might begin to wonder whether at some point the police department hadn't done precisely the same thing to him.

So I always felt the amusing irony about Harrison's character would be that he was, in fact, a synthetic human. A narrative detail which would always be hidden, except from those audience members who paid attention and got it. But Tandem felt this idea was corny. I said, "I don't think it's corny, I think it's logical. It's part of the full circle of the initial idea. Ties it off with a certain elegance, in fact." That's why, at the end of *Blade Runner,* Deckard picks up that teeny piece of foil—


PS:    —*the tinfoil unicorn origami*—

RS:    —right, the unicorn, which visually links up with his previous vision of seeing a unicorn. Which tells us that the Eddie Olmos character A) has been to Deckard's apartment, and B) is giving Deckard a full blast of his own paranoia. Gaff's message there is, "Listen, pal, I know your innermost thoughts. Therefore you're a replicant. How else would I know this?"


PS:    *But how can Deckard be an android when he's physically outmatched by the replicants, whom you've previously established as being stronger than humans?*

RS:    Deckard was the first android who was the equivalent of being human—with all our *vulnerabilities.* And who knows how long he would live? Maybe *longer* than us. Why build in the "aging" gland if you don't have to?

PS:    *Now you're bringing immortality into the equation, which is a completely different factor—*

RS:    —one I find fascinating—

PS:    *—but I must say I better appreciate the more subtle suggestions that Deckard might be a replicant. Such as the fact that he collects photographs, which you see scattered over his piano. And of course the most significant visual clue is that over-the-shoulder, out-of-focus shot in Deckard's kitchen, when you see Ford's eyes briefly glowing. Was that setup intentional?*

RS:    Totally intentional, sir. I was hoping there'd be those who'd pick up on that.

Since *Blade Runner* is a paranoid film, throughout there is this suggestion that Deckard may be a replicant himself. His glowing eyes were another allusion to that notion, another of the subtle little bits and pieces which were all leading up to that scene in the end where Deckard retrieves Gaff's tinfoil unicorn and realizes the man knows his secret thoughts.

Actually, though, my chief purpose in having Deckard's eyes glow was to prepare the audience for the moment when Ford *nods* after he picks up the unicorn. I had assumed that if I'd clued them in earlier, by showing Harrison's eyes glowing, some viewers might be thinking "Hey, maybe he's a replicant, too." Then when Deckard picked up the tinfoil unicorn and nodded—a signal that Ford is thinking, "Yes, I know why Gaff left this behind"—the same viewers would realize their suspicions had been confirmed.

PS:    *The only problem I have with Deckard being a replicant is that if he's a replicant to begin with, it rather undercuts his moral evolution as a human being. Because when the film starts, Deckard's clearly on the cusp of a change— he's trying to get out of his profession. But he's still the macho jerk. Then, as the story progresses, he just as clearly gains insight into the wretchedness of his profession, not to mention the growing empathy he displays toward the replicants. Which, to me, are demonstrably human characteristics. But if Deckard's a replicant—well, it almost wipes out his spiritual rebirth.*

RS:    Unless he's a more sophisticated replicant and has had a spiritual implant. And is a Nexus-7.

PS:    *Interesting thought! What do you mean by that?*
RS:    Well, it's not exactly an action-oriented idea. Because now we're getting into the notion of a world and a situation which at some point is going to fail us. But that's the value of science fiction, going into these interior philosophies.

PS:    *Expand on this idea of Deckard being a Nexus-7.*
RS:    If Deckard was the "piece de resistance" of the replicant business—"more human than human," as Tyrell would say—with all the complexities suggested by that accomplishment, then a Nexus-7 would, by definition, have to be replication's perfection. Physically, this would mean that the Tyrell Corporation would be prudent in having Deckard be of normal human strength *but* extended lifespan—resistance to disease, etc. Then, to round off their creation, the perfect Nexus-7 would have to be endowed with a *conscience.* Which would in turn suggest some kind of need for a faith. Spiritual need. Or a spiritual implant, in other words.

PS:    *That sounds like the perfect idea to pursue in a* Blade Runner *sequel. A course I understand you're thinking of taking, because, in a* Newsday *article (dated October 6, 1992), you're quoted as saying: "I'd really like to do that. I think* Blade Runner *made some very interesting suggestions to the origins of Harrison Ford's character, addressing the idea of immortality. I think it would be a very intelligent sequel." What are the sequel possibilities for* Blade Runner?
RS:    Well, that's partly a game. The Hollywood thing. It'll cost a lot of money to buy the title off the original producers, and the question remains, is the title worth it, or should I prepare another project that's along the lines of the same genre? Notwithstanding the question of using an actor named Harrison Ford. Because by the time you end up paying $2 million just for the bloody rights and another $15 to $20 million for Harrison, it's kind of crazy, you know? I don't know yet—it's something I'd certainly like to do, and science fiction is certainly something I want to get into again. Because as we all know, the arena of science fiction, if you attack it correctly, or whatever way you address it, is an area in which anything can happen.

PS:    *Despite it's potential cost, the proper* Blade Runner *sequel could, I think, be immensely profitable. You wouldn't have to fight the same battles in trying to get the audience to understand the picture, for instance*—Blade Runner*'s now a well-known piece of entertainment history.*

RS:    Well, I definitely feel that if I went back to a sequel, any such project would have to further perpetuate and explore the idea that Harrison Ford was a replicant. And if he is a replicant, maybe we'd explore the idea that instead of a four-year lifespan, he has an indefinite lifespan.

There could also be the idea of a *Blade Runner* sequel which contains a situation where they've perfected the process of cryogenics to prolong lives—in a world that has a big population problem. Following that line of thought, the next thing you'd have to develop would be the Off-world angle—you certainly couldn't have hordes of people with extended lifespans living on an overcrowded Earth. So perhaps Off-world in a *Blade Runner* sequel really means "the frontier." A place that maybe has become so perverse that the right to die a normal death becomes the thing to seek for.

PS:    *What about this* Metropolis *picture you're planning on doing in a couple of years? Rumor has it that this is actually a* Blade Runner *sequel.*

RS:    They will say that, won't they? That sort of talk'll get me into trouble.

All I can say at this point is that *Metropolis* is indeed a science-fiction picture. We've got rather a good first-draft screenplay, which was better than I expected. But you know, like all these subjects, *Metropolis* requires a lot of preplanning. Big preplanning. We've got to go on one more draft, well, several more drafts. But this project actually looks more than promising.

PS:    *I guess we'll have to wait and see. . . . Two last questions. First, have you watched* Blade Runner *lately?*

RS:    You know, it ran on the BBC in mid-1995, when I was home for a short time. And I thought, "I'm going to sit down and watch this thing, to see if I can last twenty minutes." Which is what usually happens after you've made a movie—you bail out. You think "Oh God, I've seen this." So when you hear that people never watch their movies again, there's a very good reason for that.

Anyway, I watched my so-called Director's Cut. And you know what? I was absolutely stunned by how clear it was in terms of story. The removal of the voice-over also makes a tremendous difference.

But my final impression was of how much of *Blade Runner* was Hampton Fancher's movie. I think you've got to lay it with Hampton, because the script is his. David Peoples did some colorful stuff with Hampton's blessing, and these two guys get on very well. But really, it's Fancher's motion picture.

*Blade Runner* works on a level which I haven't seen much—or ever— in a mainstream film. It works like a book. Like a very dark novel. Which I like. It's definitely a film that's designed *not* to have the usual *crush-wallop-bang!* impact.

PS:    *Last question—what do you think is the film's most important quality?*
RS:    I think *Blade Runner* is a good lesson for all serious filmmakers to "stand by your guns." Don't listen to acclaim or criticism. Simply carry on.

Hopefully, you'll do some worthwhile work which stands the test of time.

# Stormy Weather

DAVID E. WILLIAMS / 1 9 9 6

"It's about a time in the past that will not return, the last vestiges of innocence, if you like," says director Ridley Scott of his latest film, *White Squall*, an adventurous yarn about a sailing expedition which encounters dramatic misfortune. "The rite of passage has evaporated today, so I felt it was worth refreshing people's minds that this did once exist. I hate to sound cynical, but in most walks of life today, it really doesn't anymore."

The truth in Scott's words plays well against this film's story, which is based on a real incident. In 1960, thirteen young American men joined the Ocean Academy, a rigorous floating prep school held aboard the *Albatross*, a square-rigged brigantine, and set sail into the Caribbean with their four teachers. On the journey home, after a lengthy voyage of learning and self-discovery, the ship was caught in a white squall, a freak storm which quickly capsized and sank the tall-masted vessel. "It's like a micro-burst," describes the director. "In essence it's a tornado or a hurricane over a short distance that pushes everything in its path flat. During the actual event, they went over in ninety seconds and sank in ninety seconds." Despite their training and heroism, four students and two Academy crewmembers died, including the captain's wife. The rescued survivors then had to grapple with the question of accountability. Was the captain responsible? Had he properly prepared his crew? Could he have averted the disaster?

The story's inherent combination of scope and drama offered Scott a unique opportunity to apply his skills as a visual storyteller.

---

From *American Cinematographer*, February 1996, pp. 36–44. Reprinted by permission of American Cinematographer.

Unlike many directors who have developed a signature cinematic style, Scott has continuously chosen to employ different cinematographers, a group that includes Frank Tidy, BSC (*The Duellists*); Derek Vanlint (*Alien*); Jordan Cronenweth, ASC (*Blade Runner*); Steven Poster, ASC (*Someone to Watch Over Me*); Alex Thomson, BSC (*Legend*); Adrian Biddle, BSC (*Thelma & Louise, 1492*) and Jan DeBont, ASC (*Black Rain*). On the subject, Scott ponders, "Does it make more sense to keep using the same team? If you get someone you really like and you're on the same [wavelength], like Oliver Stone and Bob Richardson [ASC], it works very well. But I've never followed that path for some reason. Working with new individuals is a challenge, so perhaps I give myself new individuals each time to sustain certain creative pressures."

But *new* does not necessarily mean *unfamiliar*, and Scott has regularly partnered with cinematographers he has previously worked with on commercials. For *White Squall*, Scott has again looked within his own team, to Irish-born cinematographer Hugh Johnson, a veteran commercial cameraman-director he has known for twenty-seven years—though this film auspiciously marks his feature debut as a director of photography.

Remembers Johnson, "I first met Ridley and his brother Tony in the 1960s while working as a trainee at a commercial house in London for Derek Vanlint. Ridley had changed the whole look of commercials and how they should be made."

After gaining experience working for the Scott brothers on many commercials, Johnson served as a camera assistant to Frank Tidy on Ridley's first feature, *The Duellists*, and later to Stephen Goldblatt, ASC on Tony's big-screen debut, *The Hunger*. The latter gig provided him with the opportunity "to photograph some second-unit stuff Tony wanted. The next think I knew, I was lighting and photographing commercials."

After many other commercial and feature projects, Johnson was convinced to join the Scotts' production company, RSA, as a director-cinematographer. Ridley Scott later asked Johnson to direct and shoot the second-unit sequences for his Columbus adventure, *1492: Conquest of Paradise*. The director subsequently brought Johnson in to shoot his planned virus-thriller *The Hot Zone*, based on the best-selling book, but the project disintegrated before a script could be finalized. The cinematographer recalls, "Ridley came to me directly after that and said,

'Do you want to have a go at another one?' I said, 'Yeah, sure.' That's when *White Squall* came up, so I read the script and came aboard."

Says Scott, "Hugh's done a lot of feature films as an assistant, been a well-known commercial director now for almost ten years and is getting close to directing his first feature. I think he figured, quite wisely, that [shooting *White Squall*] was a good way to get right in it and look over my shoulder. I thought at first it would be difficult, because he's a director and might say, 'Why doesn't she do this or he do that?' " Laughing, Scott adds, "But he never did that once, which I was very grateful for!"

Contemplating this learning process, Johnson says, "I've basically been brought up in the 'School of Scotts.' So in a way it's not very difficult to photograph for Ridley, because I know what he likes, and I like the same things—although shooting features is quite different from commercial work. You're really dealing with actors and a story."

Scott submits, "I never thought I'd go back and do another sea story after *1492*, because that was a pain in the ass. Then the script [for *White Squall*] came floating past, and we picked it up. It was the strength of the story that brought us back to revisit the sea. On *1492* we never got rough seas, but in this instance, I knew I would have to explore every avenue of water."

"If there are seven characters in a film, I treat the environment as the eighth character—or the first," says Scott. "After all, that's the proscenium within which everything will function. If the central character walks outside and you look at the city and think, 'Wait a minute, I don't believe this story could exist within this environment', then the film becomes lightweight."

One would imagine that such a focus on imagery would make life difficult for Scott's cinematographers. Confirms Johnson, "It's demanding, but if you're brought up with him and you know his work, it's possible. However, *White Squall* is not a Ridley Scott showpiece where everything is visually perfect. This movie is about young boys at sea, it's about what happens. The photography isn't waiting for this beautiful or magic light; it's very natural in an acrid way. Early on, Ridley and I felt that the film should not be cosmetic in any way. We wanted to shoot in hard light, in the weather we had, so you had the feeling of heat and warmth around the film. It's quite raw, really, especially during the boat sequences."

Johnson's descriptions in some ways recall cinematographer Dean Semler, ACS's approach on *Waterworld*. However, while that production relied heavily on Steadicam work to dampen the effect of the ocean waves, Johnson and Scott "decided not to fight it," the cameraman reports. "We went with the motion that made it look good. If it felt good in the action, in the scene, then we enhanced it or we came back on it. We never worried about the horizon. You'd probably think about it and say, 'My God, the horizon's moving all over the place.' But when you actually see it on the big screen, it doesn't worry you at all."

Another similarity between the two films is the presence of a tall-masted ship, a vertical shape that prompted Semler to shoot *Waterworld* in 1.85:1. But Johnson again took another tack, going with 2.35:1 anamorphic. He explains, "The anamorphic frame gave it a big scale, a big feeling you get with the boats. And for what we were doing, 1.85 might have seemed claustrophobic."

Says Johnson of the film-makers' other research, "We related back to some old films we both liked. We looked at *Mutiny on the Bounty* and were interested in anything having to do with boats and what has and hasn't been done."

Scott offers, "The original *Moby Dick* was really good, particularly the sea footage of the whalers with their harpoons in the long boats; I could never work out whether it was real documentary footage or whether they'd shot it. I compiled a lot of documentary footage and started to watch water, just to see how it behaved, to try and get around the curse of [shooting in] a tank. Because in a tank, even with a wind machine, you've only got three-foot waves."

Yet the cinematographer confesses, "I think we threw everything out and just got on with it. I don't think any advantage was had by looking at other movies, because Ridley always goes for what he wants."

Feeding Scott's eye for authenticity, the *White Squall* production shot almost entirely on location, beginning around the Caribbean islands of St. Vincent, St. Lucia and Grenada, which portrayed the sites that the actual *Albatross* crew visited before their disaster. The English crew then traveled up the eastern American seaboard to the cities of Charleston and Beaufort, South Carolina, where the post-storm portions of the film would be shot on practical locations and sets built by production designer Peter Hampton and his team within a converted warehouse-studio. The storm and sinking of the ship would later be staged in a huge tank facility on the Mediterranean island of Malta. Located just south of Sicily, the sprawling complex was recently utilized for the pirate adventure *Cutthroat Island*. Additional miniature work, also photographed by Johnson, would be done in post-production in order to bridge and expand on footage from both the Caribbean and Malta shoots.

However, as Scott laments, "We found no rough water in the Caribbean. It was like a damn mill pond." The director finally determined that the planned seventeen-minute storm sequence would not be convincing without authentic "big water" shots, and changed course to shoot additional footage off the tip of South Africa. Fortunately, the weeks spent in Malta and preparing a rough edit in England gave the *Eye of the Wind*, the 240-ton, 110' topsail schooner portraying the *Albatross,* time to cross the Atlantic. There, Scott says, "we found big, big sea."

While *White Squall* was shot on numerous island locations, taking advantage of the region's natural beauty, "the most difficult situation was on the boat," says Johnson. "You'd have good light up until 8:30 or 9:00 a.m., and then midday sun until about 4:00. Then it would start to fall again at about 6:00. The problems I had were actually in between those hours, and it was made more difficult for everybody because that was also the hottest part of the day—in the nineties.

"After the first four days, we'd covered the boat. We had to make it look different, but it was like being stuck in a room, really. You question some of the angles and say, 'We've done this one before.' But you make it work." Johnson used diverse focal lengths to elicit visual variation, though even that practice was restricted. He explains, "We didn't bother using long lenses, because the picture didn't call for them, and we didn't have the distance to use them on the boat. I had a set of Primos and a set of Es, but Ridley loves zooms and will ask for them all the time, so we relied on the 40–200 mm and 50–500 mm Primos, which worked quite well. We used primes sometimes but just for establishing the scene. I really liked the 40–200 mm; you could shoot the whole movie on that. I don't particularly like using zooms on interiors, though. Shooting anamorphic, you've got to build up your stop, but there were times when we couldn't, because we were only able to get a certain amount of light into the scene. So we would be on the primes. But I was surprised at how good they were at the stops I was shooting with inside—down to the bottom of the lens.

"Our favorite focal lengths were probably the 40, 75 and 100 mm. Whenever we checked the zoom, it was back to the same old sizes. I always liked putting on the 40 mm, as much as some cinematographers would hate it. For the big screen, I like a wide angle. It gives you a lot of production, so you can dress things in and get a lot of foreground and background action going on."

Johnson covered the picture's varied shooting situations—from the sunny Caribbean to the hurricane-like storm sequences—with Kodak's 5298 and 5248. "I actually did consider 45, but I don't particularly like the way it photographs in bad weather," the cinematographer notes. "I feel that it goes quite flat when you don't get hard sunshine. The 48 also works very well with the 98, which has plenty of latitude."

Johnson was flexible in how he rated the stocks. "My assistants laugh at me because I vary. I'm not one of these conventional guys," he says with a laugh. "I was brought up with some wonderful old guys, like Ted Moore, when I was a camera assistant. They always used to tell you that you should place the stop where you think it's best for you. I always find that I still work that way. It would vary partly because I was using some filters—a very light coral, like an eighth. Sometimes I would go to a quarter but no more. So I would just change my meter for that. I rated the 48 at 64 ASA [with an 85], but I varied with the 98, anywhere from 320 to 500."

Johnson added an array of filtration to offset the strong Caribbean sun. "I don't like to shoot past f8 in anamorphic or spherical," he states. "We were out there between 16 and 22½ sometimes, and most of the time I'd bring that down to about an 8. That's a nice average stop where the depth of field is pretty good and things are reasonably sharp. It also gives the camera assistant a good chance as well. I'd bring a lot of NDs in and also used a lot of Pola screens. A lot of cameramen like to give them two full stops, but I'd do 1⅔.

"I didn't use any grads, except maybe once in the storm sequence when the sky was quite hot. Ridley and Tony are definitely known for using grads, but you get to a point where you've got to change a little bit. Also while we weren't worried about the horizon moving up and down, if people saw a grad in there as well on the big screen, they'd say, *'Oh my God!'* "

The confines of the *Albatross* hampered lighting even more profoundly. Says Johnson, "The only lights I had on the boat were two 4 K HMI Pars. That's all I could have because there were only two small generators aboard. We had a 40 K and a 30 K; one powered the entire craft, and the other was for lights." (It was decided that running power from a support boat would slow down the schedule.)

"There were times when I did put up a canopy but only for a few scenes. I didn't like the look; it was almost too contrasty for what we were doing. Besides, if we were out there putting diffusion all over everything to get soft light, it wouldn't have been the Caribbean anymore. We'd have lost that feeling of ruggedness. So it was nice to get the natural shapes through the boat, get the whole structure of the boat going from light to dark and shade to light."

However, not beaten by their cramped situation, "we tracked an awful lot on the boat," says Johnson. "I suggested to Ridley that we make the camera move as much as possible. It was difficult for the crew, but it worked extremely well. We had a Pee Wee dolly and got it into very narrow places on normal track. The trouble was leveling it off all the time, because the curvature of the boat goes from one end to the other.

"On some of the boat stuff, we also used a Libra II mount, which was very impressive. Now, when I saw that being rigged up—and it takes a little time to be set up—I said to myself, 'This is going to take up all my lighting time, and we're not going to get the material we want.' But it worked really well and gave us the shifting horizon we wanted to enhance the movement of the boat."

A three-axis stabilized mount, the Libra II was used to great effect on *Golden Eye*'s car and tank chases. The mount attaches to a female Moy fitting. Using rate and pendulous horizon sensors, the Libra can allow for a variety of pan, tilt and roll effects—making it possible for Scott and Johnson to have either a slightly undulating background, with the boat itself heaving in the foreground, or a fully stabilized background.

Says Johnson, "The Libra is controlled like a hot head. I think [the manufacturing company Megamount] is building one for the Panaflex, but the one we had was designed for the Arri III, and it worked extremely well. The camera itself was modified to use all our Primo and E lenses."

In their search for new ways to shoot the action aboard the *Albatross*, the filmmakers resorted to other measures as well. Finding some extra time in their schedule, Scott decided to try to shoot interior scenes on the ship, rather than wait to use the set built on Malta. "The boat downstairs was great-looking, but photographing it was extremely difficult," Johnson recalls. "Ridley would come down and say, 'Hang on, let's look at a 40 mm here.' And I'd say, 'Yeah, put a 40 on, where do I put my lights?' You know, a 40 mm in anamorphic is about a 20 mm in spherical. But Ridley would say, 'Let's go for it, Hughie.' So we'd do the shots, and we'd look at dailies. That was the other thing: we'd never get dailies until five or six days later, but Ridley would always check out the footage and say, 'See, it looks great!'"

After five weeks in the islands, the company traveled to Charleston, South Carolina, and shot there for about two and a half weeks. Of primary importance was a "court of inquiry" sequence in which the captain of the *Albatross* would be questioned about the fate of his crew—and faced by his surviving students. The beautiful old museums and other historic landmark buildings they were hoping to use had the usual restrictions against painting and reconstruction, so the courtroom was built in a warehouse just outside the city.

Production designer Peter Hampton, another veteran of Scott's commercial work, as well as *The Duellists* and segments of *Blade Runner*, was unexpectedly faced with a major construction effort—and the dilemma of supplying Johnson with space for his lights. Says Hampton, "That set was the biggest problem on the film, but it was the only answer after we couldn't find a real location—and at least it gave us a chance to plan the lighting a bit. That's terribly important to the design of any set. You have to know where the windows should be in relation to the camera and the scene. But the set was also important, because in the film it immediately follows the shipwreck sequence; it had to hold up against that drama, so the lighting had to be dramatic and look good."

"The roof on that particular warehouse sloped down," says the cinematographer, "so Peter built it right up to the ceiling. When I came in and saw it, I said, 'Where am I going to put my lamps?' But we worked at it together. It was the first time we really got into a set where one could move walls and light properly. In that respect, it was nice after being stuck on boats and different locations for quite a while.

"I was a little disappointed, because I expected the light in Charleston to be absolutely amazing. That light over there on the east coast of America can be fantastic, absolutely stunning—but it was like Dullsville for our week of exteriors there. Still, it worked out very well, because it brought us away from the hot sun we'd had in the Caribbean, so we wouldn't just have sunshine, sunshine, sunshine."

Scott approached the shoot in Malta cautiously, recalling the films he and Johnson had screened during preproduction. Says the director, "I noticed that everyone keeps the camera still and shoots the sea, and there you have it—three-foot waves, with wind machines going and a lot of people rushing around tip-tanks. And the storm sequences tended to develop into very swiftly-cut montages where you don't know what the hell is going on. Therefore they get the storm sequence out of the way as quickly as possible. What I wanted to do was sustain the storm sequence as a drama in itself, which of course it was."

Johnson notes, "By the time we got to Malta, the bulk of the movie had been shot. We were doing the sinking of the boat, the flooding of the boat and the underwater sets. The tank facility was built there way back in the sixties, and this was my fourth picture working there. We'd done *Orca, Sinbad and the Eye of the Tiger* and *The Martian Chronicles* there."

"The tanks are *huge*," remarks Scott of the Mediterranean Film Studios complex. "They're like two massive football fields. One was about six million gallons and forty feet deep and the other was three million gallons and only eight feet deep, with a deeper part that was eighteen feet. You don't want the tank too deep, because then every damn thing has to be moved around on scaffolding, which slows you down. So you don't need more than about six or seven feet once you get your ship in the middle pit, where your big gimbal is."

Designed by Les Tomkins and effects expert Joss Williams and overseen by Peter Hampton, the *Albatross* was reconstructed in sections. Describes Scott, "We built just over half the actual schooner with its full rig on a seventy-ton gimbal which could tip at ninety degrees in about six seconds. To continue the roll, there's another long gimbal, about forty feet long, which takes in the whole corridor running down the center of the ship. And there's the front portion of the boat where the boys are bunked, which would do nearly ninety degrees on another heavy gimbal."

Situated around the tanks were a series of towering tip-tanks, each holding up to five tons of water and several wave machines, which could churn the tank into a medium-sized surf. Built from the edges were a series of moveable catwalks for camera placement. However, the director also had a secret piece of storm-making equipment to help power the synthetic tempest. Scott recalls, "I'd done a commercial just before we started shooting, and my special effects guy had turned up with an engine from a Navy jet, which gave me a wind of six hundred miles an hour! We found two in Europe and rigged both so we could pan and tilt them. That force took the waves, which were only three and a half feet high, and whipped them up into this white foam I've never seen before. The engines had to be pulled back because they would burn you if you got too close."

Despite this preparation, the method for shooting the storm sequence still had to be worked out. Says Johnson, "Ridley and I had some long discussions about where it was going to be, how it was coming, where it was coming from, and photographically how it should look. He wanted a storm nobody had ever seen before. So we decided to do some tests."

The trials would also determine whether the scene would be shot at night or in daylight. As darkness would obviously help hide the tanks' limitations, the first were done at night.

Says Johnson, "I put up a couple of big Wendys, and we did some tests with the actors. But it was too theatrical and too much of a contrast from what had been done before. So we decided to do some tests during the day, in the latter part of the afternoon. When we got the dailies back, we decided that the day was more interesting and a lot better for photographic reasons. Besides, it can be quite cold in Malta at nighttime during that time of the year."

The tests also helped determine how to overcome the limitations of the relatively puny curls produced by the wave machines. Says Scott, "In heavy seas, if you're in a thirty- or forty-foot wave motion, the walls of water have waves on *them*. So what we discovered was that by gimballing and generally moving the cameras, the three-foot chop created by the wave machines looked like chop on the sides of walls of water. So we kept the horizon changing all the time. Consequently, there are shots where we run for ten or fifteen seconds, with no problem at all."

Says Johnson of shooting the storm, "We had the cameras on dollies, we did handheld stuff, we had them on rigs, on cables; we used every device you can think of. We also had a crane set up to get in close into the boat, a Titan arm, with a very long extension and a hothead. It was a lot more controllable than any kind of flotation for the camera."

Yet despite their efforts, Johnson says that the filmmakers always found themselves "coming back to the same angles on the boat, primarily because we had a land mass to the right and left of the tank as we looked out to sea, our natural horizon. We used quite a lot of smoke, rain and water effects just to hide it, because we didn't want to get into too much expensive CGI work. So we didn't have a lot of clarity there or a lot of depth. You'd be looking through the camera and not seeing a thing! But I just went for it, and as we saw the dailies, we learned more. Photographing something you can't see with the bare eye is difficult, but you know you're on to something when Ridley's there saying, 'Loving it!'

"Still, photographing through all of that was tricky, with our exposures fluctuating anywhere between f22 and 11. As far as lighting was concerned, I just used some lighting effects. I would bank in some Brutes at the end of the day, when the light would start to go a little bit, just to give an overall form to the sequence. But they weren't doing that much. Again, the tank situation was restrictive, because moving lamps and equipment around the boat would take up too much production time. But the sun would break through every now and again, so I was getting enough fill from that.

"We'd probably do three setups a day, which was pretty good considering what we were going through. Just to move one of those big tip tanks or a wave machine could take anywhere from a half-hour to three hours: we had to be very positive about where we wanted one. Fortunately, we were working with a very good assistant director, Terry Needham, and he was very much in control of that."

Underwater portions of the storm scene, in which the students are trapped below deck and try desperately to escape death, were shot in the deeper tank. Scott recalls, "The internal boat sets were built on gimbals that would roll three hundred and sixty degrees. As they turned over, they filled up. We would shove the guys in there and shout 'Action!' It was very successful and truly claustrophobic."

Johnson adds, "Those shots were quite difficult in the sense that you're dealing with actors in the water with a lot of practical lamps. I let the practicals do all of the lighting, and I kept it very low-key. We had an excellent underwater guy from Los Angeles, Pete Romano [of HydroFlex], who did a wonderful job. You're quite restricted in what lenses you can use on the underwater camera. I think all we could use were the 30, 35 and 40 mm close-focus Es."

During the five weeks spent shooting the storm sequence, the issue of keeping camera equipment functioning became increasingly important. Johnson says, "We brought one of our technicians out from London, whom we desperately needed because we were really beating up the equipment. The cameras were not only getting wet, but they were *in* water, with tons of water coming down on top of them. Panavision came up with a lot of sophisticated stuff to keep things dry, but it never really worked. So we went back to basics: plastic bags. [Laughs] It's a bit of a pain to reload cameras or change lenses—you have to strip it all down, take the bags off, undo all the gaffer tape, and then do it all over again, but it works."

Equally important was that the actors and crew could stand up to the same degree of stress. As Johnson reports, "Every day we'd fill the place with smoke; we had jet engines, we had lots of water effects. They were put through hell. You can't imagine what those jet engines can do in the water and how it affects you."

"The jet engines saved the day," counters the director. "In fact, I'm buying them for [Shepperton Studios in England, which the Scott brothers recently purchased]. Propeller fans are good for certain things, but if you really want storm stuff like this, you've got to have the jets. But what we got out of Malta was terrific. It's very much a studio situation, and it's the best water facility I know of."

The calm weather encountered during the Caribbean shoot was in fact a disaster of sorts for the *White Squall* production, which was counting on some rough seas for the storm sequence. "It's Murphy's Law," admits Scott. "We had wrapped the ship, and the skipper was going back to Portsmouth, but we said, 'Listen, here's the bad news. We want you to go down to the Cape of Good Hope." He said, 'Oh, no,' but he did it.

"It would take him three months to get to South Africa. So after a month in Malta, I went off to Shepperton to edit for two months while he was chugging down the coast of South America. He arrived six days before we did with a small camera unit. And since we had a good edit by that time, we knew exactly what we needed."

"The first day we went out was probably our best," says Johnson "It was really the kind of weather conditions we wanted—dark skies, breaking sunlight, high seas, the boat rolling. . . . It was fantastic, but everybody got seasick. Ridley, my first assistant, one of the grips and I were the only survivors. Still, we were very lucky with the light down there, and we got some spectacular footage. Using the Libra made the waves seem even higher."

Says Scott, "Because the crew was so well-versed by then in terms of leaping around this boat and getting camera positions, we actually dealt with it pretty easily. We got some big, big water for what I call the intermediary stuff, and then the big storm was entirely created in the tank [in Malta and at Pinewood] and with models.

"The biggest problem at sea was all the actors on board. You're on the high seas, and if somebody goes overboard, you just never pick them up. By the time you turn around there's just this little head bobbing around in the water. We were very careful about that. We only experienced maybe thirty five- to forty-foot waves, and they weren't curlers, so they rarely broke on the deck.

"But I think we were even more successful than we could have been, because the storm was always a worry. It's one of those things you stick in the back of your head, thinking, 'Well, experience will tell if we'll be able to pull it off.' But I was always worried about it."

Enthused about his trials on *White Squall,* Johnson concludes, "This is the first movie I've photographed all the way through, and it was a great team of people, a great team of actors, and a big experience for me. When I went to directing commercials, I thought that was it, that I'd never get a chance to photograph a movie. But Ridley and I are talking about shooting another feature, which should be quite interesting. It's a totally different subject altogether."

That project is the thriller *G.I. Jane,* starring Demi Moore as the first elite female U.S. combat soldier. "I've photographed some beautiful women in my time, and it'll probably be a lot more controllable than rocky boats," Johnson quips with a laugh.

# *White Squall* Director a Visionary without Visual Strategy

## MICHAEL WILMINGTON/1996

Ever since his 1979 and 1982 science-fiction classics *Alien* and *Blade Runner*, Britain's Ridley Scott has been regarded as a filmmaking visionary.

And while his new film, the exciting rite-of-passage film *White Squall*, released February 2, might not have won many critical hearts or box-office scores, it has a similar visual magic and excitement.

There's a sense of the ocean's vastness and danger breathing through almost every shot of *White Squall*. Most impressive is the picture's hair-raising squall re-creation: a sudden microblast that hits a ship with the force of a hurricane.

Yet if you compliment the fifty-eight-year-old Scott on his famous eye or ask about his visual strategies, he says: "You know what? I have no visual strategy. I see things in a certain way. . . . I was born with a certain kind of photographic memory. I'm like blotting paper. I just soak it all up."

Scott now thinks that in *Blade Runner*, the inspiration for the film's dark and rainy evocation of a futuristic Los Angeles is not anything from the real L.A. nor from the Philip Dick novel on which the movie was based (*Do Androids Dream of Electric Sheep?*).

"[What] came out strongest for me doing *Blade Runner* was the fact that twenty years of my life were spent among steelworks and coal mines and shipyards. I saw beauty in that," he says.

Scott—a partner these days with his six-years-younger director-brother Tony (*Top Gun*, *Crimson Tide*) in a movie company called Scott

From the *Chicago Tribune*, March 15, 1996. Reprinted by permission of the author.

Free—was a graphic artist before he entered films and an art director for the BBC. Ridley says he painted "incessantly from the age of nine."

"[I] would go out every day and sketch and paint," he says. "I saw beauty in places where other people would see mostly filth. That's so bred into me—I tend to gravitate toward dark stories and dark treatments."

In contrast to *Blade Runner* (the future) or his 1990 film *Thelma & Louise* (the present), *White Squall* is set in 1960–61 and based on a true story of thirteen teenage boys on a doomed school ship, the four-masted brigantine *Albatross*, commanded by Skipper Sheldon (Jeff Bridges).

If some detractors have condemned the movie's story as Hollywood cliché, the real-life survivors take a different view. Central character Chuck Gieg (played in the film by Scott Wolf), calls it a faithful re-creation of the experience and insists the original script, before studio-requested changes, was even more accurate.

And screenwriter Todd Robinson, who researched and wrote the script (with Gieg's help), says of the film's reviewers: "We were sort of staggered at how cynical some people are. Nearly every scene in the movie [except the climactic competency hearing] really happened."

But, mixed as the movie's reception has been, almost everyone has praised *White Squall's* hair-raising set piece: a re-creation of the sudden storm that overturned the *Albatross* and killed six of its crew and students.

Scott, who knew the squall was a movie-stealer, says he put it "on the side burner" for most of the shoot. "It's a bit like *Alien*. I said 'yes' to the script. But the thing that worried me most was, how do I do the monster?

"In *Blade Runner*, I said yes to the idea. But, then, how the hell do I do the world that will support the notion that replicants [artificial humans] exist?"

For *White Squall*, the challenge was the storm. "It was sitting and waiting for me at the end of the movie. . . . Like a big monster," Scott says. "I didn't want it to be a four-minute, crash-wallop-bang and everybody's in the water. I wanted to experience the whole process of what it means to be shot out of the blue like that, to be trapped, to see people that you got to know quite closely just taken away from you. Because that's what life does to you. Right?"

The solution came from Scott's other career, as one of the world's most prolific and highly regarded TV commercial directors. In a Miller

Beer spot he recently made, Scott tried jet engines for wind effects, instead of the usual wind machines. Then, in Malta—in the same tank that earlier housed the disastrous *Cutthroat Island*—Scott brought back his jets. "We imported two [jet engines] and basically blew the s--- out of the set—six hundred-mile-an-hour winds."

The effect on screen is devastating. The real-life ninety-second squall is stretched over fifteen minutes. The wind crashes down. The boat tips and sinks. People die. The ocean closes up. The images of chaos and turbulence burn into your mind.

So, how do you become a filmmaking visionary?

Scott's path was a curious one. As a teenager, he soaked up movies. His favorites, he says, were American genre movies, especially westerns. His favorite western was John Ford's *The Searchers*. "That's the best. And if I were ever going to do a western, which I'd love to do, that would be the one I'd re-examine."

Other Scott favorites include David Lean's *Great Expectations* and Orson Welles's *Citizen Kane*. Later, at art school—where Scott was a classmate of David Hockney's and Ron Kitaj's—Akira Kurosawa's *Seven Samurai* became a favorite.

Yet despite these film interests, until he was in his twenties, war baby Scott seemed destined for a painting career. It was his London teachers who discouraged him. "I think I was a bit of a loner as a kid. I painted a lot. In fact, my parents used to worry a bit, that I was so much of a loner. My dad decided that I should go to art school . . ."

Scott was surprised by the vehement controversy aroused by *Thelma & Louise*. As he says: "[Screenwriter] Callie Khouri is a smart enough writer to want to make her writing constructive and not destructive. My intuition was to keep [the movie] humorous and light—and gradually increase the threat.

"Because I'm European, because I think I have one foot halfway into the truth behind documentaries and non-mainstream movies, I can't quite shake that mud off my feet. . . . Some people call it perversity. It's not perversity. Life isn't a bed of roses. People die. People get cancer. And therefore one is always reminding the audience that there's a dark side to life. That attracts me.

"Because it's the truth."

# Joining the Club: Ridley Scott on *G.I. Jane*

PAUL M. SAMMON / 1998

By this point it's clear that Ridley Scott is a filmmaker with the talent to do anything. The question is, does he have anything to say?

That query has dogged Scott throughout his career. From the staggering French Dordogne landscapes of *The Duellists* to the claustrophobic spacecraft corridors of *Alien,* through the rain-lashed urban canyons of *Blade Runner* to *Gladiator*'s blood-soaked Coliseum sands, Scott's films have been uniformly praised for astonishing visual virtuosity. Yet, just as often, they've been criticized for what some perceive as a lack of an individualized worldview or an absence of an artistic voice.

To which this writer replies—hogwash.

Since the early 1980s, I have been privileged to periodically interview Scott regarding his work. That access has resulted (so far) in three books: 1996's *Future Noir: The Making of Blade Runner,* 1999's *Ridley Scott: Close-Up* (my book-length monograph on his early life/first ten motion pictures), and 2000's *Alien: The Illustrated Screenplay* (which reprints the script of Scott's blockbuster while teasing out its thematic threads). This ongoing immersion in the world of "Ridleyville" has naturally led me to question whether any substantive aesthetic or artistic concerns are discernable in Scott's work. My answer to that inquiry, as you've probably guessed, is "yes."

However, the arguments sustaining my belief that Ridley Scott is more than a technically gifted filmmaker whose Hollywood projects occasionally evidence art-house sensibilities lies within the pages of *Ridley Scott: Close-Up*; therefore, those interested in the themes, obsessions and commonalties of Scott's films should consult that book (there simply isn't enough room here to buttress my opinion). Suffice it to say that this is a director who, throughout his career, has repeatedly managed to expand upon (or subvert, depending on your POV) the strictly commercial concerns driving most big-budget studio films.

One way Scott has pulled off this delicate balancing act is by inserting ironic cultural critiques where you'd least expect them. *Alien,* for example, features a telling scene wherein the working-class stiffs responsible for maintaining the *Nostromo*'s engines argue pay bonuses with the crisply-dressed "suits" who run the ship's flight-deck. Yet this discussion is not solely prompted by blue-collar grousing but by the unexpected discovery of an extraterrestrial signal, beamed from a barren planetoid. Thus, instead of infusing this "first contact" scene with the obligatory sense of awe or terror common to the genre, Scott reduces man's initial encounter with intelligent E.T.s to the level of a contract dispute. Moreover, a strong undercurrent of spiritual enrichment flows through the supposedly formulaic crime thriller *Black Rain,* as Japan's ethics-and-community-oriented culture transforms Michael Douglas's selfish, abrasive New York cop into a humbled, morally-aware team player. And then there's *Blade Runner*, Scott's most deeply subtextual effort, which not only challenges urban indifference, slavery, overpopulation, environmental pollution, and the militarization of the police, but simultaneously poses a prickly existential riddle—what, exactly, does it mean to be human?

In point of fact, then, there often *is* more to the cinema of Ridley Scott than what meets the eye. Surprisingly mature nuances resting comfortably alongside big budgets, big stars, state-of-the-art visuals, and multiplex-friendly plots—this strategy is Scott's trademark, and nowhere is that approach more transparently evident than in his 1997 ode to the first female SEAL, *G.I. Jane.* A film which, while ultimately relegated to the lower tier of Scott's catalog, nonetheless also reveals this perpetually underrated director's ongoing (and canny) method of fusing personalized art with mainstream artifice.

The following interview (which encompasses both *G.I. Jane* and Scott's preparations for the aborted *I Am Legend,* a proposed 1999 big-budget science-fiction film set to star Arnold Schwarzenegger and based on the novel of the same name by Richard Matheson) is the result of two talks I conducted with Ridley Scott on August 24, 1998, and

October 26, 1998. These took place at the office of Scott Free Films in West Hollywood. The resulting material was then meant for inclusion in *Ridley Scott: Close-Up.*

However, I was unable to include the majority of Scott's views on *G.I. Jane* in *Ridley Scott: Close-Up* due to that manuscript's length limitations. Therefore, the bulk of those interviews appear here for the first time.

PAUL M. SAMMON:    White Squall *was released in 1995;* G.I. Jane *came out in 1997. I realize that's not much of a gap, given that two years is the usual amount of time it takes to mount a studio film, but what were you involved with between these projects?*

RIDLEY SCOTT:    Between *Squall* and *Jane?* Sometimes when I take time out between films, I'll use it to develop other projects. In this case, after *White Squall,* my partners and I were moving into the creation of a more serious Scott Free. That's our features production company. It was mostly organizational stuff; we were redefining and redesigning Scott Free in terms of generating low-budget movies as well as high-budget ones, and I was hiring a new head of the company (Chris Zarpas). So a bit of time was taken up with that.

PS:    *A major partner in Scott Free is your brother Tony Scott, who, of course, is a director in his own right (*Beverly Hills Cop II, Crimson Tide, *etc.). If it isn't too personal a question, what's your relationship like?*

RS:    Oh, the best. I've been in business with Tony thirty-seven years. We've been working together since my first film. That was *Boy and Bicycle,* a little black-and-white short I did in 1961. Tony starred in that, and he was a teenager then. In fact, I think *Boy* was probably the moment Tony first thought making movies was interesting. He then went to art school for a fairly extended period, like I did—about seven years or so—and when he was ready to work, I convinced Tony to join me instead of the BBC, which he'd originally intended. We've been together ever since. So, yeah—Tony's a very important part of Scott Free.

PS:    *What I find interesting is that, even though you're brothers, the two of you make very different kinds of films. Your work tends to be personalized and offbeat, whereas Tony seems to lean towards more glittering, big-budget, "Hollywood"-style films.*

RS:    I think Tony always shot that way, even when he first began doing commercials. We've rarely competed for the same work. Which is probably a good thing (laughs).

PS:    *Getting to the matter at hand, who brought* G.I. Jane *to you?*
RS:    It was Demi Moore. What's interesting is that *Jane* wasn't the first project she'd brought to my attention. I'd met Demi on a couple of prior occasions, where we'd swapped ideas; in fact, she'd tried to offer me one film I didn't go for. And with Demi it's always better to be frank. So I'd said "no." This is why, I think, she came back later with something that was more appropriate for her and me—*G.I. Jane.*

PS:    *What initially attracted you to the project?*
RS:    First, I thought it was a good film for Demi. I'd also always wanted to work with her—I think she's one of the best actors we've got. And I loved the idea. I'd never done anything connected to the military before *Jane,* and that appealed to me.

PS:    *In what sense?*
RS:    In the sense that, at one stage in my life, I almost joined the Royal Marines. I was very curious about them when I was about twenty. But then my dad, who had been in the British army, stepped in and said that although it was up to me whether I went into the service or not, I really should go to art school instead. Looking back, I think what he was trying to do was to get me to, ah—

PS:    *Follow your bliss?*
RS:    Exactly. And I chose the Royal College of Art. But I was and remain curious about the military. So when Demi offered me *G.I. Jane* to direct, I was drawn to the military subculture it took place in. I also liked the fact that *Jane's* subject matter was so provocative. A woman entering combat training in a very rarefied area of the military, and how she fares against the obstacles placed in her way, seemed a challenging topic.

PS:    *That topic was ubiquitous in the mid-1990s. The popular media had turned the basic women/military idea into a hot-button issue, and, at the same time, the Navy was being scrutinized for its handling of the Tailhook scandal (wherein a group of female Naval pilots-in-training had accused their male counterparts of sexual harassment).*

RS:    Absolutely. In fact, when we began prepping *G.I. Jane,* the Tailhook affair was fairly recent, only about ten months old. Then, a week before principal photography started, another story broke about the resistance a young woman was encountering after she'd tried to enroll in the Citadel, this all-male military academy in Charleston, South Carolina. The whole notion of the problems women were having in the military became very on-the-nose at the same time we were doing the film.

PS:    *Making* Jane *a cultural mirror, reflecting then-current concerns.*

RS:    Yes. It was all moving in that direction anyway—the necessity of women receiving military parity. Most of the publicity was being generated by groups who were in denial of this wave. That's one thing *Jane* was addressing, you know. The fact that if a female wants to join up, she has to be accepted. Eventually.

PS:    *If it was* Jane's *central thesis that made you want to make this particular picture, then what, in the broader sense, prompts you to direct any film? In other words, is this decision influenced by a recognition that the latest offer shares a certain thematic commonality with your other films? Or do you simply choose each picture on a film-by-film basis?*

RS:    To be honest, I think that, on the surface, it tends to be project-by-project. I sign on to whatever interests me. Particularly if the script involves a genre I really haven't tackled before, as was the case with the military and *G.I. Jane.*

PS:    *Wasn't* Jane's *screenplay originated by Danielle Alexandra? I understand she not only came up with the idea for the film but also convinced Demi Moore to become involved. At which point Alexandra specifically wrote the part of Lieutenant Jordan O'Neil for her.*

RS:    That's right. Danielle also wrote the first drafts of the script.

PS:    *So, to quote the film's press kit,* G.I. Jane *was written "by a woman, for a woman, about a woman"?*

RS:    Yes.

PS:   *Interesting. I also understand that, in addition to being a novelist, sce-narist, and TV producer, Alexandra had cultivated a number of professional relationships with military officials working inside the Pentagon, as well as congressmen working in Washington D.C. That background must have invested* Jane*'s political and military elements with a certain degree of informed realism.*

RS:   It certainly didn't hurt (laughs).

PS:   *On the other hand,* Jane*'s script is co-credited to David Twohy. Now, Twohy cowrote the screenplay for the Harrison Ford version of* The Fugitive *and directed an interesting little science-fiction picture called* The Arrival. *So my question is, in regards to Twohy and Alexandra, who wrote what for* Jane?

RS:   First you have to understand that I came onto the project after Danielle Alexandra had done her drafts, so I never actually worked with her. David Twohy was the writer I worked on the film with. I think it would be fair to say that Danielle Alexandra came up with the plot, drama, and characters. David Twohy came up with the action, as well as integrating my concerns into the script. He did a great job of grafting all that onto a good story with humorous and intelligent dialogue. The real issues and politics that were in the *Jane* screenplay also attracted me. I felt they gave the film another dimension, one that, perhaps, audiences weren't expecting.

Working with the writer is an important step in the process, you know. In fact, it's always been my feeling that one of the hardest things to get right in filmmaking is the script, because story is so important. Sometimes I get knocked for not caring about story—mostly by the press—but I really do believe that the script is everything. Once you've worked this blueprint to the point where it feels right, everything else falls into place behind it.

PS:   *You just mentioned* Jane*'s political subplot. I'd like to return to that topic a bit later; for now, I'd rather address the overall "look" of the film, which I found unusual. It's very steely, and dark. Why did you choose that particular palette?*

RS:   I always have a little trouble answering that one, because I think people assume that the very specific look and quality of my films is a con-scious decision. It's not—actually, it's a very *sub*conscious decision. When I start making a film, it's as if there's this little, invisible computer in the back of my head. That switches on and presets the overall look of the film at the very beginning of the process. It's not easy to articulate: I tend to think pictorially. Something just drops into place and rolls down a chute, and I follow it.

If you pressed me on it, I guess I'd have to say that because of its military context and because the subject matter of *G.I. Jane* was rather somber and austere, we decided to make the film look somber and austere. That's why there are so many harsh blues and earth tones—I felt the visuals synched up with the story.

PS:    *I know you often operate your own camera during production. I also know you work very closely with your directors of photography. Any comments about Hugh Johnson, G.I.* Jane's *D.P.?*
RS:    Well, once you get to that part of the film where O'Neil is training at the Florida Navy base to be a SEAL, it quickly becomes apparent, or at least I hope it does, that the SEALs are not just a group of specialists. They're also very severe, very spartan. It was important to me that Jane's color and shooting style reflect that point. That's why I went with Hughie. I knew he could stay on my wavelength and catch lightning in a bottle.

PS:    *How could you be sure of that? Because Johnson had previously served as your cinematographer on* White Squall?
RS:    Partially. Hughie and I have known each other forever. He worked with Tony and me during the early days of RSA (Ridley Scott Associates, the international commercial firm Scott founded in 1968). He was a camera assistant on *The Duellists*, my first feature, and on *The Hunger*, which was Tony's first feature. Hughie also worked as the second unit director on *1492 (Conquest of Paradise)*. So we have a long history. What's interesting is that Hugh has spent the last twelve years directing commercials and videos. That's one of the reasons he decided to go back to being a cameraman on *Squall* and *Jane*, oddly enough.

PS:    *How so?*
RS:    Basically, Hughie told me he wanted to work on a feature again and that he wanted to stand alongside me and watch, in the closest way possible, the process of making a film. I think he probably wanted

to learn more about directing, right? So I told him, "The best way of doing that would be for you to act as a cameraman." He did, and I think he enjoyed it.

PS:    *Let's continue to talk about your directors of cinematography for a moment. I would assume you pick them very carefully—how do you go about that? Do you just constantly watch films to know who is out there, or do you select someone with whom you've already worked?*
RS:    Don't forget, I've come out of advertising, and many companies now do advertising and rock videos. Commercials and rock videos are a format I'm very familiar with—we even have a company, Black Dog Films, that my son Jake founded, which only does rock videos. RSA and Black Dog are pretty well-known.

Consequently, we have a very excellent, very carefully chosen group of directors working for us in commercials and videos, both here and in the U.K. And much of this material features style over content. But style is, in turn, shaped by a piece's visual aspects, which directly connects to the cameraman. So I keep up to speed by watching who's doing what. Although sometimes it's not as simple as that. If you're doing a film, which involves a big canvas, you can't just assume that you can take a kid from a commercial or a rock video and have him shoot your picture. Features have a different size. You need a cameraman who's had the experience, if you like, of someone who knows how to cover that larger canvas. It's a technical thing, really.

PS:    *In other words, it's just a matter of properly matching up the right person to the right project, because you're already professionally plugged-in in terms of being aware of the D.P.s who are out there.*
RS:    Yeah. For instance, my very first film, *The Duellists*, was shot by a cameraman who had never done a film before (Frank Tidy). But he was definitely the right person for the job.

PS:    *Staying with cinematography for a moment, almost all of your features have been shot in anamorphic (widescreen). Is this your preferred frame ratio?*
RS:    You're right, I do prefer widescreen. In fact, only one of my pictures has been shot in a different aspect, and that was *The Duellists* (shot at 1:85). By the time I moved on to *Alien*, my second film, I'd realized I

liked the proportions anamorphic gave you. I like the shape of that frame; I enjoy placing things within it, and the visual dynamics of the anamorphic frame. Now, some people have a problem filling that particular ratio. I don't seem to. I've found that if you arrange things carefully within it, it's more naturalistic.

There is one problem with anamorphic you can't work around, however. That's the fact that there's more glass in front of the lens, which means you lose about two exposure stops. It then becomes more expensive to use anamorphic, because you need more lights for a scene, and more lights means more time, more personnel, and, eventually, more money. So anamorphic's definitely a more expensive process than 1:85. On the other hand, the fact that you have a shorter depth of field when you use anamorphic is something I like—I think that lack can actually contribute something subtle and interesting to a film. Really, though, it's just a matter of preference as to whether you like widescreen or not. I do.

PS:    *Tell me about* G.I. Jane*'s production designer, Arthur Max. Didn't he have the same job on Fincher's* Se7en?
RS:    Yeah, Arthur was the production designer on that. He also worked as a stage lighting designer for bands like Pink Floyd, when they did live concerts in the 1970s. Did you know that?

PS:    *No. I sure know Pink Floyd, though.*
RS:    Yeah, great band. Anyway, *G.I. Jane* was the first time I'd worked with Arthur as a production designer in the context of a feature. I did work with him on several commercials before that. Arthur's great. Very talented. His background is as an architect. That came in handy on *Jane*.

PS:    *In what way?*
RS:    One of the first design decisions we made regarding *G.I. Jane* was to use as many authentic locations as possible. But then, when Arthur and I started looking at reference photos of real naval bases and buildings, it became pretty apparent pretty fast that these facilities looked pretty dull. So we were constantly trying to make the locations and the few sets we built visually interesting, while not making them seem excessively unrealistic. Arthur's architectural background really saved us there.

PS:    *I imagine your own early training as a production designer came in*
*handy as well.*

RS:    Sure, but some people might think that my coming from a production design background and then applying that as a director would
be difficult for the rest of the crew. Actually, it isn't. I can draw, right?
So I use drawing to communicate my ideas to the crew—the first A.D.,
the head of the props department, the art director, whoever's relevant.
It's very helpful. I can scribble something down, hand it to someone,
and say, "Right, I want it something like this." That cuts right to the
chase. They then can get on with it and do their own thing.

So those little drawings are invaluable during production. Sketching out
my ideas is also cost-effective, because then the crew has a concrete idea of
what we have to do. They can immediately begin to schedule and produce that work, instead of trying to figure out what you verbally said, in
which case they might over-allow for a scene. That's dangerous. Over-
allowing is one of the problems of our business—it's over-allowing that
causes budgets to shoot up. Over-allowing causes huge amounts of waste.

PS:    *Your mentioning having to communicate and coordinate your design*
*intentions throughout many different departments reminds me that most*
*civilians, you know, people not involved in our industry, really aren't aware of*
*how complex a director's job is.*

RS:    Tell me about it. A director's expected to be the expert on everything. You are expected to be the expert on sound, cameras, wristwatches, shoes, contact lenses, lighting, casting, you name it. When
you're making a film, everyone asks you every conceivable question all
the time, because you're the conduit through which everything goes.
And you'd better be able to either enjoy or tolerate that. Otherwise,
don't do the job. Because it can either stress the hell out of you and
drive you crazy, or else you learn to deal with it and take it in stride.

PS:    *Let's move on to some specifics.* Jane *opens in Washington D.C. with a*
*session of the Senate Arms Committee, one of whose members in Anne*
*Bancroft, who's addressing the issue of women in the military. Why did you*
*cast Bancroft? Because of the strength her characters usually convey? I'm*
*thinking of her appearances in things like* The Miracle Worker *and* The
Elephant Man.

RS:   I picked Anne to play a senator named DeHaven because, frankly, to me she already seemed like one. Anne's an incisive, smart, elegant woman.

PS:   *Then that onscreen power she projects is part of her actual character?*
RS:   Yes. We were very lucky to get her because, after Demi, my two major casting concerns were DeHaven and Master Chief Urgayle, the SEAL instructor who instructs Demi. I didn't want either of these characters to be caricatures. That's why Anne Bancroft was always my first choice for the senator, who's a representative of strength and intelligence and woman's rights. Anne's very good at that. She's quite capable of pulling off the tricky balance of being sympathetic while, on the other hand, being tough.

PS:   *Although* G.I. Jane *now begins in Washington, didn't you initially intend to open the film with an entirely different scene?*
RS:   That's right. We did shoot a different title sequence. It was designed to show that Lt. O'Neil was a pretty physically adept naval officer, by opening with Demi practicing this very fast, very dangerous winter sport called luge. The credits were going to run over her doing a very fast luge run.

PS:   *Luge? You mean that variation on one-man bobsledding?*
RS:   Exactly. We shot a whole sequence of her doing that up at Lake Placid in New York State. The idea was to portray O'Neil as being so physically capable that she was almost Olympics material.

PS:   *Why was it cut?*
RS:   Because it set up her character as too much of a superwoman. We also filmed a little scene that was going to follow the luge run, of Demi putting on her uniform. We dropped that too. Basically, after we'd shot the run, I thought it would be more interesting to open directly on the woman's rights issue, by having the audience immediately meet Senator DeHaven, who seems to be the main supporter of those rights in the film. Then you're introduced to O'Neil a bit later on when she's working at Naval Intelligence.

What was ironic about that luge sequence was that, while we were filming it, I slipped on the ice in Lake Placid and banged up my knee. Weeks later, when we were halfway through shooting in Florida, where the SEAL training sequences were set, that knee gave out. Shooting then had to be suspended while I got a fairly serious operation. So all that was for nothing—the luge scene isn't even in the film!

PS:    *Earlier you mentioned the fact that* Jane *was mostly shot on location. Were Florida and Washington D.C. your two principal sites?*

RS:    Yes. There weren't too many sets built for this film, so our primary locations were Washington and Florida. It's difficult to shoot in Washington, though. It is a beautiful city but, for obvious reasons, you have a lot of bureaucracies to go through to get your various filming permits. I must say that the Washington Film Commission was tremendously helpful to us, but it was still tough.

Anyway, besides D.C. and Florida, we also shot at the state capitol building in Richmond, Virginia. We used that structure to stand in for the Senate in Washington. Then we were in Beaufort, South Carolina— that's where we shot the war games exercises and the stuff where O'Neil is captured during her SEAL training and interrogated. We went to a few other places as well. One was Lone Pine, California, where George Stevens filmed *Gunga Din.* We used Lone Pine for the scenes set in the Libyan desert. Those come at the end of *Jane,* when the SEALs have to help retrieve a Department of Defense (DOD) satellite that's crashed in Libya and O'Neil finds herself in a real combat situation.

PS:    *What about the Naval Intelligence Center, where we're first introduced to Moore?*

RS:    That's one of the few sets we built; obviously, we couldn't shoot in the real Naval Intelligence Center. In fact, we couldn't even find any references as to what the real NIC looks like. So Arthur Max built a set down in Florida we called the Hexagon, as sort of a takeoff on the Pentagon. The Hexagon was our biggest set—there were about two hundred monitors and projection screens in there. I liked what Arthur Max did there. He kept that set believable but, at the same time, he gave it this slightly fantastic, almost Bondian edge.

PS:    *I have to say that the decision to introduce O'Neil in the Hexagon rather than on the luge course was a good one, because it allows viewers to first meet the character when she's using her mind, as opposed to her body.*

RS:   Yeah. O'Neil's not just athletic. She's intelligent. The NIC scene shows that O'Neil's a good lateral thinker—she tends to put herself into the position of her antagonists, in order to understand what their plans and procedures should be. Which is interesting, because the subtext of the NIC scene—that O'Neil has particularly good intuition, if you will, although that's not really the proper word—we use later in the last act of the film, when she saves Urgayle.

PS:   *From* The Duellists *onwards, your films—particularly* Alien, Someone to Watch Over Me, Thelma & Louise, 1492: Conquest of Paradise, *and now* G.I. Jane—*have consistently featured strong female characters.*
RS:   I'm drawn to strong, intelligent women in real life. Why shouldn't the films reflect that?

PS:   *One feminist grace note in* Jane *is fairly subtle, but I found it amusing. That's the fact that the senator in this film is a woman, and her assistant is a man.*
RS:   John Michael Higgins, yeah. He's the actor who plays DeHaven's chief of staff. I thought that was an interesting character. What's fascinating about these kinds of people, assistants in general, is that they're not only among the handful who get to speak with persons of power privately, they're also able to tell them exactly what they think. So these people are never just "secretaries," quote unquote. They're much more than that.

PS:   *Your mentioning not being able to research the real NIC reminds me that the Navy didn't exactly support this film.*
RS:   That's an understatement (laughs). We were trying to get the cooperation of the Navy and the DOD for the film. But although they did go into extensive talks with us and were very curious about *G.I. Jane* at first, they also said there were certain things about the script we'd have to change. Some of those were puzzling—for instance, they told us that naval officers didn't swear.

PS:   *Really?* (laughs)
RS:   Yes.

PS:    *Well, as someone who grew up in the Navy—my father spent over thirty years in the military—I can tell you that that response is a little, uh, suspect.* (laughs)

RS:    They also had problems with the scene where Demi shaves her head—they told us she would never cut her hair that short. Now, I'd already researched things well before we presented the project to them, because obviously we wanted the cooperation of the DOD. Once I had their blessing, I would have had all the equipment I'd needed and any base I wanted. So right there you're talking about saving money. Also, it's much more interesting to go into a highly active, polished base, which would give your scenes a sense of efficiency and reality that is impressive.

But then everything turned into a face-off. I didn't want to change certain things; they wanted them changed. It later became clear that the Navy and DOD didn't want this film to happen. I just thought they were picking on us. God knows why.

PS:    *Is it true that Demi Moore actually called up the White House and tried to use her political connections to get President Clinton to allow the production company to get access to a real training facility?*

RS:    Yeah. That didn't fly either.

PS:    *That's an interesting anecdote.*

RS:    More like frustrating, really, because certain operational bases we could have shot at were fabulous.

Eventually, we decided to do it our own way. We'd located a place in northern Florida, a military compound that the Navy had pulled out of seven years ago. It's being used by the National Guard now. Somehow we managed to negotiate our way in there. Then we overhauled the place and used it as our primary location for *Jane*'s SEAL training camp, naval base, and obstacle course.

PS:    *That was Camp Blanding, correct?*

RS:    Correct. It's located between the cities of Jacksonville and Gainesville at a place called Kingsley Lake. I think Camp Blanding was an important Army base during WWII, but then it was turned over to the National Guard as a training facility. Basically, though, it was a nonoperational base when we were filming there. So we had to detail it ourselves.

PS:    *What did you do?*

RS:    When Lt. O'Neil first arrives at the base we called the Catalano Naval Facility—that's Camp Blanding—she passes through a main gate, and you see two cannons, mines, anchor chains, and such. Those were ours, added purely for decorative purposes. Then Arthur did more substantial detailing, like completely changing the parade ground by changing the color of the sand on it and painting the hut-like structures surrounding the parade ground black. We also used an actual commanding officer's office that we found at Camp Blanding for Scott Wilson's office in the movie; Scott plays the commander of this SEAL training camp. The real office was empty, of course, so we had to dress it ourselves. But it's close to what the real thing looks like: comfortable, yet masculine. And then Arthur did things like add the bell on the training courses that the SEAL candidates ring if they want to drop out of the course—that wasn't there before.

PS:    *You mention not getting any support from the DOD, yet there are certain shots on a beach during O'Neil's training sequences where you can clearly see naval ships and an aircraft carrier in the background.*

RS:    We had a bit of good luck there. Across the water from the beach where we chose to build our training camp in Florida was a real naval facility, the Mayport base, in Jacksonville. With that across the way, I could get real military craft, including super-carriers, into the backgrounds of some shots. So I did. Whenever I could, I used this base as a background to whatever was going on.

PS:    *So much for the DOD.*

RS:    Yeah (laughs).

PS:    *When O'Neil is assigned to Catalano for SEAL training, she immediately butts heads with her primary instructor, Master Chief Urgayle. Now, I felt Viggo Mortensen really shined in that role—it's almost a breakthrough part for him. How did you go about casting Mortensen? I mean, he's been around for years, mostly doing character parts, but* Jane *was the first time I'd seen him take on anything this high-profile.*

RS:    Urgayle was a nice role for a male; that was obvious. But as I said earlier, I decided to go a little against the grain when I cast the part, because I didn't want whoever took that role to be your typical Navy chief. The reason I went with Viggo *(Portrait of a Lady, Daylight, Carlito's Way)* was because I'd been very impressed with him after seeing him in a film Sean Penn directed called *The Indian Runner* (1991). Viggo was designed never to say that much in that film, but I loved his presence. Viggo's character there exhibited a certain strength which was offbeat, and because it was offbeat, it was quite threatening, which I wanted Chief Urgayle to be. However, that just goes to show how screen personas can be so utterly different from the real person. Viggo's essentially a gentle man, but what comes across on screen is another character altogether.

That's one reason I went with Viggo, because I'd had my eye on him since *Indian Runner*. Then my brother Tony used him in *Crimson Tide,* where, funnily enough, Viggo also played a Navy man. I asked Tony about Viggo and liked what I heard.

PS:    *Could you elaborate on what you meant about your wish to not cast a "typical" Navy chief?*

RS:    I just didn't want to go down the usual route of presenting a loud macho bully. That's too traditional, and it's already been done. I'd also met a few real master chiefs by this point, and I'd actually found them to be the antithesis of what you'd expect. They were quiet, composed, and had a certain gravity to them. They were also reserved and, I don't know, faintly dangerous. There was just something subtly threatening about them. That's what I was aiming for with Master Chief Urgayle.

PS:    *Mortensen certainly nails Urgayle's talent for intimidation, but what's interesting about the character are his other qualities. I mean, Urgayle even likes poetry (laughs), which isn't the first thing that comes to mind when you think of a SEAL instructor.*

RS:    Yeah, but Urgayle's taste for poetry wasn't just thrown in for effect. I mean, I always saw Urgayle as dedicated *and* intelligent. He's not just macho. On the other hand, Urgayle genuinely believes that the SEALs are only as strong as the weakest link in their chain, and the primary reason he treats O'Neil harshly is because Urgayle's not quite sure Demi isn't that link.

What I wanted to do was reveal something surprising about this guy, show that there was another side to his character you wouldn't expect. That's why I was excited when Viggo came up with the idea of Urgayle quoting fragments of poetry during the training sessions—it suggested other dimensions in the man. Urgayle's definitely a special kind of individual.

PS:   *It was Mortensen's idea for Urgayle to quote poetry?*
RS:   Yes. We'd had something else written for Urgayle to say that didn't work for me, so I told Viggo, "It would really be interesting if we could find something real for Urgayle to recite." Viggo said, "How about a poem?" And I said, "Fine, but it's gotta be short. So short it's almost like a slogan." What I then discovered was that Viggo Mortensen is a poet, who's been published and done recordings on CD. He's very familiar with poetry. So Viggo came up with several different works, and we chose the ones that wound up in the film.

PS:   *According to Jane's end rollers (end credits), those poems are "Self Pity"* and *"Sea in Sardinia" by D. H. Lawrence, and "XLIX" by Pablo Neruda.*
RS:   That sounds about right. Viggo found all of those.

PS:   *What type of research or training did Mortensen go through, since Urgayle has such a specific profession?*
RS:   In terms of observing real master chiefs? I think he went down to the Coronado naval station in San Diego, where Viggo watched some special ops training, you know, the real thing SEALs go through. I'm fairly certain he also talked to as many active and retired SEALs as he could.

PS:   *One of the film's primary hooks, of course, is its depiction of the SEAL training curriculum, which is tremendously challenging, in both the physical and mental sense. How much of that is genuine?*
RS:   The SEAL training you see in the film is a bit of the real and the fanciful mixed together. For instance, to research what SEAL trainees go through, first I observed the real thing, and then I went to bases at Parris Island and Pensacola [Florida] to watch basic training exercises. So I'd already picked up a lot of the actual SEAL training methods when

we first started the film. But in a funny kind of way, those weren't very photogenic—they were more repetitious than anything else.

PS:    *By that do you mean the usual obstacle courses we've seen in other war movies? The running, climbing, and crawling courses?*
RS:    Yeah. We've all seen those before, those huge climbing structures you have to go through. What's interesting is that photographing something like that doesn't look very difficult until you actually try to do it. Then it gets pretty tough. And it doesn't transmit to film. That's why, when it came to the training sequences, I decided to mix fact with invention.

PS:    *Which sequences involved genuine training techniques?*
RS:    Various things. For instance, the stuff with the recruits hauling their rubber rafts in and out of the sea? That was real. So were the scenes when the trainees had to stand for hours holding the same rafts over their heads, and the scene when they had to scrounge through trash cans for their breakfasts. Also, the idea of these guys only getting about an hour and fifteen minutes of sleep after being up for a couple of days was authentic. They really do that. Actually, that's the thing I found most perverse about the SEAL training and at the same time so inspired. To not let them get any sleep for such a long period and to then, after all that physicality, expect the recruits to complete a complex mental exercise. I very consciously put that routine into the film to show how serious and vital this training is. I mean, once a SEAL graduates and gets into a real combat situation, that's going to be much worse than anything he experienced while he was training for it.

PS:    *You sound sympathetic towards these extreme methods.*
RS:    Maybe "realistic" would be a better word. These guys who seem to be bullies, the instructors on the SEAL courses, are really the candidates' best friends. They're preparing them for something that's going to be much tougher later on. To me, it's entirely logical that you would crank up the stress on a SEAL course. You're not trying to create boy scouts, you know. You're training professional killers.

PS:    *Which, again, I always felt was one of* Jane's *more interesting aspects, the details of that process. In any event, are genuine SEAL instructors as hard-bitten as they're portrayed in the film?*

RS:    Oh, yeah. I mean, when they finally allow the recruits to get their hour and fifteen minutes of sleep, after keeping them up for days? The instructors wake the trainees up by going into their barracks and firing blanks into the ceiling or setting off a stun grenade. That'll get your attention!

PS:    *What training methods did you embellish?*

RS:    One thing I came up with involved the scene where Demi and the other recruits carry those black rubber rafts out of the water and have to hold them over their heads. Like I said before, that really happens. But at the last minute, I came up with the idea of also having those rafts filled with water, to increase their weight. And a lot of the stuff on the live fire course, where Demi and the guys are having real explosives chucked at them, was exaggerated. Not by much. It was not unusual on real training courses of this sort some years ago to use high explosives and real live rounds, which they would shoot over the recruits' heads. That was dropped from the military as being too extreme.

PS:    *I understand that the course where* Jane's *recruits are fired upon was actually designed and built by the production.*

RS:    You're right, we did that about five miles from Camp Blanding, on this sort of unofficial motocross course that ran through the woods. It was going to be torn up for a shopping mall. We laid down gas pipes for fire effects, put in water obstacles, explosive zones, just tons of shit. So even though we were only simulating the real thing there, it was still pretty hairy. We had real barbwire, for instance, in some shots, and these enormous tractor tires that the Navy uses to protect ships berthed at docks. In fact, we had some officers drop by this set while we were shooting a scene there one day, some real military guys, and they said, "Goddamit, we like this course. Can we move it and use it at Parris Island?" (laughs)

PS:    *One last question about SEAL training—how high is the real drop-out rate?*

RS:    Tremendously high. It also increases as the program goes on. But, you know, if the drop-out rate was total, there'd be no candidates left at the end of it. What the instructors are really looking for are the recruits who can stick it out for about three or four days. They've learned, through experience, that those survivors then have a good chance of completing the training. In other words, if you can just get through three or four days, you're going to tend to start hanging in there.

On the other hand, being a SEAL isn't just about being a physical superman either. SEALs are known to be highly skilled specialists in communications, mapping, field medicine, ordinance, you name it. Whatever particular field they've trained in, they're the best. So it's a mental as well as a physical discipline.

PS:   *Obviously,* Jane*'s performers had to be in pretty good shape just to survive this shoot. In fact, quite a few reviewers mentioned how amazingly fit Moore was in the part. How did she go about getting physically up to speed?*

RS:   Well, those training scenes involved a lot of other actors besides Demi. There were about fifty guys, in fact, who played the class that went through the SEAL training with her. We had a core group of eight performers who were key supporting characters—we called those guys the Great Eight—then we had forty extras we called the Top forty. Now, even though these guys didn't individually have a lot to do, cumulatively they're there in the background or interacting with O'Neil throughout the story. So they were all important to the film.

PS:   *Was casting that many supporting characters difficult?*

RS:   The casting process for these guys is always difficult, because I'm always trying to find new people. This is my opportunity as a director to introduce new faces, you know? I also of course was looking for a potential star in each one of them.*

PS:   *Where did you find them?*

RS:   The Great Eight were cast in L.A. and New York. The rest of the guys were either locals, guys from Florida who were ex-SEALs or ex-Marines, or actors who hadn't made the cut in New York and Los Angeles. All of them were very dedicated—they gave 100 percent, just like Demi. They

---

*Scott did discover one such rising star in *G.I. Jane* in the form of Jim Caviezel (*The Thin Red Line, Frequency*) who plays "Slovnik," one of the Great Eight.

were also very fit. That was a good thing, because even though *G.I. Jane* was make believe, making it was murderous.

PS:    *You once told me proper casting was half of the battle in getting a good performance. Do you still believe that?*
RS:    Oh, now I'd say that casting is 90 percent of the battle. I mean, if you cast imaginative actors for a part, you usually discover that you don't have to tell them what to do. They already know what to do, because they've done their homework. A creative performer brings a lot to the table. Casting is a crucial part of the process.

PS:    *To get back to my original question, how did Moore and her classmates get into shape for the picture?*
RS:    We put all of them through this intensive two-week training period before shooting began.

PS:    *Walk me through that.*
RS:    Well, it was done in Florida at Camp Blanding under the supervision of Harry Humpheries, our chief technical advisor. Harry was an actual SEAL officer for a good portion of his life, and he took the cast through this sort of accelerated boot camp during a period that dovetailed between preproduction and rehearsals. Demi went through that two weeks too. Viggo was also there, but as an observer, mostly, watching at first, and then he gradually got involved. So these guys had already had two weeks training by the time we started filming. I knew this was going to be a demanding shoot. I also knew I had to make damn sure that all of these people were as fit as they thought they were.

PS:    *What were some of the specifics of this actor's boot camp?*
RS:    Things like running thirty miles in one hundred degree heat, learning weapons handling, and learning how to put up with being constantly yelled at while doing it. Harry made sure the cast went through the same type of verbal harassment real SEALs have to put up with.

PS:    *You said Moore participated in this too?*
RS:    Absolutely. Demi was doing push-ups and sit-ups and running around obstacles. She completely submerged herself into doing everything the men did. In fact, some months before filming, Demi had

already started dieting and working out under a program cooked up by a personal trainer named Greg Jou Jon Rouche, who's very knowledge-able about diet and exercise. So she was already in a very healthy state before boot camp.

PS:   *Does that mean she did most of her own stunts as well?*

RS:   There were very few times a stuntwoman or double stepped in for Demi. That was commendable, you know? *G.I. Jane* was enormously tough, yet Demi really did almost all of what you see in the movie. She was rarely doubled. In fact, Demi put on about twenty pounds of mus-cle for the part, much to her horror. She kept insisting she looked like Atlas from the back. I thought she looked fantastic. That's how she was able to do those one-handed push-ups in the film. That really is Demi. She's really doing those. Remarkable.

PS:   *Did sharing these punishing experiences help Moore bond with the actors playing the other recruits?*

RS:   You bet. In fact, there's a story about that. One of the require-ments for the guys who played the SEAL recruits was that they get a Special Forces haircut, which is very short, about one-eighth of an inch. But a lot of these actors showed up with long hair and mustaches. So after they'd all trained together for awhile, Demi threw a "Shave Your Dome" party for them at a local club, on the day the guys had to get their hair cut. They all ordered a lot of beer and pizza and used electric razors to shave each other's heads. Demi couldn't shave hers yet, of course, because that was a major story point. She had to save hers until later.

PS:   *Sounds like fun.*

RS:   Yeah, but the hair-cutting process really was a nuisance, because hair grows back so fast. You'd have to send the cast to hair and makeup almost every other day, just to maintain that buzz cut.

PS:   *You mentioned the scene where O'Neil cuts her own hair—could you explain why that was so important?*

RS:   That's the turning point for O'Neil. It's the moment she decides that she is going to stick with this training no matter what happens. The hair-cutting scene is pivotal—at that moment, O'Neil decides she's going to join the club.

PS:    *O'Neil also cuts her hair as a symbol of defiance.*

RS:    Right. She does that because she's upset that the commanders are applying a double standard to her during training, making her sleep away from the guys and giving her special treatment and so on. But O'Neil doesn't want that. She wants parity. So she shaves her long hair down to a buzz cut like the rest of the guys.

PS:    *How long after the "Shave Your Dome" party did Moore cut her own hair, and how did you film that?*

RS:    It was about six weeks later. And she really did it. That's really Demi's hair. You can't fake this stuff. You can't do it with a wig, and you can't have someone else cutting off her hair. Demi had to do the whole thing herself. Actually, she got through it pretty well. The trickiest part was making it look effortless.

Basically, I just planted three cameras around her, one above and one on each side, and took her through it until Demi was having a hard time reaching the back of her head. Then I cut, we moved the cameras, and she just finished off. So we got O'Neil's hair-cutting scene in two setups with three cameras.

PS:    *My wife Sherri saw* G.I. Jane *with me, and I remember her letting out a little groan during that sequence.*

RS:    Oh, yeah. When we premiered the film in London, you could feel women in the audience tense up when they realized what O'Neil was about to do. Hair is very important to women—psychologically and metaphorically. It's their crowning glory.

By the way, the guy that comes into the barbershop after Demi shaves her head, the man who bangs through the door and almost bumps into her? That was my production designer, Arthur Max. He had a cameo there.

PS:    *Arthur's little walk-on.*

RS:    Yeah. (laughs)

PS:    *After she cuts her hair, O'Neil eats and sleeps with the men. Were you afraid this action would be perceived as a form of exploitation or titillation?*

RS:    Not at all. I wanted to present this cohabitation without any sign of sexuality or harassment. O'Neil eats and sleeps with the men purely as a reflection of her own capability. Besides, the usual male/female sexuality issues wouldn't be an issue. These people would be so stressed and exhausted by this point they'd just want to get through the goddamn course. Sex would be the last thing on their minds.

PS:    *I understand you filmed, but cut out, a scene of O'Neil showering with the recruits.*

RS:    I did shoot that. It showed Demi coming in to the same shower facility as the men, dropping her towel, and bathing. But, again, it was gender-free. Totally nonsexual. In fact, in that scene some of the men became embarrassed, covered themselves up with their own towels, and left the shower room. I thought that would be a realistic reaction to that situation. But then I cut the communal bathing scene out and did a reshoot showing Demi showering alone.

PS:    *Why?*

RS:    Because the first version upstaged the real meaning of that scene. In the context of the narrative, that sequence showed O'Neil going about her daily routine—in this case, showering—when she's told another recruit has just dropped out of the course. Because of that, O'Neil will be promoted and given a group of men to command. It sort of hit me after the fact that the true emphasis of this scene involved her promotion, not O'Neil showering with men. So I rethought, reshot, and cut the first bit.

PS:    *Continuing in this vein for a moment, Jane's most disturbing scene— and potentially risky one, especially for a studio film—has to be the sequence when, during a war-game exercise, O'Neil is captured and interrogated by Urgayle as if she were an enemy POW. That's a brutal, very intense moment.*

RS:    Yes. It's meant to be. We had a prerelease screening of the film in London, and some women in the audience were covering their eyes through that. But it's not gratuitous.

PS:    *Before we address your intent, where, exactly, in Beaufort, South Carolina, was the interrogation scene shot?*

RS:    I think it was at a local state park [Hunting Island]. The place had a great landscape, very tropical and exotic. Like somewhere in Vietnam. Once we'd detailed it with a little hut and such, it was quite convincing.

PS:    *I know your work well enough to realize you habitually shun exploitation, but if there was any one scene in the film that became a critical football,
the interrogation is. Which is understandable, to a point, since Urgayle beats
O'Neil badly, and then almost rapes her.*
RS:    He doesn't, though. I wasn't about to go that far; Urgayle only
uses the threat of rape. And O'Neil definitely gets her own back. Breaks
his nose, among other things.

I think the problem there was one of perception. Perhaps some
viewers—some critics, certainly—didn't know that Urgayle's interrogation
was based on reality. This intense form of questioning really goes on during SEAL training. I based what I showed by doing a lot of research and
talking to a number of trainees and supervisors who'd gone through the
real thing. Historically, these mock interrogations can become very brutal, and from time to time there have been accidents. So this part of the
program, in fact the whole SEAL course, is constantly being adjusted.
Because some accidents have proved fatal, or certain people have been
given too much power that they can't control, as happens with Urgayle.
And if they're not in control of themselves, it can get dangerous.

The other misperception there, I think, was the actual intent of the
interrogation scene. Real SEALs have been ordered by the Navy to stay
silent for twelve hours after they're captured by an enemy, even if
they're being tortured during that period. That's so that any information they've been carrying before they were captured can be quickly
changed if an enemy gets them. During my researches, I'd also come
across two different cases of men who'd had to drop out of the SEAL
program, because they couldn't take the same kind of POW interrogation training I showed Demi going through. And a real SEAL commander probably would select someone he perceived to be the weakest
trainee during such an exercise, then try to break that person. In doing
so, he'd also break the resolve of the other captives. So I thought it was
only realistic to show Urgayle interrogating O'Neil that way.

PS:    *O'Neil's interrogation is quite violent, but neither Moore nor Mortensen
were really injured during its filming, were they?*
RS:    Nope. They came out fine. You have to be very careful when
you're shooting this stuff—apart from not wanting to hurt the actors,

which is primary, you don't want the film to be shut down because of some stupid piece of planning. So their confrontation was all careful camera angles and padding and sound effects.

There was a moment when Viggo was holding Demi's head under water though. They'd worked out a prearranged signal when Demi would tug on Viggo's trousers, to let him know it was time for him to pull her back up so she could get some air. But Viggo was so into the moment that Demi was like, "Tug, hey, tug, let me up, tug, I'm drowning here!" He finally did, and Demi was fine. Probably a little annoyed though.

PS:    *I'll bet (laughs). Dramatically speaking, the interrogation climaxes with what I've always felt was the film's high point. Urgayle has tried everything he can to break O'Neil's spirit. But not only does he fail, O'Neil tells him to—*
RS:    "Suck my dick." Yeah (laughs).

PS:    *Yeah (laughs). That's a terrific comeback. Very comical. Given the film's feminist subtext, it's also highly appropriate. Almost surreally so.*
RS:    It's the perfect reply. That line always gets a very positive response, particularly from women (laughs). But, again, it's dialogue that's signifying something else for this character. When O'Neil yells, "Suck my dick," that's the moment she's earned her rights to join the club. And she definitely does join the club, which really is a requirement for these types of armed services. It's all about making that decision—if you want to achieve a certain goal, you must join the club.

PS:    *Urgayle says something interesting to one of his men after that interrogation; "She's not the problem, we are." What were you trying to put across there?*
RS:    I was worried that the interrogation scene might play a little too strongly and that concern provoked a rewrite of the scene following it, the one you're referring to. We changed it to what you now see in the film. Urgayle's bathing his wounds and a companion tells him, "That sort of thing won't happen again." Meaning the sort of abuse Urgayle's just put O'Neil through. Urgayle agrees that it won't happen with him or these men, but it could happen somewhere else, in a real combat situation. And then Urgayle says, "She's not the problem. We are." In other words, it's not the woman who's the problem here. It's the men.

PS:    *Ah, I see.*

RS:    That's the whole point. The men are the problem.

PS:    *Yet even though O'Neil survives her interrogation, she still has to deal with the maneuverings of Senator DeHaven, who's always expected O'Neil to fail the SEAL course and to then use that failure for her own political ends.*

RS:    Now we're back to politics. I always liked the political element in *Jane's* script, because I felt it gave the story another realistic shading. I mean, on a certain level, O'Neil is being used by the system. Certainly by DeHaven, who seems to support this idea of women in the military but really doesn't, because she doesn't want to be associated with women coming back in body bags, especially since she's a woman herself. DeHaven is engaged in a subterfuge from the beginning. She thinks O'Neil will not make it through the SEAL course. Then, when it becomes apparent that O'Neil is not going to drop out and this becomes an embarrassment to DeHaven, the senator sort of turns a blind eye to this obviously false accusation that crops up late in the film, that O'Neil is a lesbian. It's not until Demi confronts her that DeHaven relents and agrees to put O'Neil back into the program.

PS:    *Using lesbianism as a smear device seemed your not-so-subtle way of commenting on the manner in which the armed forces were handling the issue of gays in the military at the time.*

RS:    I didn't want to comment on lesbianism per se with this plot element, but, yeah, I do think it reflected the way the military was officially addressing that issue. Which was to basically ignore gays and lesbians until it became something you couldn't ignore. You know, the "don't ask, don't tell" policy. That definitely was another hot-button topic at the time.

PS:    *What's your own personal take on this?*

RS:    It's a nonissue.

PS:    *Bancroft really comes into her own during her scene with Demi.*

RS:    They were both great. You know, I originally wanted to model DeHaven after Senator Anne Richards of Texas. But once Anne was cast, we decided that although modeling her on Richards might be a good starting point, we should just step back and let Anne get on with it her-self. But we still went in that general direction, of making DeHaven this sort of grande dame character. Bancroft was a grande dame too. She might not like to hear that, but she really was great.

But that's the way it always goes. I always find that actors who are prepared to contribute and who regard the process as a collaboration are a pleasure to work with. I definitely don't believe in modeling my actors like clay. My job is to cast the best person for the role. Then I can sort of become a barometer, gauge their talents, and react to what they bring to the part. Basically, I view the whole performance relationship as a partnership. I certainly don't believe in bullying my casts. Some directors do, because they think that if they can make an actor feel insecure that will make them give a better performance. I don't. I believe in creating a safety net, where performers feel they can do or try anything, and it won't matter—it will either be right or it will be wrong. And if it feels wrong, then we will cover ourselves and try to do something else.

PS:     *Still, when you have two high-profile performers of the caliber of Anne Bancroft and Demi Moore working together in the same scene, a director has to feel a little anxiety about going into that situation.*
RS:     Funnily enough, the main thing I remember worrying about when we were shooting the scenes between Demi and Anne was the fact that their husbands (Bruce Willis and Mel Brooks) showed up. They hung around the set watching these scenes being shot, and at first I was a lit-tle uncomfortable with that, because I wasn't sure what would happen. But they were fine. In fact, I remember them mostly asking me directo-rial questions. One was, "Why don't you ever get angry?" (laughs) I said because it wasn't worth it, being a screamer. I'd learned that lesson on *Blade Runner.*

PS:     *Since we're moving on to more uncomfortable topics, let me ask you this—didn't anyone ever point out that the term "G.I." (Government Issue) is an army phrase not a Navy one? I mean, if you were going to be completely authentic, the film should have been titled "Swabbie Jane." (laughs)*
RS:     Oh, we knew. That just fell under the heading of "dramatic license." *G.I. Jane* made for a better title. It got the point across.

PS:    *True. On the other hand—and this is more of a personal reaction having to do with the script rather than the way you mounted the material—my main criticism of Jane lay within its final sequences, the ones where O'Neil goes into Libya, engages in real combat, and rescues Urgayle. I thought those scenes were superfluous. To me, the real heart of the drama lay in Moore proving herself in the training sequences. I understand that there probably was both an audience expectation factor you had to satisfy and a marketplace necessity to get O'Neil into a real combat situation, but by the time we got to Libya I felt O'Neil had already won her battle.*

RS:    Yes. Well, first, in terms of the original script, we basically readjusted the entire third act from the point when Senator DeHaven puts O'Neil back in the program to the end of the film.

PS:    *Do you mean it was completely rewritten?*

RS:    Basically, yes. The way the last act in the screenplay first played, O'Neil won her way back into the program after having beaten the senator at her own game. Demi simply rejoined the course, and Urgayle took her back into combat training. Then we cut to a helicopter training sequence, where a chopper Urgayle was riding on accidentally lost power and went into the sea. It wound up on the bottom in about fifty feet of water. Urgayle survived, but he was trapped down there in an air pocket with a dead pilot.

Now, Demi had been in a following helicopter and seen Urgayle go down. At which point she joined a group of frogmen and managed to rescue Urgayle, using her own training to actually bail him out. Then, as O'Neil was taking him back, Urgayle said, "I'll never live this one down," and O'Neil told him, "Shut up. Save your strength." And that was the end of the film.

I had a number of problems with that. I was uncomfortable because I'd felt that we'd already seen how good she was on the course, and to put O'Neil back into another training scene, even ones with helicopters, seemed redundant. Especially after seeing how she'd handled the interrogation in the POW camp, which had come out much stronger than I'd anticipated. I was also frustrated because, after all this training, I wanted to see what SEALs really did for a living. So I took them into that with the Libyan sequence.

PS:    *But isn't such a large-scale rewrite prohibitively expensive, especially when you're already in production?*

RS:    That became *the* big question—where are we going to get the money for this upgrade, to make it more exciting? Well, I found that to be a positive challenge. The kind that exhilarates, you know? Basically, we just culled our collective experience to cheat things a bit.

For instance, that whole bit with the SEALs in the nuclear submarine towards the end of the film? We didn't use a real sub at all. The interior of the sub was just an old 1942 troop-carrier ship moored down in Long Beach, California that we cleaned up and dressed out to look like a sub. That was much less expensive than building a new set. But that's one of the benefits I've gained from shooting commercials, learning practical ways of cost savings. Then, for those shots of the sub surfacing and diving, I simply called up my brother Tony and said, "Can I use three sub shots from *Crimson Tide?*" He said fine, and that's what we did.

PS:    *You've already indicated that you shot the Libyan desert battle scenes in Lone Pine, but where were the shots of the SEALs landing on the Libyan beach filmed?*

RS:    On a beach about a hundred miles north of Santa Barbara. I had Arthur construct a recreation of a fisherman's mosque that I'd once seen in Morocco on that beach and started shooting.

PS:    *Did your decision to change* Jane's *ending force any kind of production hiatus while you worked out the details of this revised climax?*

RS:    Yeah, but it wasn't time wasted. When we decided we'd go with a new ending, I wrapped the first unit for about seven weeks and got on with my editing, while also prepping this new shoot and location. Then we picked up filming again. We shot for about two weeks; in the prior seven weeks, I'd actually scouted some real locations in North Africa, Morocco being one of them, but I just thought the California location was more appropriate. So that's where we ended up. All I needed to do was add a couple of camels and some bedouins to the Lone Pine valley, and we had Libya.

PS:    *I hadn't realized* Jane*'s last act was so extensively reworked. Knowing that now, and knowing the economic imperatives that must have been imposed, was that why you shot the final battle with handheld cameras?*
RS:    Documentary-style? Yeah. It was definitely cheaper to go that way, because we didn't have any big action pieces scheduled for Lone Pine, just smaller, covert skirmishes. But I also thought a documentary approach would make the final battle feel more realistic. So I used a lot of handheld camera while we were shooting that and a zoom lens.

PS:    *I'm glad you mentioned using a zoom, because* G.I. Jane*'s final battle is punctuated by some unusual, jittery, staccato-like zoom-ins that are very dynamic. Did Hugh Johnson come up with those?*
RS:    No. Because the beach and desert stuff was shot seven weeks after we shut down principal photography, I lost Hughie and hired another D.P. for the Libyan scenes, a guy named Daniel Mindel. Danny had been a camera assistant on *Thelma & Louise.*

PS:    *I noticed you also used an actor who'd appeared in* Thelma & Louise *as a character in* G.I. Jane.
RS:    You're right. Jason Beghe, the actor who plays O'Neil's boyfriend in *Jane*, also played the cop that Geena Davis and Susan Sarandon lock into the trunk of his police cruiser during *Thelma*. You know, the cop who starts crying.

PS:    *The cop who's later forced to inhale marijuana, when a biker blows reefer smoke through the bullet holes in his trunk.*
RS:    That's the one (laughs).

PS:    *What about those zooms during* Jane*'s final battle?*
RS:    Those just came about through experimentation, while I was lying on the ground with a camera waiting for the next setup. I was operating one of the cameras that day—we had four of them rolling—and I started experimenting with the zoom. When we later rolled playback on what I'd shot, the other operators saw what I was doing and thought it looked great. So we shot a lot of the final battle using that very quick, rough-looking zoom on all the cameras.

PS:   *In other words, you invented that "shaky zoom" on the spot.*
RS:   Yep. I was lying on the ground thinking, "Jesus, this stuff looks dead. I need something more documentary-like." So I just started screwing around with the zoom, manipulating it with my hands, and that's what came up.

PS:   *What I don't think many viewers realize is that you shot two endings to* Jane.
RS:   That's correct. The ending you see was pretty much the same, until just before they're all picked up by a helicopter and flown out of Libya. Then I filmed an alternate ending where Demi caught a stray bullet just before they were picked up and died on the floor of the helicopter next to the chief, who watches her fade away. . . .
We tested both endings but, interestingly, although the version where O'Neil died came out with a lower score, it scored pretty close to the one where she lives. The difference was minimal, just a few points either way. I guess O'Neil's death came as such a shock and such a downer to our test audiences that we just couldn't go with that.

PS:   *You almost sound unhappy with that decision.*
RS:   Eventually, you come up against the marketplace. The reality is that filmmaking is an increasingly expensive proposition and, while I'm not saying you should trade what you feel are legitimate concerns for an increased box office, you do have to keep in mind that what you're involved in is a business, as well as a creative enterprise. In this case I actually thought the eventual ending of the film, the one where O'Neil lived and Urgayle gave her his Navy Cross medal, was a pretty good one. It signified both his respect for O'Neil's perseverance and abilities and Urgayle's gratitude for her pulling him out of a lethal situation. So it was a nice wrap-up.

PS:   *I noticed there was no dialogue during that moment.*
RS:   Yeah. I liked the way Urgayle went about this silently. I thought that his gesture reflected the manner in which actual SEALs, the guys who really do this job, go about their work. They do it with a certain devotion to the process and an overall modesty. So *G.I. Jane* essentially ended with no words because the Master Chief really wasn't up to that

display of emotion. Instead, he decided to honor O'Neil with a symbolic, nonverbal gesture. That's his way of saying thanks. I just felt that's how it would have played out in the real world.

PS:    *How long did principal photography take, including the new ending?*
RS:    About sixteen weeks.

PS:    *And then of course you went into post. Now, you mentioned editing . . . I noticed that this was the first time you'd worked with* Jane's *editor, Pietro Scalia, who won an Oscar for cutting Oliver Stone's* JFK.
RS:    Yes. Pietro edited *Wall Street*, too. What I like about him is that he not only cuts according to story and performance, but he's particularly good at visual cutting. By that I mean he's got a tight grip on editing in the imagistic sense. Pietro has a good eye. A very special one.

PS:    *Another first-time collaborator for you on* Jane *was Trevor Jones, who scored the film.*
RS:    Trevor's interesting. He's really done the gamut, you know, from low-budget films like *Brassed Off* to big-budget movies like *G.I. Jane, Excalibur,* and *The Last of the Mohicans.*

PS:    *Jones also did* The Life of Brian, Labyrinth, *and* The Dark Crystal.
RS:    Right. I'd had my eye on him for awhile, but Trevor prefers to live and work in Britain. So when I decided to edit and mix *Jane* in England, it seemed the perfect opportunity for us to finally work together.

PS:    *It surprises me that more critics haven't commented on this, but music always seems an integral, important part of your films. I mean, you just don't lay in a string of sales-friendly rock songs. The scores in your movies are often quite distinctive.*
RS:    Oh, yeah. But don't forget, I did have some rock songs in *G.I. Jane*. For instance, I got Chrissie Hynde of the Pretenders to specifically write a couple of new songs for us. That was a great experience. I like her music, and I thought she came up with some good stuff. One of those songs, in fact, is playing on a radio when Demi shaves her head. Because I always thought if O'Neil could sing, her voice would be the voice of Chrissie Hynde.

PS:    *You seem unusually well-versed in popular music.*

RS:    That's probably because I have children who are very aware of what's going on out there; they tell me things, you know? I prefer a good Bach concerto. Although, having been involved in that whole London, Swinging Sixties thing, paisley shirts and all that, I do have a taste for a good rock tune. In fact, *Jane*'s music tracks were recorded at Abbey Road, the old Beatles hangout, which is still regarded as having three of the best rooms in Europe, acoustically speaking.

But as far as my thoughts on working with soundtrack composers go, and on scores in the general sense, music is always a difficult choice for me. It's also a critical one. I almost regard music as the last dialogue track. Because the sound and the music are usually the things you nail down last in the process, yet they're terribly important. I mean, a score is not only feeding you information. If it's doing its job properly, it's pressing emotional buttons. It's adjusting you. So it's a very, very important element when telling a visual story.

PS:    *I must say that I was disappointed by* Jane*'s soundtrack release, because it focused on the rock songs that underscored the story, instead of on* Jane*'s original compositions. In fact, there were only three tracks of Trevor Jones's score on the official soundtrack CD. Yet, as I remember,* G.I. Jane *had a lot of original music.*

RS:    It did. There *was* a lot of music in *G.I. Jane*, about ninety-eight minutes worth. Our main difficulty in coming up with that lay in trying to find a theme for the film without it sounding overly martial. However, I think Trevor was very successful with the soundtrack. He worked it out over a period of some weeks, then laid down all that music in only about four-and-a-half days. That's very tough, and impressive.

But I know what you mean. There is a tendency these days to release soundtracks that are made up of preexisting songs. I prefer working with original composers, though.

PS:    *Like Jerry Goldsmith and Vangelis and Hans Zimmer and, now, Trevor Jones.*

RS:    Yeah. Great musicians, every one. Incredibly creative.

PS:    *Despite my reservations about* G.I. Jane's *final Libyan sequence, my wife and I enjoyed the film when it was first released. We found it to be very entertaining. The audience we saw it with seemed entertained too. Yet Jane only reaped fair-to-middling grosses. I was surprised by that—I found the film very audience-friendly and thought it would pull in a much larger box office. How much did it make?*

RS:    About $80 million worldwide, I think. Not great. That surprised me, too. I thought we'd do better with a story highlighting a woman in the lead doing a man's job; I felt that sort of thing would generate high curiosity in women and hyper-curiosity from men, who'd go into a film like this thinking, "A female SEAL? Right—prove it." The context of *G.I. Jane* was also very current then. I mean, it dealt with real issues and events that were happening on the news at the time. But then it under-performed. I thought we'd do better.

PS:    *What happened?*

RS:    God knows. There did seem to be a bit of audience resistance to Demi at that time, a bit of a backlash, which I think she experienced unfairly. I mean, I certainly had no complaints with Demi. I just can't put a finger on why *Jane* wasn't more popular.

PS:    *You've mentioned a fascination with the military early in your life. Now that you've made your first military film, what are your feelings on the military in general, and the SEALs in particular?*

RS:    Maybe I can roll both of those questions into a single response. If you were to ask yourself, "Do I think the military is necessary?" and then came up with "Yes" for an answer, then the idea of a covert group like the SEALs is a practical one. Because units like the SEALs are state-of-the-art spearheads in terms of avoiding warfare. These groups can infiltrate enemy territory months before a confrontation. They do that in order to pinpoint the coordinates of essential strategic positions, so that when and if a confrontation happens those targets have already been mapped within the meter. In that sense, the SEALs actually save lives. Ultimately, I think that's what the concept of the military is all about. *Saving* lives.

PS:    *What did you find most satisfying about having done* G.I. Jane?

RS:    I was quite pleased with the film. I think we got a fairly good sense of really being inside the military and of how hidden agendas motivate politics. As for its so-called feminist angle, I thought *G.I. Jane* just reflected the way the world is really working.

PS:    *"So-called" feminist angle?*

RS:    What I meant was, many people misread this picture. Despite the fact that the film dealt with a manufactured political event, one that capitalized on a hot-button issue, *G.I. Jane* was pro-women not anti-women. It was basically a parable of a woman trying to make it in the most manly of male worlds, (a story of) a woman fighting back and refusing to be beaten down. Essentially, with *G.I. Jane* I was trying to show what a woman has to do just to have the same chances as a man.

PS:    *That seems a good point to close our discussion on this film. However, I would like to briefly touch on the project you were developing right after* Jane, *which unfortunately never reached fruition. That was* I Am Legend.

RS:    Right, the Arnold picture.

PS:    *Yes. Before we start, however, I should probably point out that I'm going into this phase of our talk with a bias. I have read the source novel on which that was based, the Richard Matheson book of the same name, and I've also seen the two prior adaptations of that novel, which were* The Last Man on Earth *(1960) and* The Omega Man *(1970). And frankly, Matheson's book stands head-and-shoulders above the films, even though the book was written in 1954. So, now that you know this, let me ask—did you read the book?*

RS:    No, just the *I Am Legend* script, by, uh—

PS:    *Mark Protosevich (who also wrote the scripts for 2000's* The Cell *and 2002's* The Imposter*).*

RS:    That's it. He'd written a very good screenplay. Have you read it?

PS:    *Yes. I agree, Protosevich's* Legend *script was surprisingly good. My primary objection to it was one of focus.* I Am Legend, *the book's basic plot, shows the last normal man on earth trying to deal with a biological warfare event that's turned everyone else into vampires. Matheson then dealt with that idea by keeping it small-scale, interior, and realistic. His take on the material was essentially character-driven and suburban—it showed how the*

*protagonist, Robert Neville, dealt with the isolation he was suffering, and how*
*he went out every day to kill the vampires in his own neighborhood. Protosevich,*
*on the other hand, amps the material, pumps it up. His Neville is a bit of*
*a super-warrior, incredibly fit, incredibly adept at technology and weapons*
*handling, a guy who's trying to kill all the vampires in San Francisco.*
RS:    Protosevich didn't call them vampires. He came up with a new
label: "Hemocytes."

PS:    *Hemocytes, right. Super-vampires. Anyway, my point is, Protosevich's*
*script seemed more of a remake of* The Omega Man, *the Charlton Heston vehi-*
*cle, than an adaptation of Matheson's novel. The Omega Man on steroids.*
RS:    How did you feel about that one?

PS:    The Omega Man? *I thought it was dreadful. I know it has something*
*of a cult following these days, especially among younger viewers, but really,*
*it's painful to watch. Silly and dated. The only thing I cared for was the score*
*by Ron Grainer. Then again, I did warn you I was biased. (laughs)*
RS:    Yeah. Well, as much as I liked the *I Am Legend* script, I did feel it
needed work. That's why I was working with another writer named
John Logan on it before I left the project.

PS:    *Isn't Logan currently rewriting* Gladiator, *the film you're working on now?*
RS:    Yes.

PS:    *How did the* I Am Legend *script initially come your way?*
RS:    Through Warner Brothers and Arnold Schwarzenegger. Warners
asked me in to a meeting, and they just popped the question—"Would
you like to do *I Am Legend* with Arnold?" I thought "Wow, doing a film
with Arnold would be great." Then I met with him, and my initial reaction proved right. Arnold's great, a doll.

PS:    *Why were you eager to work with Schwarzenegger?*
RS:    Well, first, the parameters of the book and the script contained a
fascinating idea. That man's arrogance in dealing with genetics and disease and success with research had backfired on him and resulted in a
mutated, airborne virus that had gotten loose and couldn't be controlled.

That virus then spreads to the point where it essentially devastates the world. Now, part of the beauty of this central idea, where Matheson really came up with something, was the fact that *Legend*'s story starts after the fact. You come in after the plague, into a whole different world. That really appealed to me.

PS:    *Many films and novels have co-opted that idea since Matheson's book, of course, including George Romero's* Night of the Living Dead *and* The Stand *by Stephen King.*

RS:    But I connected *I Am Legend* most strongly with *Robinson Crusoe*, the story of a man who suffers terrible isolation until he meets his Man Friday. That was the strongest parallel for me, and that's why I was eager to work with Arnold on this. I felt I could take his usual screen persona into a new area, one that dealt with this suffering. But that didn't happen.

PS:    *True. You spent almost a year on this project, reworking the script with Logan, casting Arnold, and designing the look of this post-holocaust environment, which I understand you relocated from the San Francisco of Protosevich's script to contemporary Los Angeles.*

RS:    *I Am Legend* was going to be set in Los Angeles, yeah.

PS:    *How far along were you and Logan with the rewrite before the project shut down?*

RS:    I felt we'd licked the first two acts. We were still working on the third one. There was a lot of talk, of course, of coming up with an ending where Neville would find his Eve, or another group of normal human beings. I resisted that. I wanted the ending to emphasize the idea that, among all other animals, the human race is unique—whatever the problems, it will always carry on. So even though Neville has an awareness that he may be the last normal person, he perseveres. I liked ending on that. He *is* the last person. I mean, that's why it's called *I Am Legend*, right?

PS:    *I always preferred the climax of the novel. Neville is killed by a third race of beings, an offshoot of the biologically mutated vampires, and his death results in his becoming mythologized as yet another type of monster to this third race. Come to think of it,* The Last Man on Earth, *the first adaptation of Legend, has Neville die at the end too. But that's also a terrible film. Did you see that one?*

RS:   Oh, yeah, with Vincent Price. I drank six packs of beer.

PS:   *That sounds like the best way to get through it (laughs). Besides script problems, I understand budgetary concerns were another reason you didn't do the film.*

RS:   We never really licked the script and to do this kind of film today, which shows one man living in a desolate, deserted city, costs a certain amount of money. You just can't do it on the street with the budget I was given. I said, "Look, it can only be done with *this* budget." Interestingly, we weren't that far apart on the question of how much was needed to do this properly. But then Warners suddenly said shut it down.

PS:   *Could that have been due to the fact that* Waterworld, *the Kevin Costner vehicle which reportedly cost around $200 million to make, had failed and become a hot potato while you were prepping* I Am Legend?

RS:   It could have been. I think Warners also had recently had a bad experience with a lot of huge over-expenditures on films like *Batman and Robin* and *The Postman.*

PS:   *Wasn't* I Am Legend's *budget going to be around $100 million?*

RS:   A little less than that. Anyway, I think they'd had some bad experiences, and our project came along when they were going through a nervous point of low confidence. I did fight for our budget, because I thought it was correct, and, you know, I have a good reputation about being accurate about costs and for bringing projects in on budget. I just felt that I couldn't lie. I could have said, "Yeah, I'll remove $15 million (from the budget) now." But the costs would've gone right back up there. So that's what I told them. Rightly or wrongly, I stuck by my guns.

PS:   *One final question regarding* I Am Legend—*it's my understanding that you also were having difficulties designing the Hemocytes.*

RS:   The tricky thing is that you cannot start illustrating vampires by having them running around in monk's robes and sunglasses, as they did with *The Omega Man.* That's not the way to arrive at what I'd call an A-class movie. And God knows I didn't want *I Am Legend* to be a "fang movie," where you have people with pale faces and long white teeth. I was a little uncomfortable with that. I did want the vampires to look monstrous, but we had difficulty with making them look monstrous without humanizing them. Then they started to become too human-looking, which became a huge problem. So we let that one go.

PS:    *To summarize, then, Ridley Scott's* I Am Legend *never materialized because of matters relating to budget, script, and creature design.*
RS:    All of the above.

PS:    *Then I think we're finished here. Thanks for your time, as always, and good luck with the* Gladiator *project.*
RS:    Thank you. *Gladiator* should be interesting; I'm looking forward to spending time in ancient Rome.

# Commercial Break

RICHARD NATALE/1999

The Van Nuys airport is deceptively quiet, with only occasional reminders from ear-crunching private jets landing and taking off outside the cavernous hangar in which commercial director Marcus Nispel is shooting inserts for a new Air-Touch cellular phone spot. With a kind of mellifluous choreography the late Jerome Robbins would have envied, Nispel's crew seamlessly sets up shots with a rapid succession of "types" who are lined up in front of a red velvet (and later a black velvet) backdrop—a little girl in pajamas with a teddy bear, a silver-haired Wall Street magnate, an Asian businessman, a farmer in a brown plaid wool jacket. Lighting banks are shuffled in between shots to lend a slight variance to each setup. Artificial tree branches are added for texture and depth. Nispel's seasoned crew anticipates his every move. There's no yelling, no pushing, no hysteria. A slight cock of the head from the director, and everything falls into place. Nispel doesn't waste much film. One take, two takes, he's out. If these inserts are used at all, he explains, they will be almost subliminal split-second flashes in a minute-long (as well as a shorter thirty-second spot) commercial. The crew moves on to a giant blue screen, banked by massive lighting arcs. On a large platform two "suits" holding briefcases twirl around on a turntable and quickly step away. A jazz trumpeter takes their place. The background will later be filled in with an array of urban backgrounds. The jagged, makeshift pieces will become an integrated, expertly timed whole. Hundreds of individual shots will be compressed into a dizzying succession of images, all intended to promote the universal appeal of

From *Madison*, May 1999, pp. 74–77. Reprinted by permission of the author.

cellular phones. It's an average shoot for the workaholic Nispel, who has clocked more than six-hundred commercials and music videos over the past several years. The German-born director is surely a prime candidate for the "hardest working man in show business" award.

It all began with "1984," Ridley Scott's groundbreaking Orwellian Apple commercial. Scott was already renowned as a commercial and film director. But his eerily futuristic and heavily stylized Macintosh ad created a sensation in the advertising world. Shown only once—during the 1984 Super Bowl telecast—the daringly innovative spot has had an overarching influence on the look and feel of advertising over the following years similar to the impact Scott's *Alien* and *Blade Runner* had on virtually every science-fiction film since.

RSA is the "house that Ridley built," according to its handpicked exclusive cadre of in-house directors. The name may not be familiar to the average consumer. But RSA has been a prime contributor to our visual vocabulary. RSA's commercials (and even its music videos for the likes of Madonna, REM, Janet Jackson, Mariah Carey and Sean "Puffy" Combs) are easy to spot: high gloss, stunning cinematography and conspicuously fast-paced editing. There have been hundreds of variations on two basic approaches: a barrage of highly charged, sophisticated images creating a contemporary visual tone poem (any Nike commercial), or a series of sensuous dissolves, exotic, dreamlike and provocative (Calvin Klein's Obsession ads).

While RSA is hardly alone in advancing this kind of kinetic visual style (its chief competitors include Propaganda and HSI), it is certainly one of its more consistent and successful practitioners. The corporate images fostered through the company's television ads have become synonymous with the consumer perception of certain products. It's hard to think of Obsession perfume in color. Or Nike without the heightened thud of sneakers on a gymnasium floor and giant beads of slo-mo sweat.

With offices in Los Angeles, New York and London, RSA and its music video division, Black Dog, were founded by Ridley and brother Tony Scott. The current stable contains about thirty directors, evenly split between the two continents. Like any other successful, groundbreaking company, RSA is having to navigate the treacherous waters of maturation while still trying to hold on to its cutting-edge reputation.

The fact that commercials and music videos are both highly evolved marketing tools has made maintaining that balancing act all the more difficult. Add to that the founders' overstocked plate. Ridley is off in Morocco filming a big-budget period piece, *Gladiator*. Brother Tony is in Toronto on the set of the Showtime series *The Hunger* (based on one of his early films), which he produces, and has a thriving movie career of his own—from the definitive eighties high-concept movie *Top Gun* to the recent hit thriller *Enemy of the State*, starring Will Smith. In addition to RSA, the growing Scott empire also includes a feature film division, Scott Free Films; England's Shepperton Studios; and The Mill, a London-based computer-graphic imaging company.

The brothers may not always be accessible, but they are not absentee landlords, either, says Tom Dey, one of the company's young directors who is about to cross over into feature films. "Tony and Ridley may not always be around, but I know I can get them on the phone if I need to. I feel protected." Dey has reason to be grateful. While most RSA directors are courted from other companies, he was plucked from obscurity by Tony Scott based solely on a short reel of sample commercials Dey had shot nights and weekends while trying to earn a living loading film.

Dey will make his film debut this year with *Shanghai Noon*, starring Jackie Chan. Like fellow RSA director David Dobkin (who directed his first film last year, *Clay Pigeons*, starring Vince Vaughn and produced by Scott Free), Dey hails from film school. But many of the other RSA in-house directors are from other disciplines. Nispel started as a commercial illustrator. Randee St. Nicholas and Dean Karr were still photographers.

But the one thing they all had in common was a desire to join RSA's selective club, crossing back and forth between commercials and music videos. "There's total creative freedom here," says Dobkin. "If they like my ideas, I'm not held back." So eager were some directors to join the RSA family that they left their own profitable enterprises. Nispel shut down his own production company, and St. Nicholas walked away from an independent shop run by her closest friends. "I feel at home here. There's a lot of people who believe in you and give their all," says St. Nicholas, one of the few women working in what is still largely an all boys club.

RSA promotes itself as a family-run company. And it's more than just an illusion. In addition to the elder Scott brothers, RSA boasts a new generation of Scotts, Ridley's sons, Jake and Luke, and daughter, Jordan. Jake Scott, the eldest and most seasoned of the siblings, heads the Black Dog film and music video division. He has also recently made the leap to feature-film making with *Plunkett & MacLeane,* a period adventure starring Liv Tyler and Robert Carlyle.

The day-to-day aspects of the company's U.S. business operations are overseen by Bruce Martin and Linda Ross, who spend most of their time in the Los Angeles offices. RSA's West Coast headquarters are located in West Hollywood, adjacent to the higher profile interior design show-rooms. They are situated at the hub ("office central," they jokingly call it) of RSA's rambling office-loft space, comprising large and small offices, a melding of form and function with warm wood paneling to make it inviting. An indoor-outdoor café with a full-time cappuccino server lends a collegial touch.

Out of the hundreds of reels Martin and Ross cull through every month, few are chosen. They are always on the lookout for new addi-tions to the roster: a director who is good at humor, one who has a strong feel for written material, someone with a unique visual style. "The only requirement is that they be innovators," says Ross. Bringing new talent into the fold is only the first step in the nurturing process. "There is such intense competition in the business today," says Martin. "The days when a director could sit and wait for work to come in are gone. You have to be very proactive, ferociously aggressive."

At the same time they are mindful that talent needs to be cultivated, encouraged. As in any other creative medium, it takes time to guide directors up the ladder by surrounding them with top producing and technical talent. Dey recalls many a lean time before he earned his stripes as a commercial director. Many other companies would have cut him loose. But RSA hung on, promoting him to clients, until he finally broke through.

Cultivating their directors, allowing them free reign, however, can-not come at the cost of pleasing the clients. "You want to keep the bar up creatively, but can't forget you're selling a product," says Ross. They have secured the more powerful directors like Nispel the right to pres-ent a director's cut of a commercial or a video. Newcomers have to fight harder. After all, in the end the client owns the negative. "Sometimes the planets align," Ross laughs. But it's clear that sometimes is definitely a sometime thing.

Upstairs, under the eaves of the office, above the exposed air-conditioning tubing, are the younger brothers Scott, who are situated in adjoining but distinctly different work spaces. Jake lives amid a swirl of monitors and music players, while Luke's place next door is an almost monastic, attic-like space. Their environments reflect the sensibilities of two of RSA's heirs apparent, who, along with sister, Jordan, commute between the company's American and European operations.

Having taken time off to direct his film, Jake Scott has recently jumped back into the fray. His pet, Black Dog, he admits, is in the same rut that all music videos are in today. The economics of the music business have changed. The big record companies have consolidated. The larger talents increasingly control the content and style of their videos. And the form itself has become less adventurous than commercials, says Jake. Ten years ago it was the other way around. "The language that's developed in music videos has been hard to get rid of," he says. "They've lost their edge, whereas advertising has gone the other way. Commercials are accelerating creatively."

Jake is looking to grow Black Dog into the one arena that RSA has not yet entered—low-budget independent films in the $2 million to $5 million range. He sees it as a logical progression from commercials and music videos into big-budget filmmaking. Having just spent the better part of three years on *Plunkett & MacLeane,* he says the learning experience was daunting. The difference between creating an effective thirty-second commercial or a three-minute music video doesn't necessarily mean one can automatically stretch into the demands of a two-hour narrative.

Mindful of that, his uncle Tony has been encouraging directors in the RSA stable to take advantage of his series, *The Hunger,* as a training ground. Though some RSA directors consider the vampire series too lowbrow ("some of them think they're Terrence Malick," Jake says), others, like his brother Luke and Dey, have used it to stretch. "It's a great forum to make that next step," says Luke. "Commercials can be a difficult language to get rid of, especially in the way you deal with actors." But the transition to bigger films (hopefully produced and developed at Scott Free) would be eased by the ability to play in the low-budget independent field. It's all part of RSA's one-stop-shop objective, a way to keep everyone creatively happy and fertile as well as maintain a level of excellence for the company—which wouldn't hurt the commercial side of the business one bit.

Though the company purports that it maintains an open-door policy for directors to surf between commercials, music videos and motion pictures, such interdisciplinary jumps can be disruptive to the main income flow—i.e., commercials. "We're known as a melting pot for the hottest directors" says Tony Scott. "I'm always begging Jerry Bruckheimer [the ultra successful Hollywood action film producer—*Top Gun, The Rock, Armageddon*] to stop chasing my directors," he adds, only half kidding.

The much in-demand Nispel is a good example. He has been actively courted by the motion picture industry but has thankfully begged off movies for the time being. Considering that he brings millions into RSA every year (about $20 million last year alone, according to one source), he is holding the fort while Dey, Dobkin and Jake Scott take off for a year or more at a time, not to mention the elder Scott brothers' frequent forays into filmmaking.

But that's the nature of the beast, says Ridley Scott: "We are always looking for ways to help our directors develop their careers, challenge their talents and evolve their style. I believe that in a well-balanced career, the different forms are complimentary and not exclusive to each other." Brother Tony admits that this philosophy may not be the best way to run a business financially speaking, but creatively the cross-pollination is "a blast. There are juggling acts in every business. If you look at the personalities in the company, there are no rigid rules and regulations. It's very individual. We give them an opportunity to mix and match their lives. The growth of the company will ultimately come from the creative growth of its directors."

For Ross and Martin, who, along with Ridley, are the bottom-line keepers, the many faces of RSA have to be maintained without the entire ball unraveling. The inevitability of growth is fine, but not if it gets out of hand. "Our value is only as strong as our directors' contracts," says Ross. "Once you go corporate, you're dead. You have to maintain your identity."

Identity, however, is a shape-shift term, says Tony Scott. RSA's image is so well established that it's in danger of becoming, well, "establishment." And truly, the company's style is so influential, so widely imitated, that what was once envelope pushing now is in danger of appearing old hat (if you'll excuse the mixed metaphor). "We're going through some changes," he admits. "I personally don't think RSA should get any bigger. There's only so much you can do and still maintain the look and feel of a creative family."

Creative stagnation is the ultimate bugaboo, impacting on the company's reputation and ultimately on its business. It's already happening in music videos. It could happen with commercials, too. Fortunately, he says, there is always new talent to supplement and challenge their directors. "The established guys are moving up. Now I'm looking for us to break the mold."

And that goes not only for RSA as an entity, but for himself personally. As a director of slick, fast-paced action films, he has been wildly successful. He could continue to coast on that reputation. Instead, he's embarking on a new film project that will be radically different, much less slick, shot on video and downloaded onto film. "I think people will be shocked. It's going to be a performance movie. But you need to make a big change. Otherwise the spontaneity is gone."

# Veni, Vidi, Vici

## DOUGLAS BANKSTON / 2000

Director Ridley Scott doesn't simply direct feature films; he creates cinematic worlds. All of these worlds—which have included the distant future in *Alien*, the Napoleonic era in *The Duellists* and ancient Rome in the newly released *Gladiator*—bear Scott's indelible aesthetic imprint and benefit from his keen photographic instincts. They also demonstrate Scott's unquenchable craving for atmospheric smoke.

Another trait that all of Scott's films share is an acute attention to set detail. After establishing deep roots in television and commercial production design during the '60s, Scott blossomed into a truly inventive visualist. Later, he became increasingly involved in cinematography, operating the camera himself while directing highly influential thirty- and sixty-second spots that revolutionized Britain's television advertising industry.

In addition to having a brother and three sons who also work as directors, Scott is able to harvest cinematographic talent through his production companies: Black Dog for music videos, RSA for commercials, and Scott Free for feature films. Many of Scott's music-video and commercial collaborators eventually photographed features for him. Frank Tidy, BSC, lit Scott's first feature, *The Duellists,* and Derek Vanlint illuminated *Alien*. (Scott storyboarded and operated principal camera, including handheld shots, on the dark and claustrophobic science-fiction thriller.) Scott has also worked with Jordan Cronenweth, ASC (*Blade Runner*); Alex Thomson, BSC (*Legend*); Steven Poster, ASC (*Someone to Watch Over Me*); Jan DeBont, ASC (*Black Rain*); Adrian Biddle, BSC (*Thelma & Louise* and *1492: Conquest of Paradise*); and Hugh Johnson (*White Squall* and *G.I. Jane*).

From *American Cinematographer*, May 2000, pp. 46–52. Reprinted by permission of American Cinematographer.

Scott took some time between mixing sessions at Todd-AO Studios to light up a cigar and invite *American Cinematographer* to peer into the directorial stratagems he brought to bear on *Gladiator.*

AMERICAN CINEMATOGRAPHER:    *How did the* Gladiator *project come together?*
SCOTT:    I was approached by Walter Parkes and Dream Works. Walter, one of the great story pitchers, preceded his remarks by presenting a reproduction of a nineteenth-century painting by the artist [Jean-Léon] Gérôme. It showed a Roman arena from the level of the sand, where a gladiator holding a weapon was standing over his vanquished foe, looking up at an emperor who was staring down at them and preparing to give the thumbs-down gesture. Walter really had me the second he showed me the painting. I honestly hadn't thought about that world before, and it's a tricky one to address because of the "toga/gladiator syndrome" [in film history]. I just thought it was a good pitch, a great story, and a great world to explore.

AC:    *Was it the time period or the story that appealed to you most?*
SCOTT:    After many years and millions of feet of film, including lots of television commercials, I've discovered that I have an artistic side, and that I really like creating worlds. That's one of the things I bring to bear when I do a movie. Something clicked in the back of my head, and I thought, "Damn it, I hadn't thought of doing this one before. This is really interesting." That's what really got me going. In this instance, the world came first, then the story. Usually, it's story and character first, and then the world finally rolls in.

AC:    *What led you to choose John Mathieson as the project's cinematographer?*
SCOTT:    One of my sons, Jake Scott, had already directed his first feature film, the seventeenth-century piece *Plunkett and Macleane* [a 1999 release that was shot by Mathieson]. Jake happened to be in London editing it at the time, and he would show me cuts of his film. I thought it looked absolutely wonderful on every count. John Mathieson and Jake had worked together a lot doing rock videos and commercials, and John had already done several movies. So I said to Jake, "Do you mind if I ask John to do my next movie?' That's a reversal, isn't it?" [Laughs.]

AC:    *What skills did Mathieson bring to the table?*
SCOTT:    Not all cameramen are artists, but John is. He's [also] extremely knowledgeable technically, partly because of his background in rock videos and commercials, where he could experiment. If anything, people making rock videos *expect* you to experiment; otherwise, the band isn't interested. Each of these three- to four-minute pieces are essays of creativity [set] to music. That's why I have Black Dog—we see it as a great beginning for young filmmakers. John had been through a lot of that, and therefore is very inventive.

For instance, I didn't want to just shoot the battle sequences for *Gladiator* in a traditional manner, so we adopted various styles, which John and I talked about, for the different stages. We used various techniques in terms of cameras and camera speeds. When you've got two thousand soldiers in the field at any one time, and you're planning to experiment, you'd better make sure you're right, because you can't go back and reshoot it. I like the fact that John had been down those [experimental] routes, whereas others, I think, might rather play it safe. John would go for it, and mostly, thank God, he was right.

AC:    *When it comes to cinematography, you've been known to be very hands-on. Was that also true on this film?*
SCOTT:    I'm a reasonably practiced operator, so I like to get in there and line up the shots. I know that certain cameramen don't like to work with me or my brother, Tony, because we both came up [through the industry] the same way—primarily from the visual side into long-form work—and we both like to be on the camera. I always think the best job on the floor is the operator's job, because that's where you see the bells going off. I came out of TV commercials, which I feel have very much to do with a director and his eye. On those types of shoots, the director ought to be looking through the camera, and I did a lot of that.

Now that video-assist has become so sophisticated, of course, I don't have to look past the operator's left ear to see what I'm getting through the viewfinder; I can just talk to them very accurately using the monitor. It's not simple; it's hell, actually, but you can move pretty fast if you know what you want, and I always know what I want. I think for the most part, cameramen enjoy the experience with me, even though they sometimes go into it with great trepidation. I believe that the process should be fun and inventive, and I can be influenced by anything or anyone.

AC:    *Speaking of influences, what did you use as references for* Gladiator? *A film like this could draw comparisons to classics such as* Spartacus, Ben Hur, The Fall of the Roman Empire *or* Quo Vadis.

SCOTT:    I probably drew from the same references those filmmakers did—paintings and drawings. The greatest photographers were the painters who represented those historic times, particularly [artists] from the nineteenth century. [Sir Lawrence] Alma-Tedema, who was painting Greek, Roman and Egyptian environments with great perception and accuracy, was a big reference; he created beautiful representations of an ideal world. It then fell to me to say, "Rome was the Golden City, but it was probably dirty and grim in parts, despite the beautiful architecture." For me, the process mainly involved looking at the illustrations and paintings and then reinterpreting them based on what I wanted.

AC:    *Did you make a conscious effort to avoid similarities to previous films about ancient Rome?*

SCOTT:    Yeah, but *Spartacus* is a good movie. *Ben Hur*'s got some great stuff in it, and so did *The Fall of the Roman Empire*. There's a lot of accuracy in those representations [of the era]. The question is, when you bring a different eye to the time period and [shoot in a] different decade, will the picture look different than previous films? Absolutely. I think through the production design, we got an interesting view of Roman life that I'm very happy with.

AC:    *How extensive were your interactions with production designer Arthur Max during preproduction?*

SCOTT:    When I'm in prep on a period film, the people I probably do the most work with are those in the art department—partly because I come from that discipline myself. I love the process. I always make sure I've got the best storyboard artist I can get my hands on, as well as the best production designer. This is my second film with Arthur; we did *G.I. Jane* together, and I've also done commercials with him. Arthur is an architect, so he's very conscious of architectural details. Naturally, there were endless discussions.

The biggest thing Arthur was doing for *Gladiator* was [the Colosseum set] in Malta. I had once used the water tank in Malta [for *White Squall*], and I remembered one lunchtime when I was wandering around the studio. I walked up to a ruined barracks which had been used by the British Army [during its war] against Napoleon in 1803. The whole military infrastructure was built in limestone. There is a prevailing wind in Malta that blows sand all the time, and this limestone is soft, so it has aged beyond its two hundred years. I thought if we could put the Colosseum in the middle of one of the parade grounds, we could dove-tail our sets into all of the existing architecture. Arthur and I got the original 1803 plans [for the site] from the city. We made a scale model of the actual site, which was enormous, and we started to play chess in that with model pieces to see how our additions would fit within the structure. By doing that, I think we saved ourselves a lot of money.

AC:    *You shot* Gladiator *in Super 35 with spherical lenses. How did you exploit that format to enhance the film's "epic" look?*
SCOTT:    If I think about the very epic directors, the one that would spring to mind first would be David Lean and *Lawrence of Arabia*. We couldn't really [shoot in the standard 1.85:1 aspect ratio] because we were attempting to tell an epic story. I don't know why, but psychologically, an epic tends to feel as if it ought to be widescreen with landscapes as opposed to portrait photography. That probably means anamorphic, which can be hard to do within time constraints. We knew that if we shot with spherical lenses, it might save on lights, because you've got a minimum difference of two and sometimes three stops. Lights mean time, and time means money. Therefore, we ultimately elected to go spherical, which would give me what I needed and give John [Mathieson] what he needed, which was speed in working.

Of course, we still went for what I call the "epic quality"—it's that combination of how you see the landscape and which lenses you put on the camera. I don't use a lot of wide-angle lenses; my widest lens tends to be around 75 mm. I'd rather move back and use a 75 mm, because the image is more powerful. With a wider-angle lens, you see more, but it's less powerful. It's a funny effect. If I want a wide view of a scene, I'll move back, which is also quite good because the actor doesn't have a lump of glass stuck in his face. The camera and crew are further away from him, so in a sense, he's on his own.

AC:   *Did the film's period dictate a particular photographic style?*
SCOTT:    If anything, I shot it in a rather modern way. A lot of the battle scenes, of course, were done with handheld cameras. We employed a lot of techniques we learned from videos to enhance the speed and violence of certain sequences. When you're dealing with a bunch of guys wearing muddy skirts and carrying swords and spears—and they're not on horseback and everything is flat—it requires a lot of energy to get the footage you need; you have to use a lot of cuts to keep the action moving forward. We worked out a proper strategic battle plan in order to illustrate the formidable might of the Roman military machine. The infantry were engaged in the front, and there were war machines like catapults and arrow launchers to the rear. The arrows were really thick and would impale whoever got in their way; if you got off a really lucky shot, you could nail four blokes together, like a kabob. The Romans would also catapult Greek oil, which is basically a kind of kerosene, in these large, earthenware pots. They would saturate the ground with black oil, then fire flaming arrows that would ignite the whole battlefield. The Romans were very clever strategists.

AC:   *How difficult were the logistics of filming such large battle scenes?*
SCOTT:    Nothing's difficult if you've got a good team. It all has to do with planning and discussion, and finding ways to shoot things in a way you haven't seen before. People get tired of watching [the same kinds of] medieval battles, or any battle scenes that have run dry. I think Steven Spielberg did an incredible twelve minutes [in the opening scene of] *Saving Private Ryan;* that sequence felt absolutely real and documentary. He raised the stakes in terms of the film interpretation of what that experience might be like. So now *we* have to go and raise the level. [Laughs.]

What I discovered is that with a big unit, or any unit, the less you move the better. I went to Brataslava [Slovakia] and looked at the military base there, but once I got into it, I thought, "You know what? I'm staring at pine trees. I know there are pine trees around London." We found that they were about to burn a forest [in Gatwick]. Half of the valley is all pine trees, and they'd already ripped up the middle. In this valley, I also found that I could put the Roman encampment just out-side of the battle area, because the encampment logically wouldn't be on the spot. I never had to move the camera more than a quarter of a mile, and I was really happy about that.

AC:    *How effects-heavy is this film?*
SCOTT:    The number of effects shots started off quite low, at around forty. We ultimately wound up with about ninety shots, but they're very complicated. It's a very neat jigsaw puzzle, particularly in terms of Rome itself. We planned with Arthur to go for a giant scale version of what he built, meaning that a column with a diameter of eight feet would be up to thirty-five or forty feet high. When I jump back to do a wide shot, I'll add another eighty feet to the column [via digital effects]—the entire upper part, along with the [rest of the] city. There were a million people in Rome, and because it was on seven hills, I wanted it to feel very dense, as if you could never see sky. I noticed that the other Roman period films were always done with two-story structures, and it all looked a bit provincial. I wanted this to feel like a New York or Wall Street of the time, particularly in the palace district and the Colosseum district.

AC:    *Were the gladiator/tiger combat sequences a mixture of live action and CGI?*
SCOTT:    Tigers don't do what they're told to do. The biggest problem with a tiger is that half the time, it lies on the ground purring or staring at you. We had six Bengal tigers that were about ten feet long, weighed six hundred pounds and could move as fast as a small cat once they decided to. But half the time you're poking at the animal, saying, "Come on, do something." That's the moment when you must watch out, because you've got a cat lying on the ground with its tail swishing, and you want to go over and pat it. When you watch [the trainer] hit the deck, he's feeding it with his right hand. In his left hand, he's got a little handle of a sword [with] no blade, and he has to "stab" the tiger. CGI will drop in the glint of metal that goes into the fur and out the other side with blood on it. All of that action was cheated and helped by CGI.

AC:    *You also used the Wam!Net service, which was used to digitally transmit footage of the film for production purposes and test screenings. How did that go?*

SCOTT:    We previewed only twice, I think once in Orange [California] and once in San Diego. We were on four channels on the Internet. Fortunately, the channels were really great. Needless to say, however, that could easily be negative [in terms of security]. I'm doing *Hannibal* right now, and somehow a guy at Yahoo! got hold of the script. There are only three *actors* who have seen the bloody script, so how he got it, God only knows. In fact, he's already written a critique of the script! Fortunately, he loved it and said [Jodie Foster] should have done it. [Laughs.]

AC:    *Did Wam!Net speed up the production process?*

SCOTT:    The quality isn't that good yet, so it's a work in progress. But it's a great sketchbook to show where you are and how far you've developed. It also helped when I did the music in London, because Hans [Zimmer] likes to record at Air Studios, which is George Martin's place. I got to take a firsthand look every day as they fed me the developments over Wam!Net. Eventually, it won't matter where the various studios and effects houses are—you'll be able to work from anywhere.

# Great Scott: An Interview with Director/ Adventurer Ridley Scott

## ELIZABETH WEITZMAN/2001

"What stone can I turn over that hasn't been lifted before?" demands director Ridley Scott, contemplating the motivations that urge him to forge an apparently boundless series of adventures. We've followed him to the darkest depths of outer space (*Alien*) and the most liberating stretch of the open road (*Thelma & Louise*). We've explored the sweeping past (*The Duellists*) and the suffocating future (*Blade Runner*), and the reason we're always ready to tag along is because, unlike many Hollywood directors, Scott—who is actually British-born and bred—finds the personal within larger-than-life stories.

Of course, when you turn over stones for a living, you're bound to find something squirmy underneath. For many audience members, that unwelcome surprise was *1492: Conquest of Paradise*, Scott's loudly scorned follow-up to *Thelma & Louise*. His next projects, *White Squall* and *G.I. Jane*, received a similar snub.

But the beauty of living big is that while you may fall hard, you're always primed to come roaring back. And so, last year, Scott swooped us up and dropped us right in the middle of ancient Rome, characteristically honoring both the glorious grandeur and the humanizing minutiae of a gladiator's life. With barely a pause for breath, he then decided to revisit a certain Dr. Lecter, whom, he felt, had been quiet for too long. *Hannibal* arrives in theaters this month, because if there's one thing this director can't stand, it's silence.

ELIZABETH WEITZMAN:   *Each movie you've made has taken audiences on a new kind of adventure. Do you look at them that way?*
RIDLEY SCOTT:   Yes, but ideally, *all* movies do that. Every film you see should at least bring you on a psychological adventure.

EW:   *Your films are all so different. Do you think of them as having any common link?*
RS:   Only in the sense that there's no link. Each time, I search for a fresh experience and a fresh meaning. They say that nothing's really new anymore, that there are only seven stories in the world, which sounds rather depressing, but I've got a funny feeling it's more or less accurate. Fundamentally, you've still got the good guy or the bad guy. So it's got to be about the way you look at things.

EW:   *You've blown out the boundaries of several genres now.*
RS:   Definitely. But what you finally realize is that nothing matters more than characters and story. The trickiest thing of all is the script. Creating a "genre" world, whether it's sci-fi or period epic, is relatively easy once you've figured that out.

EW:   *How do you go about creating those worlds?*
RS:   Well, it's dressing, but dressing I love to do, because I'm good at it. I sit there and think about what life would be like for a Roman general in 175 A.D. What's it like to be standing in a coliseum, about to confront five thousand people who think you're a barbarian? I get inside the battlefield. I think that's how it becomes real. Once you've really felt it, you can start to melt it down into textures and smells—and usually a lot of dirt! Then you mix the dirt with the emotion.

EW:   *You chose to make a sequel to Jonathan Demme's* Silence of the Lambs, *and of course you've seen other directors continue a thread you started. What was your opinion of the second and third* Alien *movies?*
RS:   I mean, all the sequels were good. But you can never repeat the original essence of that creature once it's been seen. The key to the first one was that the beast was so unique; it was heart-stopping. Although, would I have done the sequel? Absolutely, I would have. I created *Alien,*

so I was surprised when they planned to make another one and I hadn't heard about it.

EW:  *Did that experience give you any particular insights coming into Hannibal?*
RS:  Nah. *Silence* was so good I couldn't forget it, of course. But *Hannibal* takes on a life of its own. It's not really picking up where *Silence* left off. It's ten years later and the character's entirely different. I didn't even think of it as a sequel. It goes in such a different direction.

EW:  Hannibal *has been pretty shrouded in secrecy. Can you tell me a little about it?*
RS:  It's ten years later, and Hannibal is on the loose. There's been silence from him for a decade, so we're meeting Clarice in a new part of her life. It's really more of a psychological thriller and even a love story, I think.

EW:  *A love story? Between Hannibal and Clarice?*
RS:  (laughs) Maybe "love" is too specific. Affection and respect is probably more appropriate.

EW:  *Were you concerned about being loyal to the book?*
RS:  I was fascinated by Tom [Harris]'s details. But of course, you're looking at a six hundred-page novel, which was taken down to roughly one hundred pages. I did ask him if he would insist on keeping his ending.

EW:  *Did you change the ending?*
RS:  "Change" sounds like a completely different tack. We *adjusted* the ending, while capturing the essence of the book.

EW:  *When you make a film, is your goal to look for personal answers, to make a great piece of art, or to entertain?*
RS:  You just listed my three prime motivations. Certainly, part of the process of making the size of the films I do is to be an entertainer. I know Hollywood films elicit a certain amount of disdain, but there are

some pretty good mainstream movies out there. When you think about it, Hollywood is actually this tiny community, and out of it comes this giant wealth of material. Then there's that whole outside world of independent films. As a director, if you're very strict about retaining your creative freedoms within the confines of a low budget, you accept that you'll have a smaller audience. But the kind of material I like to do, unfortunately, isn't inexpensive. Therefore, I have to put on at least three hats in pulling it together.

EW:   *Three hats being?*
RS:   Creative, commerce, and probably, somewhere in there, artistry. (laughs)

EW:   *I imagine that can get complicated, and Hollywood is not exactly a town known for being amenable to risk. Do you worry about that?*
RS:   My whole job is based on risk. My life is based on risk. And I like it that way. But risks gradually shift, as you become more experienced, into judgement calls.

EW:   *Have you ever made a compromise onscreen that you regretted?*
RS:   No. Never. Well, yes. But only driven by myself. You get impatient with your own material, so the danger is to shave it down so fast and hard that you remove the heart of the character.

EW:   *When did you do that?*
RS:   *Legend.* And I think I compromised on *Blade Runner* in certain areas, which I shouldn't have done. It was *film noir,* and you can't pull back from that and have a happy ending. Or get into voiceovers trying to explain things. Because during the film, the audience will find out, and if they don't then they're stupid, and they shouldn't be watching the film anyway.

EW:   *With* Blade Runner *you did have a difficult time convincing executives to share your vision for the film, didn't you?*
RS:   I think I wasn't used to sharing a vision at that point. Because by then, I'd done *The Duellists* and *Alien,* which, for two first films, were

pretty good. I got the prize at Cannes for the first one, and *Alien* was fairly unique science fiction. But I hadn't shot in Hollywood. I was stepping out of the team I used in Europe and into a place where, essentially, I was the new kid on the block. And therefore I found that I had to go through the irritating process of having to prove myself all over again. I wasn't used to working that way.

EW:    *How did you feel about the film's initial reception?*

RS:    *Blade Runner* was kind of hugely disappointing for me, because I was really, really initially stricken by the fact that I thought I'd made a pretty special film, and, fundamentally, only a few die-hards got it. So at that particular moment, you tend to definitely get a touch of giant insecurity.

EW:    *Do you now blame the studio for the changes in* Blade Runner?

RS:    Oh, no. There isn't a "them" and an "us" as far as I'm concerned. I have enormous respect for the studios. They're paying me to go away and have a jolly good time making my version of what we've agreed on. All creative minds have to deal with the people who are paying the bills, and I've never had a problem with it. I've always had respect for the fact that they are entrusting in my hands a certain amount of money to deliver the best piece of material I can.

EW:    *You don't hear that attitude very often from directors.*

RS:    Well, I'm a businessman. When I did my first feature, I'd already made about two thousand commercials, for everything from Coca-Cola to Apple. So by the time I entered the world of film, I was a relatively responsible fellow.

EW:    *How did you bounce back after the disappointment when* Blade Runner *was released?*

RS:    I went down another risky route, because I had it in my head to do a live-action fairy story. I did wonder if audiences were ready for it, because that was the experience I'd been through with *Blade Runner*— basically, people weren't prepared for the presentation. But then I slowly saw it rebound.

EW:   *What do you mean?*

RS:   MTV happened. And in those early years, MTV was more oriented in the direction of storytelling than in performance. I started to notice that the videos were getting darker, it was always raining, the streets were always shining, and there was smoke coming off them. So I thought, "Ah hah, it's finally struck ground." I was watching *Blade Runner's* influence appear.

EW:   *That must have been rewarding.*

RS:   I was amused by it. I thought, "Oh, well, if that's the final reward, then that's fine, that's good enough." But taking the next step from there was doing *Legend*. It was a huge risk. Did I think the film worked? Absolutely I thought the film worked. Did people get it? Again, no, they didn't, even though there was an enormous amount of absolutely brilliant work in it.

EW:   *Did that experience re-shape your approach to filmmaking?*

RS:   It did. I thought, I've got to adjust something here, because what I'm doing isn't working. So then I made more normal films with more normal worlds.

EW:   *So your stance isn't defiant—like, "I'm honoring the vision inside my head whether they like it or not."*

RS:   Well, it definitely was, until then. My attitude was, "Audience be damned, I'm gonna make what I want." Listen, my first four movies were *The Duellists, Alien, Blade Runner,* and *Legend*. That's a pretty diversified group of films. And I'm still really pleased I did them.

EW:   *Have you regretted any films you've made—maybe the ones with a more commercial intent?*

RS:   I'm still sorry I went on a sidetrack for almost ten years.

EW:   *Which films are you referring to specifically?*

RS:   I don't want to say, because I think they're fine. Actually, I don't think I've ever *really* made a mistake. They're all my babies. Have they all played? No, they haven't. But as a group I wouldn't mind owning the library. (laughs)

EW:   *Do you plan to always make mainstream films in the future?*
RS:   I'd be very happy to always have a mainstream audience in mind, yeah. That's really the nature of the beast, isn't it? Filmmakers are not doing a piece of theatre that may run for three weeks for an audience of two hundred. Between making a movie and advertising it, it's the most expensive form of entertainment there is. Apart from running an American basketball team, anyway.

EW:   *Your movies immediately after* Thelma & Louise—*like* 1492—*were received rather negatively. Did you go through any periods of insecurity during those years?*
RS:   Yeah, absolutely. Why *1492* didn't play, I really don't know. But I learned not to let anything overwhelm me. You can sit and dwell on something and let depression consume you, or you can just shut it out. You don't allow doubt in. You can't.

EW:   *Still, did* Gladiator's *success feel like any kind of validation for you?*
RS:   Oh, sure. And I knew where we were headed about three weeks into it. I thought, shit we've got something here!

EW:   *What would it mean to you to win an Academy Award for* Gladiator?
RS:   (laughs) Well, I'm British, and we don't think that way. When something sounds too good to be true, we have to wait and see. Of course, if it occurs, great, absolutely fantastic, couldn't wish for anything better.

EW:   *You did some interesting technical experimentation in* Gladiator. *Do you get excited about trying out new techniques in filmmaking?*
RS:   Always. Because somebody's always laying down the gauntlet, like Steven Spielberg did with the opening battle scene in *Saving Private Ryan*. And that raises the stakes. Filmmakers are very competitive, which is good, because the audience reaps the benefits. But it's important to remember that the technical is just a means to an end. CGI is a tool. When you're looking at stunts that are physically impossible, there's no drama. It's always about trying to keep yourself within the realms of reality.

And you know, the medium that still does that best is a book. Because if you have a good book, then you have the best screening room in the world—you've got your brain. Nothing can compete with the brain. I think the more internalized one gets as a director, the better. Say with *Thelma & Louise*. I was preparing it, and I started thinking about figures in the landscape, and the car, and how this really was the last journey, though the audience wouldn't know that. But the last journey ought to be spectacular in some way. That's why the landscape started to kick in like a character. And then with the landscape comes the score, and that's how I start to build.

EW:    *We know that you direct big. Do you play big, too?*
RS:    My brother [*Top Gun* director Tony Scott] tries to get me into mountain climbing, and I hang off the cliff thinking, "What am I doing here? I could kill myself!" I'd much rather get on the tennis court with a good pro.

EW:    *So off the set, you're not a danger-seeker?*
RS:    I think the job is enough, thank you very much. I'm about to go to Rabat for sixteen weeks to do *Black Hawk Down*. The last thing I want to do is go on holiday when I've finished a movie. I like to muck about in the garden. Play tennis. Read. That's it, really. The job's got everything else.

EW:    *Cinematically speaking, what's left for you to conquer?*
RS:    I'm looking at a pirate movie right now. But I'm also thinking about going back to my first love, which is Westerns. I know it's odd, because I'm European, but I was obsessed with cowboys and Indians when I was a kid. And I was a very keen horseman. I learned to ride when I was nine. I even started hunting. Of course, I never saw a fox caught in my life. The little bastards are too clever. It's all about the chase. But then I fell a couple of times and thought, "Wait a minute, this is daft!"

EW:    *Did you do a lot of risk-taking when you were a kid?*
RS:    Well, I was always outside, falling into the sea or climbing on rocks. It makes me slightly concerned that you see kids sitting in front

of a screen tapping buttons now, when I'd be out waving a wooden stick around as a rifle, defending a pile of mud. Of course, times change. But I hope computers aren't the only option today.

EW:   *Movies are, too.*

RS:   That's no alternative either. Experiencing adventures in your own imagination is what's key.

EW:   *Do you look at directing itself as being an adventure?*

RS:   Oh, totally. You've no idea how lucky I consider myself. We're going off and creating other worlds. In a way we're really the last explorers.

# Eat Drink Man Woman

## JILL BERNSTEIN/2001

The only person watching Clarice Starling more closely than Hannibal Lecter is director Ridley Scott. In a Los Angeles sound studio, Scott, his weathered face somewhat at odds with his baby-fine, strawberry-blond hair, sits behind a console as the opening scene from his new movie, *Hannibal,* plays on both a large screen across the room and on a nearby monitor. "Pretty busy today," Starling mouths, via hidden mike, to a fellow FBI agent at a fish market, where a sting operation is about to go tragically wrong. "Pretty busy today," comes the simultaneous voice of Julianne Moore, who is in New York on this November day, taking part in a bicoastal looping session to ensure that the scene's background noises do not drown out her dialogue. Scott presses a lighted square atop a little black box. "That was good," he tells her in his quietly authoritative British accent. "It's going to be quite loud. Project as much as you dare, considering what your face is doing." He takes his hand off the button and whispers, "Can I get some coffee?" as the footage is cued for replay. Three beeps indicate when to begin speaking. "Pretty busy today," Moore says again.

Sound technicians scrutinize the playback, making sure the words match the lip movements, and give Scott a nod. The director sits back in his chair. For the next few hours, he will remain supremely attuned to the nuances of Starling's voice, the logic of her actions, the nature of her character. Everyone connected with *Hannibal* knows there is much at stake. Three months from now, Moore will appear before millions of fans who have waited ten years to see Lecter and Starling play cat-and-mouse again.

---

From *Premiere,* February 2001, pp. 59–61, 106–7. Reprinted by permission of the author.

Italian is the first Language spoken at Martha and Dino De
Laurentiis's production office on the Universal lot in the Hollywood
Hills. Dino, the eighty-one-year-old veteran of such films as *La Strada,*
*Ulysses,* and *War and Peace,* is a short man sporting large, dark-rimmed
glasses and a coral shirt, with the first few buttons opened, under a
tweed jacket. His wife and partner, forty-six-year-old Martha—a slim
woman in a cornflower-blue suit, with long blond hair and dainty, san-
daled feet—sits beside him. Nearby, a dark wooden desk, big enough to
roller-skate upon, is covered with awards. But today they are talking
about the one that got away.

Back in 1985, the couple bought the rights to Thomas Harris's best-
selling thriller *Red Dragon,* from which they produced the 1986 movie
*Manhunter,* directed by Michael Mann and starring William L. Petersen
and Joan Allen. The film, which features the first, brief screen appearance
of the serial killer Hannibal Lecter (played by Brian Cox), was inventive,
frightening, and well-reviewed, but it grossed a paltry $8.6 million, less
than the cost of its print ads. The De Laurentiises were disappointed.
"*Manhunter* was not *Red Dragon,*" Dino says. "*Manhunter* was no good."

And so when Harris completed *The Silence of the Lambs,* neither Dino
nor Martha bothered to read it, even though they owned the screen
rights to the Lecter character (who figured much more prominently in
this new novel). "Big mistake" is how Dino now characterizes this lack
of interest. Harris and director Jonathan Demme came to him, wanting
to set the project up elsewhere; Dino said yes and lent the now-defunct
Orion Pictures the character of Hannibal Lecter—for free. "Well, we
were afraid to make the movie," Martha explains. "You could be terrible
and say no, or you could demand money, which was kind of, 'Why be
greedy?' Or you let them use it, and if it's successful, your asset has
value." *The Silence of the Lambs* was released on February 14, 1991. It
grossed $131 million and received five Oscars, including Best Actor for
Anthony Hopkins, Best Actress for Jodie Foster, and Best Picture.

The De Laurentiises suddenly found themselves sitting on *quite* a
valuable asset. Even before the movie came out, there was maneuvering
for a stake in a potential *Silence* sequel. Tom Pollock, then-chairman
of Universal Pictures (and a former attorney who represented De
Laurentiis while he was making *Manhunter*), asked Dino, who still
controlled the Lecter character, to make the sequel at Universal, if one

should develop. The De Laurentiises felt that Pollock was using other films they were partnering on as leverage for this request; Pollock felt they had reached an oral agreement to do the sequel. A conflict ensued, and the producers filed a $25 million lawsuit against Universal. The parties ultimately settled; the studio got the participation it had wanted.

All of this planning was still hypothetical, of course—the notoriously unprolific Harris was years away from finishing the next installment. Every year, the eager De Laurentiises would fly down to Miami, with their personal chef in tow, and have dinner with Harris. ("Tom is a great gourmand," Martha says.) "Finally, I receive a call from Thomas," Dino recalls in his gravelly voice. "'Dino, I did it.' He finish." *Hannibal* picks up ten years after *Silence* left off, with Lecter on the loose (he spends a chunk of time, to the De Laurentiises' delight, in Italy) and keeping a watchful eye on Clarice Starling—who will be used to smoke the serial killer out. The novel received mixed reviews but pushed *Harry Potter and the Chamber of Secrets* out of the number-one spot on the best-seller list. Dino purchased the rights for a record $10 million.

Before publication, the manuscript went out to Hopkins, Foster, and Demme, who had expressed interest in directing the sequel. Dino and Martha flew from Malta, where they were filming Universal's *U-571*, to New York to meet with Demme and begin structuring a deal. Later, however, Dino received a call from Demme's agent, CAA's Rick Nicita. "He say to me, 'Dino, I have-a no good news for you. Jonathan Demme pass.' I say, 'Rick, when the Pope-a die, we create a new Pope-a. Good luck to Jonathan Demme. Good-bye.'"

It wasn't long before a puff of white smoke appeared in the air, signalling that a new leader had been chosen. Ridley Scott (*Blade Runner, Alien, Thelma & Louise*), who had worked with Dino briefly on 1984's *Dune* before pulling out for personal reasons, was in Malta filming *Gladiator* next door to *U-571*. He invited Dino in for a cup of espresso. Five days later, Scott recalls, Dino brought him "a giant manuscript that said *Hannibal*," which prompted this classic response: "I said, 'Dino, I don't want to do elephants coming over the Alps. I'm doing a Roman movie *now*.'"

But after reading the book (which features vicious boars rather than elephants), Scott accepted the job—although not without some hesitation. "My first question was, 'What about Demme?'" he says. "I couldn't understand. After I did *Alien*, I would have definitely done a sequel. But in those days, I was never asked, right?" And he had qualms about the ending of the book, in which Clarice and Hannibal ride off amorously (and, to many readers, inconceivably) into the sunset. "I couldn't take that quantum leap emotionally on behalf of Starling. Certainly, on behalf of Hannibal—I'm sure that's been in the back of his mind for a number of years. But for Starling, no. I think one of the attractions about Starling to Hannibal is what a straight arrow she is." (Universal, too, was wary of the ending.) "I said to Dino, 'I'd really like to talk to Tom [Harris] to see how much license we've got.' Tom said, 'Well, what would the interpretation be?' I said, 'I really don't know.'"

Figuring that out meant hiring a screen-writer. Ted Tally, who'd won an Oscar for his *Silence* adaptation, passed on the sequel. An offer went out to Steven Zaillian (*Schindler's List*), who also turned it down. "I was busy," Zaillian says. "And I wasn't sure I was interested, basically. You can almost never win when you do a sequel, particularly a sequel to a successful movie." David Mamet then whipped up a version, but according to Scott and the De Laurentiises, it needed major revisions, and he was about to begin directing *State and Main*. Dino and Scott went back to Zaillian, who at that point was willing to reconsider. "I had found out that David Mamet was working on it," Zaillian says, "and I started to feel like, 'What sort of a jerk am I?' You know? 'Who am *I*?'" Besides, he says, "it's hard to say no to Dino once, and it's almost impossible to say no to him twice."

Still, Zaillian would not commit to the project until the ending was sufficiently resolved. Somehow, Dino convinced the reclusive Harris to fly to Los Angeles, where the author spent four days brainstorming with Scott and Zaillian in his Beverly Hills Hotel suite. "Tom had said, 'I don't really do this, you know?'" Scott recalls. "But after four days of sitting around the table, his comment was, 'This has been really fun. I'll do this again.'" (Harris would remain closely involved with the project, even sending handwritten notes to Universal Pictures chairman Stacey Snider on issues such as casting.) Zaillian then went off to write; both he and Mamet are credited with the final screenplay. "I think the ending is more tonal as to what could possibly be in her mind at that moment," Scott says, shrugging and lighting a small cigar. "He's quite specific. She is more enigmatic." The film, he adds, contains "an interesting postscript, which, if nothing else, I think is fun. Some people think it's sick."

The character of Clarice became an obsession for the entire production, for two reasons: first, when the De Laurentiises passed on making *The Silence of the Lambs*, they also passed on the rights to Clarice. To get her, they would have to go through MGM, which acquired Orion's properties after the latter company folded. Inevitably, a coproduction deal, including equal shares of the profits, was struck between Universal and MGM. (MGM is releasing the film domestically, and Universal is handling foreign rights.) The second problem? What Snider calls "a hiccup with the casting."

As far as Lecter was concerned, "everybody felt like there was nobody [but Anthony Hopkins] who could play him," says Kevin Misher, Universal's president of production. The actor came aboard happily. "I never thought a sequel would come up," Hopkins says. "And then it did, and I thought, 'Okay, fine. Let's see what it's like.' I tend to be low-key about things like that." Hopkins had recently returned from a brief, self-imposed exile from Hollywood, following a trying experience making *Titus*. He read Harris's manuscript but formed no opinion of it. ("I go into neutral. I don't make very much of things," he says.) Then he read the screenplay. "I liked the script. I didn't know what the problem was. I said yes. It was as simple and matter-of-fact as that. It's a living. It's just work." The kind of work that would net him $11 million in salary alone.

Foster reacted differently, for reasons that are widely speculated upon by those close to the situation. (She declined to be interviewed for this story.) Some say she had sequel-itis. Others say she either disliked the book, didn't want to do it without Demme, and/or was slated to direct the circus-world love story *Flora Plum* (a project that, ironically, was later sidelined when star Russell Crowe injured his shoulder). A final possibility is that when she saw the film's back-end points (percentages of the gross profits) already being divvied up between Harris, Dino, Hopkins, and Scott, she got her back up. "I call the agent of Judy Foster," recalls Dino, who chronically mispronounces the actress's name. "He say to me, 'I have instruction. She no want to read the script if you no give her an offer of $20 million and 15 percent of the gross.' And I say, 'Give my love to Judy Foster, good-bye.' That's a crazy demand." Besides, he says, "I don't believe Judy Foster from day one was right when I read the book." (Foster's agent did not return calls.)

Universal took Foster's decision much harder. "We went back to her, like you go back to any actor who has passed, and said, 'Come on, this is Clarice Starling. This is the character that really was yours. Can't you do it?'" Misher says. Scott, who worked with the actress in the early '90s on the never-produced adaptation of Richard Preston's *New Yorker* story "Hot Zone," spoke with her too, but to no avail.

Hopkins stayed out of it. "I think that actors who get involved in that stuff must need a good psychoanalysis," he says. "Just give me my plane ticket, and I'll show up. I keep my life much simpler that way."

"It was one of those moments when you sit down and think, 'Can Clarice be looked upon as James Bond, for instance? A character who is replaceable? Or was Jodie Foster Clarice Starling, and the audience will not accept [anyone else]?'" Misher says. To find out, Universal quietly floated the possibility around town, and soon several A-list actresses (Cate Blanchett, Angelina Jolie, Hilary Swank, Ashley Judd, and Julianne Moore) had shown interest. "I think it emboldened us," Misher says, although they knew that they "had this enormous bar to live up to. We really had to pick well."

Moore quickly rose to the top of the list. She was someone with "impeccable credentials who was also a star," Misher says. "She was kind of it," adds Scott. Before offering her the role, however, Scott consulted with Hopkins, figuring that the franchise "was more his than mine. He said, 'Oh, yes. Jolly good.'"

Moore was hired for a reported $3 million, and she opted out of *Unbreakable* as a result. Even the Internet rabble-rousers seemed pleased. Scott considers her a fitting successor to Foster, seeing in her "a certain kind of gravitas, an intelligence which is very similar. But you know, honestly most good actors are really smart. Some producers will say that's nonsense," he adds with chuckle. "No. I've got to work with them."

Lecter's mind may be a creepy place, but Hopkins had no trouble moving back into it. "I just learned the lines and showed up and walked around as Hannibal Lecter," he says. The actor did, however, pop in a tape of *Silence* before shooting began. "I thought, 'Do I repeat that performance, or do I vary it?' Ten years had passed so I changed it a bit. Because I've changed." Today's Hannibal is "a bit mellower," Hopkins says. "He's probably a much richer character."

Rivaling Lecter in the villainy department is Mason Verger, a pedophile and the only victim of Hannibal the Cannibal who remains alive (but, unfortunately, not quite intact). Verger uses his enormous wealth to search for Lecter and plot a gory revenge. The role required hours of prosthetic makeup, and Scott found his man in the chameleonlike Gary Oldman, who goes uncredited in the movie. "We had a funny situation with Gary," Martha De Laurentiis says. "He wanted a prominent credit. Now, how can you do a prominent credit with *Hannibal*? The characters are Hannibal and Clarice Starling. So we really couldn't work something out [at first]." For a while Oldman was out, then he came back, asking to go unbilled. His casting was announced by Dino at a press conference in Florence just prior to the start of shooting, "so we couldn't deny that he was in the movie," Martha says. "They [Oldman and his camp] got really pissed off. And to have a pissed-off actor . . . " She changes tone abruptly. "You'll have to see the film to see if it's Gary Oldman or not." (Oldman's manager declined to comment.)

Even then, audiences might not recognize the actor. Oldman (who zooms around in a wheelchair, unlike his bedridden character in the book), has been completely transformed, thanks to a translucent type of silicone that makeup artist Greg Cannom says he and his associate, Wesley Wofford, invented for *Bicentennial Man*. "I knew we could get away with more with him than some other actor," says Cannom, who was part of the Oscar-winning team that did Oldman's makeup for *Bram Stoker's Dracula*. "The first thing he said [regarding *Hannibal*] was, 'Can we stretch my eye open?' " No lips, no cheeks, no eyelids. "It's really disgusting," Cannom says. "I've been showing people pictures [of Oldman as Verger], and they all just say, 'Oh my God,' and walk away, which makes me very happy."

Verger wants Lecter dead. Most of all, he wants to watch him suffer. To this purpose, he has been breeding an especially vicious pack of wild pigs, "hip-high to a man," Thomas Harris writes, "intelligent little eyes in their hellish faces . . . capable of lifting a man on their great ripping tusks." Animal coordinator Sled Reynolds (who worked with Scott on *Gladiator*) looked at more than six thousand pigs across North America before finding what he calls "the biggest ones I could," fifteen three hundred and fifty to six hundred pound breeding boars from a

Canadian dealer, who ships about two hundred a week to Japan. After some blood work and a quarantine, the tusked, long-haired beasts, with teeth four or five inches long, arrived to train with Reynolds on his California ranch. "They're supposed to look very violent and mean, but they're also supposed to stand around in a crew of one hundred and fifty people and have Gary Oldman lying among them and not eat him," Reynolds says. "So, obviously, their aggression has to be trained, not spontaneous." He quickly discovered the animals to be very intelligent. "I really grew fond of the little buggers."

Cinematographer John Mathieson, another *Gladiator* vet, says the "rather charming" creatures would "come up and wipe their noses on the cameras and get pig shnoz all over the front." One "particularly nasty" task, Mathieson recalls, was left to an animatronic boar, which "grabbed [a dummy's] face and ripped it right off," Cannom says. "The other one grabbed his entrails. People were getting sick. I don't think they will be able to show much of that."

Another of the movie's stomach-turning set pieces involves a cozy little dinner that Hannibal arranges for himself, Clarice, and Clarice's Justice Department nemesis, Paul Krendler (Ray Liotta). "He has the opportunity and the know-how to make [Starling's] life miserable," Liotta (*Goodfellas*) says of Krendler, "so that's what he does." Liotta used a little know-how of his own to nab the role: he caught Scott off-guard, at a Gold's Gym in L.A., before production began. "He was walking out," Liotta recalls, "and, like two or three movies that I've gotten, I just went up to him and said, 'I'd love to work with you.' "

"*That* worked," Scott says, still amused by Liotta's tactic. "I was struggling at the gym, and he was sitting on a bicycle, reading a newspaper. I had never met him, but I knew he knew who I was. I was walking out in the car park, and he said, 'I know what you're doing. Is there anything in there for me?' I thought about it and said, 'Well, why not?' "

A $70,000 animatronic dummy of Liotta was created for the climactic dinner scene, which gave the actor an unusual opportunity to stand off-camera and "watch myself acting with [Hopkins]. They had all kinds of wires and things, levers they're pushing, opening the mouth. It was the oddest thing." Liotta, who endured a full head and body cast, and shaved his head for the role, says he had a ball playing someone who's "filled with drugs yet is still awake while all this is happening. I think

people will definitely remember this scene." Those who've read the
book certainly do. But even they may be in for a surprise. "If anything,
it's more explicit than in the book," Liotta says.

It's the morning after Halloween. Taped to the door of an editing
room is a reduced copy of the *Hannibal* poster, which has been doc-
tored with a strip of paper near Hopkins's mouth that reads: TRICK OR
TREAT. DO YOU HAVE SOMETHING I CAN EAT? Ridley Scott emerges
from a chat with editor Pietro Scalia and Dino De Laurentiis and goes right
into a meeting with members of a Manhattan design studio, who've come
to pitch ideas for the film's opening title sequence. They present Scott
with storyboards offering a tour through the chambers of Lecter's mind
and discuss using the aptly named type font Chianti. Scott seems
pleased but warns against making the sequence "whimsically gothic."
He suggests that instead of music—or in addition to it—the journey
could be accompanied by "the sound you get from blood when it
moves through the vein," or "old secrets whispered over books."

With *Hannibal* nearing completion, Scott's got a few things on his
own multifaceted mind. Back in his office, he has an easel full of
panoramic snapshots showing possible locations in Rabat, Morroco, for
his next film, *Black Hawk Down*, based on the true story of American
soldiers who got caught in a ground battle in Somalia in 1993. "I'm
already drawing some helicopter sequences," he says. As he drives from
one postproduction facility to another in his black 1987 Bentley, a call is
patched through from Bonnie Timmerman, the casting director on
*Black Hawk Down*, who is calling to express her delight at Scott's having
offered a role to Tom Sizemore (*Saving Private Ryan*). "I don't know what
he wants," Scott says, referring to Sizemore's salary request. "I don't
really even want to know." In a few weeks, he will sign on to direct
Disney's upcoming pirate movie *Captain Kidd,* and Dream Works's big
Oscar push for *Gladiator* will commence.

And he may not be through with Hannibal Lecter quite yet. The De
Laurentiises have announced plans to capitalize once more on their
investment and remake *Red Dragon* at Universal; the studio's Stacey
Snider says it will include new, Lecter-related plot lines. It is unusual,
to say the least, for a story not written by the likes of Shakespeare or
Austen to be made into a movie twice within some fifteen years. One
can only guess how *Manhunter* director Michael Mann (who declined to

be interviewed) feels about it. "Mann was informed that we were doing this," Snider says. "We didn't want to be disrespectful of his earlier work." Many directors, she adds, have raised their hands for the job, and "I'm sure Dino spoke to Ridley. They're very close."

Hopkins, who has verbally agreed to play a cameo, now waits to see the script, which *Lambs* scribe Ted Tally is writing (it's due to be delivered to Universal this month). He is delighted and surprised by Lecter's continuing appeal. "He seems to be a popular cult figure," says Hopkins of the character he enjoys playing with tongue firmly in cheek. "I don't know if that makes the whole of the world crazy, but . . . there are dark sides to all human nature."

# Ridley Scott Discusses Making His Oscar-Nominated Movie *Black Hawk Down*

## TERRY GROSS/2002

TERRY GROSS: *This is* Fresh Air. *I'm Terry Gross. My guest Ridley Scott is nominated for an Academy Award as best director for the movie* Black Hawk Down. *The film also has Oscar nominations for best cinematography, film editing and sound. Last year Scott's film* Gladiator *won an Oscar for best picture. Ridley Scott also directed* Alien, Blade Runner *and* Thelma & Louise. Black Hawk Down *is based on the best-selling book of the same name that tells the story of one U.S. military mission in Somalia in October 1993.*

*Special Forces were dropped by Blackhawk helicopters in the middle of a Mogadishu marketplace on a busy afternoon. Their goal was to surprise and arrest two lieutenants of the Somali warlord Mohammed Farrah Aidid. But what was intended as an in-and-out, quick mission turned into an eighteen-hour street fight with Somalis. Two Blackhawks were shot down and convoys were sent in to rescue the soldiers who were trapped and to bring back the bodies of those who died. Eighteen American soldiers were killed, seventy-three injured. There were over a thousand Somali casualties.*

*Ridley Scott, welcome to* Fresh Air. *There are a lot of shots in the movie that you might not get a second crack at because something's going to be destroyed or blown up, and you got to do it right the first time around. Why don't you describe one of those shots and what you did to make sure you got it right the first time?*

---

From *Fresh Air,* aired on March 6, 2002. Copyright "Fresh Air with Terry Gross"; produced in Philadelphia by WHYY. Reprinted by permission of WHYY.

S:    Well, filming is always based on repetition. I never do anything that I can't repeat. So everything that you see that is about to get blown up, it wasn't really blown up. When you see those RPGs that fly—that's a rocket-propelled grenade—they're basically a cylinder that is turned on a lathe in polystyrene with a small weight in its nose and a radio-controlled rocket on the back that's triggered by radio. It runs along a wire like a model. And, of course, you can't see the wire, so when somebody's standing off on one side with his radio switch, at this given moment I can fire it at Ewan McGregor, say, who turns and sees it as it becomes a glancing blow on a column, ricochets off and comes at him, blows half the building out above his head, and I can do that three times in a row. I could do that ten times, it just takes twenty minutes each time to reload.

G:    *Well, about the building blowing up? How can you keep doing that again?*

S:    Well, it was just cork. You could actually stand there two feet off it, turn your back to that seemingly huge, high explosive, and all you do is get covered and showered in cork and a bit of dust. I then put the sound on afterwards, and you think it's a huge bang.

G:    *So you could rebuild the building made out of cork to do the shot over again?*

S:    Well, I choose a corner, which is actually a little inlet in the building, which is actually somebody's garage. I build a tin box, which is about the size of the mouth of the garage. My floor fix guys then come in. Any explosive takes the least line of resistance, so if you have a strong back to the plates, which could be wood or a tin back, any explosion there is going to blow outwards, OK?

So what my floor fix guys do is line the back with explosives, put the wadding in front of it, then pack in all the stuff that will appear to be the building particles, like earth and masonry into it, which is all light-weight stuff. It's all Jablite and cork. Then you prime it, then you're ready, and then you can just blow it. Right? It's fun. So as Orson Welles said, "Filming is the biggest . . ."—no, what did he say? He said, "It's the best toy set a boy could ever have."

TG:   *Does it ever feel kind of creepy having fun while simulating war, in which a lot of people lost their lives?*

RS:   Yes, of course. It's still a process which involves a lot of very clever people on a film set, OK? So, how do we do this without anyone getting hurt? And, of course, my target eventually is to be absolutely as close as I can get to what actually happened. But it's still my job to actually enjoy what I do. And I wouldn't be honest if I didn't say that. If I said, "Well, actually I had a miserable time. I was wringing my hands for twenty weeks in Morocco," that wouldn't be true. No, I actually had a jolly good time. I love making films, and that's my passion. It's my life.

TG:   *One of the first films that you became famous for was* Blade Runner. *Now* Blade Runner *created a futuristic landscape and architecture that only existed in the minds of its creators.* Black Hawk Down *had to be as realistic as possible. What was your reaction to taking on something that had to be both very elaborate with sets, some of which were built from scratch, but also had to be very real?*

RS:   Well, to come to that part first, we found this little town called Sale, which is interesting, because Sale . . .

TG:   *In Morocco.*

RS:   Yes, in Morocco—which is a suburb—well, you could call it a suburb. It's two miles down the coast. It's across the mouth of the estuary, the river. On the other side is Rabat, which is the financial capital of Morocco. That's where the main palace of the king is. But Sale was this little village or community, a very much working-class, extremely working-class town, which was actually a really interesting representation of Mogadishu.

And so the only thing we actually built there was the town hall—I call it the town hall—which was that rather Moorish-looking building where they land the helicopters in front of, they go inside, they arrest the guys inside the building, the helicopter lands on the roof. So we built that because when we visited that street, it was a dirt football field. And I said, "All right, we've got enough here to build this building Let's make this our street."

This is all "gently does it" because you've got a community living there. So if you got Blackhawks and small birds coming in that number on any given time table, you've got to go door to door and verbally ask permission, get a sign-off, and put them in a hotel for the time that you're going to be there. It's not just a matter of me saying, "I want to shoot here," and we arrive and shoot it. It doesn't happen that way. If you think it through, you'll realize that that's the only way you can do it. You have to move people out. You can't have those helicopters anywhere near people on the ground.

G:    *Was it hard to get permission, or did they get it pretty freely?*

RS:    They were so anxious to get work—and, you know, you deal with the right authority first. You go through the mayor. You go through the king first, actually. And the Defense Department. It got up as high as Colin Powell at one point to get those helicopters. So we're dealing with a very high level to start with. And then you go through the governor of the town and then the mayor of the district. And then that melts down into the local committees, and, of course, they're nearly all Muslim, which is interesting. And, finally, it melts down to permission. That whole process can take four months while other things are happening.

You know, we are walking the streets. We're pinpointing where I want this to happen or that to happen. There's a casting process going on. There's local casting. There's casting in twenty-four African communities, which are as far-reaching as the Congo, Sudan, Somalia, and Ethiopia for extras, because I needed two thousand extras.

G:    *So did you have to pay everybody in each layer of authority from the king on down?*

RS:    Well, I don't think the king needs the money actually. But he's a very young king who has been on the throne four or five years since his father died. I'm not absolutely certain on that. He seems to be very progressive. He seems to understand what things his country has to offer. And one of the essentials, of course, has to be tourism; therefore, you need to have a successful tourist industry, and all the offshoots from that means employment. Therefore, the place has to be safe, right? If it's not safe, tourism evaporates in a flash. So he's very conscious of being very user-friendly towards such things as films. I shot *Gladiator* there.

TG:    *Oh.*

RS:    So I was in there in the desert in Wesersat(ph) for a period, where I was doing the small, provincial coliseum in the middle of the film. That was all Wesersat. That was in Morocco. So I already had an infra-structure I'd been dealing with which was trustworthy, and I felt safe. And, of course, I love the place.

TG:    *Now what kind of questions did the military ask you before handing over a couple of Blackhawks for the movie?*

RS:    I've dealt with them before. Mainly they're all these normal guys, you know. They're not this sinister bunch who walk around in black uniforms and have lots of badges and decorations. When you get down to it, they come across as the backbone of America. But these groups tend to be very straight, and, because of that, it's actually quite refresh-ing dealing with them. They say it as it is. They say, "This is what we want. If you don't want to do that, then that's fine, but then it'll be a problem for us, and that could be a deal breaker." And it starts off with what seems to be a lot of minutia, and most of it can be discarded, because if they say, "Officers don't swear," I just stare at them till they start to smile a little, then I say, "OK, next," and we keep moving down the line.

TG:    *Was that one of their requests, that no officers swear in the movie?*

RS:    Oh, of course, because officers don't swear. I said, "Yeah, sure." Then you get to procedure and process. I'm there because I want to hear about procedure and process and, therefore, I want their help in that direction. I want them to tell me, "We wouldn't do that. We wouldn't do this," because I want to make it accurate. One of the rea-sons to do the film was to make it entirely as accurate as I possibly understood it could be. All right. So I needed all that help.

But then it would finally melt down to funny little things, like the one guy saying, "Well, I'm actually really"—and he was significant enough to make a difference—"embarrassed about looking at a Blackhawk with Rangers in it, Delta in it, who are going to basically shoot a pig." And I said, "But why? It was a wild boar. They did shoot it." And he said, "Well, I don't like to know that, you know, because it's funny. This melts down to taxpayers saying, 'What's an American Blackhawk doing wasting its gasoline? And why is one of my guys putting a bullet, which is American taxpayers' money, through a wild boar so they can have it and barbecue it that night?'" I said, "Well, OK. We won't do that." And then I finally persuaded him to let me do something like that on the basis that if they saw it in context and how it came down within the context of the movie, then I'd give them the right to ditch it or not.

TG:    *So . . .*
RS:    So I actually developed a pretty open, give-and-take relationship with them. And generally the whole experience was great.

TG:    *So did you have to keep consulting the military on the script as it evolved?*
RS:    Oh, yes. I mean, I had one guy who was 6'4" who was Delta sitting on one side of me for twenty weeks and another guy who's a pilot on the other side. And both were colonels. We sat and drank coffee every morning all the way through the night, you know, fifteen hours of the day. Occasionally, we . . .

TG:    *But was it script advising or approval?*
RS:    It was not script approval so much as I would say, "Look, I want to do this. This seems to make sense to me. This process, now having studied the procedure, is the way to go. And these are the words that ought to be used here. What do you think?" So they'd look at it and go, "Well, actually, he probably wouldn't say that. He'd say this." And I would say, "OK, that's better. That's cool. But I don't like the sound of that, so how about this? You know, given the condition at that moment, in the heat of battle, is this OK?" He'd say, "Well, yeah." It was a very give-and-take experience. Actually, it was very good.

TG:    *I assume that the Blackhawks that you got from the military you had to give back to the military and the Blackhawks that were actually downed in the movie were models of some sort. Is that a correct assumption?*

RS:    Oh, yes. I mean, those Blackhawks, as you can imagine, with all their full load and compliment of technology, are very valuable, as are the little birds with their compliment of gear, which includes mini-guns, which are basically Gatling guns, which are very, very, very efficient. They all go back. I mean, one of the tricky things getting them finally into Morocco was it wasn't just the machines that I was then allowed to have, which had to come in on giant freighters with all their blades folded back like large insects. They're wheeled out of these giant freighters straight in from Kentucky, right?

And one of the tricky things that then came up—a new wrinkle which really almost made me lose the machines—was that they wanted one hundred and thirty personnel to accompany the machines. Thirty-five of them were actual Rangers. Now the Rangers were there as security really, as insurance for the machines, right? Suddenly the wrinkle that comes into it is that it has to then go through the king's departments of whatever his bureaucracy is at that moment and they're saying, "You mean we're going to have one hundred and thirty-five armed troops in here and thirty-five are Rangers? And I've got eight fully armed attack helicopters?" This is getting embarrassing.

TG:    *Well, it's almost like you're starting a military base on the set.*
RS:    Well, at particularly that moment, as we've just passed the last real tussle with Saddam, where I think we'd gone in over a period of two days and there was an air-to-ground strike, I think, and this was shortly around the time that we're trying to negotiate. And, of course, the king and his bureaucracy were actually very concerned about his neighbors thinking, "What are they thinking?" You know, suddenly this guy in Morocco has these eight attack helicopters, plus a fairly significant armed force in there, and that became very difficult for him and understandably so because he has other Muslim neighbors, right?

TG:    *So did you use military men to fly the Blackhawks during the shooting?*
RS:    Yes. Oh, yes. Those pilots that you see, none of that is special effects. All that happens where they go down the street, land in the street, and take off. That's all real. That's all live. And those big birds hanging over the top of the buildings and holding their position then

moving off, and then even the big birds when they're in trouble and they're spinning backwards, that's all flying. That's not CGI.

TG:    *What's CGI?*
RS:    CGI would be computer-generated images. So that wasn't made up. That was just good flying.

TG:    *Now what about the scenes where the Blackhawks are actually shot down, and you see them kind of spiraling out of control as they head toward the ground and finally crash?*
RS:    Now that's flying. That's a pilot flying that. And it only kicks in with CGI, which is the tricky stuff, from the moment it clips the top of the building, so it's about hundred feet above the ground, spins once, hits the ground, and then the blades carve into the dirt. There's no black top. It's all dirt in those streets. Carves into the dirt and shatters as it pulls this thing around like a big insect. But that was all CGI. Everything else was their flying.

TG:    *And then like the carcasses of the downed Blackhawks—those are models?*
RS:    Art department. You've got to remember here, I've got an incredibly sophisticated art department and floor effects department. The art department basically did *Gladiator*, so they put up everything. They put up the Roman front. They put up the stadium. They put up Rome. So, you know, to build a carcass of a Blackhawk is pretty easy.

TG:    *Sounds funny. Right.*
RS:    Yes, that's pretty easy.

TG:    *What were your concerns about how to end the movie?*
RS:    The only thing that Pietro Scalia, who I always edit films with, and I played around with was the notion of saying, "ringing the bell." There were two paragraphs we added on a crawl telling us what happened the day after, how the American forces were then removed almost immediately within days—within a practical period of time for them to get mobilized and out of there. This was all classified. It's because of that fast removal as a fiasco that the military was furious,

right? But it said that Clinton then removed all presence of ground forces, any physical presence in foreign policy. And then after that, we added, "Since then"—I'm trying to remember the words—"Since then, we have Rwanda and Kosovo, Sarajevo," and everything that entails bringing us to September 11th, right? We knew it would have to change because, you know, whatever would happen next in terms of policy would certainly be about justice and retribution.

TG:    *But you didn't use the crawl. Why not?*

RS:    Because, again, you learn to trust your own instincts. And you do hopefully, as you get older, grow up as opposed to going in the other direction. And I think, relatively speaking, in most areas I've gradually grown up. There was a little voice telling me that that's what the film does. Why do you need this at the end? I had two very discerning journalists who looked at the film and said, "You don't need that at the end," you know. "The film does it." And any smart audience is actually going to distill that one and they'll know where it's going to go next, right?

TG:    *There were scenes of complete chaos that you shot, where people in the streets are kind of rioting and shooting. You don't know what direction any-body's shooting in. And, of course, the American military men are trying to make their way through this . . .*

RS:    Yes.

TG:    *. . . and it's a horrifying, chaotic scene. How do you create that kind of chaos that looks totally out of control and yet actually control it? Because after all, you're directing the chaos. You're figuring out how the chaos is going to look.*

RS:    You know, when I'm sitting here talking about me directing it, I'm also a representative of a very large team.

TG:    *Right.*

RS:    And that team has HODs, heads of departments, and I choose those heads of departments very, very carefully. And some of them over the years have become buddies. Some are new. For instance, my HOD of the photography department was the cameraman, Slavomir Idziak.

I've never worked with him before, but I spotted him through his work and then simply called him up in Prague and asked, "Would you do this film?" And he said, "Yeah, OK."

But then I've got my old buddies on the floor. Terry Needham is a first AD that people never talk about on the floor, but the first AD is essential. A great first AD is money in the bank. First ADs have several assistants and then groups of assistants all dressed in wardrobe in crowds like this with walkie-talkies. The crowd can all go off at once or all stop at once, because you've salted into the crowd assistants with walkie-talkies. Right? So he's saying, "Right, stand by," and they're all standing in the crowd—it could be two thousand—saying, "Right, stand by, stand by." And then you say "action" and they all go into what we've just rehearsed. It's all about rehearsal and precision.

TG:  *Let me add here that it's not only chaos, but lots of people have guns. Granted, they're shooting blanks, but did things ever get out of control not because somebody was intentionally trying to hurt somebody, but just because a signal was misunderstood or somebody accidentally aimed in the wrong direction or . . .*

RS:  Yes. Well, blanks are dangerous. You have to be very careful with blanks because blanks have a wad in them which—sometimes, it is a little piece of plastic—can become a missile. So you must be very careful. There's an absolute line of where you will not have somebody in front of a gun being fired with a certain kind of blank in it. Absolutely a no-no. Otherwise, a sheet of Perspex goes up. Right? Or some other form of protection.

Funny enough, there were absolutely no accidents whatsoever. The only thing that drove me crazy was when you would shout "Cut, cut, cut!" and anybody who still had a full magazine of brass casings wouldn't stop. They'd keep firing, because they just loved to fire the guns. It's spooky how people like to fire guns. And so he wouldn't stop until, actually, he'd emptied the goddamn gun. So the casings had to be picked up every night. We had little mine detectors, and they went around and picked up every brass casing at the scene of every incident because that was the law in Morocco. They said, "We don't want any brass casings found on the ground." There are no guns in Morocco. People aren't allowed to have weapons. So the last thing they want is casings sticking around.

TG:  *Well, the casings couldn't be reused, though, could they?*
RS:  Well, you could. You could actually easily take a casing, and then you could remake a bullet.

TG:  *I see.*
RS:  You put in a little bit of powder, you put in a bit of lead, and you've got a bullet.

TG:  *Let's take one of the scenes in which the Special Forces men are trying to get through the crowds, say, in one of their vehicles.*
RS:  Mm-hmm.

TG:  *And the crowds are kind of rioting and erupting and shooting. Where are you, the director?*
RS:  I'm in the midst of it all, basically. You know, I never like to separate myself far from the camera. I did two thousand commercials as an operator, and that's a lot of celluloid. With my first four films, I had great difficulty not operating the camera because I was so used to the process. Then gradually, we had the developing sophistication of camera assist, which is where monitors now link directly through the viewfinder on the cameras. Now if I've got anywhere between two to eleven cameras according to what the setup is, if I'm operating on one, it means that it becomes pedantic, because I've then got to walk around every camera after that scene and ask, "How did you do?"

And it's odd because this played right back into when I used to do live television for the BBC. I used to do live dramas and live shows, drama series and plays where I'd sit in the gallery with six monitors because I'd have six cameras. These were two-hour drama shows. And suddenly, it's done a full circle. So I've got what I call my little video village, which is sitting there with eleven monitors because on that morning, I've got eleven cameras. And I'm usually about fifty or sixty feet away from the action, wherever we can pull the tent out of the way. Right? So then I can say, "OK"—it's all walkie-talkie. I can talk to each camera. Each camera's got a number. So I can say, "You're too wide, too tight," you know, "short-side him. Go ahead and change the lens. OK, that's better. Let's go." And then, the first AD takes over and says, "Right. Stand by. And action," and I'll watch the whole thing. I'll sit and record it, then I will say, "Right. That was complicated. I want everyone here." So everyone comes back and looks at what they just did and I'll say, "You missed that. You got that. You didn't short-side that. I think you've gotten that one. Now I want you to go for a 45-degree angle shutter, or to a 90-degree angle shutter or go back to normal speed." So you do that all the time.

TG:   *So you're watching it all as it's coming in.*
RS:   Totally.

TG:   *Mm-hmm. So do you care a lot about getting the Oscar? Do you have a lot invested in that?*
RS:   No. I mean, I'm British, you know. So British don't expect anything. We're just grateful to be here.

TG:   *OK. Thank you so much for talking with us.*
RS:   Thanks a lot.

TG:   *Ridley Scott is nominated for an Oscar for directing* Black Hawk Down.

# Bond of Brothers

BRENDAN  TAPLEY/2002

Whoever designed the West Hollywood offices of RSA USA could claim royalties. The cavernous space—part English cottage and part war room—is the perfect metaphor for the company begun by producer-director brothers Ridley and Tony Scott. Beamed cathedral ceilings remind the fifty employees of the right kind of ambition—lofty—while the non-stop intercom lets no one forget the intense business— commercials. Ads have sustained RSA USA for more than three decades, but the Scotts say the work was never more creative, never more artistic and never more interesting than right now.

"Blood and business—if it's good, there's nothing better," says Tony Scott, director of such films as *Top Gun, The Hunger*, and most recently, *Spy Game* with Robert Redford and Brad Pitt. "Ridley loves the big deals and the banks and working with the high rollers, and I enjoy the people side. The combination, I think, has been a good one."

There is much more to the Scotts' enterprises than RSA USA, their commercial production arm. They also operate a music video enterprise called Black Dog, the feature film production house Scott Free, as well as the new Top Dog, which pairs renowned television and movie directors with ad campaigns. Add to that Pinewood Shepperton Studios in England, the historic home of productions ranging from *Alien* to *Shakespeare in Love*. With the Scotts as cochairmen, Pinewood is leading a consortium that will build a major studio in Toronto by 2004.

But while business might keep the studios hopping, it's the blood that inspires the directors in them. "As a person who's worked at all the

From *Emmy*, April 2002, pp. 36–39. Reprinted by permission of the author.

production companies in town, the one thing I will say about RSA is that it's less about making money than it is about making the work viable and interesting," says John Schwartzman, a noted cinematographer and now part of RSA's elite stable of directors. "Like anything else, if you do something that you love, the success will come, and RSA has stayed that course and their business has stayed with them. This place survives on a lot of repeat business, which is very unique in the commercials business."

The passion responsible for the repeat customers comes from the top down. "Every time I walk in these doors, I never forget who inspired me," says director Angel Gracia, a Venezuelan who has been with the company for just a year.

"Art first" is an attitude the Scotts try to instill, and their young directors believe commercials are as valid artistically as longer projects. "I think with Tony and myself, the process of commercial advertising has always been creatively driven," says Ridley Scott. "It's never been about the business. It's always been about the 'film.' It's a natural ethic and it's certainly felt in the office."

"If it was old Hollywood, this place would be United Artists," says Joel Peissig, who was a creative director at several ad agencies before turning to directing. "RSA is where artists are at the top. I always compare it to art school because it's as if the students are running it. That's why it's been going on for so long."

"When Ridley and I came to Hollywood twenty years ago, there was this stupid snobbery about directors not doing commercials," recalls Tony Scott. "But I rejuvenate myself creatively doing commercials. I'm doing three days next week [of commercial shooting], and I'm struggling within myself about how I can reach and stretch and do something different and fresh."

"I have a friend who decided not to 'sell out' and just make movies," says Gracia. "He's spent six years making a film but only practiced filmmaking for two months." Gracia, on the other hand, has been working steadily since 1987, when he won a student Oscar for an experimental short film. He's logged thousands of hours for clients like Coca-Cola, Ericsson, Sega, BMW, Fuji and Fiat. For Gracia and his fellow directors, filmmaking without exposing any film does not qualify as filmmaking.

For someone like Tony Scott, who has little problem attracting feature work, commercials afford him the luxury of refusing weak projects. "I lost a film last year, and I managed because I took a year out to do commercials," he says. "I said I'm not going to do any feature films because the films that were being offered after the one I lost, I didn't like. What inspired me to say that was because I got some great spots."

An intensive year of commercial shooting gives a director a chance to experiment, something the Scott brothers and their protégés take very seriously.

"You can try out different ways to block a scene, you can try out new film equipment, you can try out a new crew. I tend to take [projects] for what I haven't done before," says Jake Scott, Ridley's older son, who along with brother Luke and sister Jordan make up the next generation of Scott directors working at RSA and Black Dog.

Tony Scott believes commercials are often where his best improvisations occur and where he plagiarizes himself for film. In preparing a spot for Italian Telecom that featured Marlon Brando, Scott used a helicopter to heighten a monologue delivered by Brando. "That scene I shot with Brando was preparation for the one on *Spy Game* with Pitt and Redford on a Berlin rooftop," he says.

Scott used the helicopter not only to dazzle the audience visually but to increase the tension between Redford and Pitt during the emotional scene. How did he know it would work? "It created anxiety for Brando," he says.

Ridley Scott adds: "Once I'd gotten past [my] first film [*The Duellists*, 1977] and discovered the process to be very similar—in fact, exactly the same—I felt confident on applying everything I'd learned from commercials into my film projects."

The digital tech seen in new feature films has been around quite a while in commercials. Peissig describes it as "bleeding edge." Tony Scott attributes the speed, the movement and the aerial moves in *Top Gun*—effects that were new with the 1986 movie—to the technological possibilities he remembered from advertising.

RSA credits the commercial industry's embrace of experimentation and creative risk for a curious trend that's emerging: noted directors taking on commercials for the artistic challenges. It's why RSA created Top Dog, its newest division, run by Kate Driver, sister of actress Minnie

Driver. Top Dog's aim is to match A-list names such as Oliver Stone, Woody Allen and Martin Scorsese with ad campaigns. All three directors have finished commercials for RSA already, and Jules Daly, president of the company, believes the step is the result of a real evolution in commercial filmmaking.

"I don't think five years ago people like Martin Scorsese or Oliver Stone would have done a commercial," Daly says. "But suddenly, they've started to say, 'God, there's some really interesting stuff on television these days, and if Tony and Ridley Scott do commercials, maybe it's okay we do too.'"

Daly has been with RSA for twelve years and running the operation for two. "The constant challenge is to reinvent ourselves," she says. "When Oliver Stone or Woody Allen do commercials for us, we hope they give those weeks the attention they would a film because to Nike, their commercial is their *Black Hawk Down* [Ridley Scott's latest film, nominated for four Oscars, including best directing] or their *Spy Game*."

"It's like when people are talking about things relating to painting, and they say one painter is illustrative and another painter is fine art . . . it all comes to the same thing in the end," says Jake Scott. A contemplative man, he likes to talk about the poetics of commercials.

"What I would like to see in commercials is more integrity and more sincerity because I think it's possible," he says. "I think with the inequities in the world and the prejudices, advertising is a place where you can actually do something to change people's ideas, because that's where most people get their ideas from. It may sound entirely pretentious, but everywhere you look, there's advertising. I believe that advertising can, at the very least, help form some clearer ideas about your fellow man."

If the philosophical musings sound out of place in the world of commerce, it's because the commercial world is changing. Aspiring filmmakers are as likely to find their heroes in ads as in epics.

"I honestly believe that whether I'm lighting Julia Roberts or a candle, the challenge is the same," says Schwartzman. "People would say to me, 'How can you go from *Pearl Harbor* to Bud Light?' and I always said, 'Easily.' Because it's still storytelling—it's not that one is more or less difficult than the other."

"It's the same challenge that you've got in films as you do in advertising," says Tony Scott. "It's a business as well as an art form. It's trying to keep the suits at length and sell their product, but at the same time create something that has artistic integrity. That's always the challenge, but it's a much bigger challenge in movies than it is in commercials."

Schwartzman echoes many of the RSA directors when he discusses the growing disparity between the benefits of commercials over the long forms not just creatively but practically. For one thing, he says, there's more time to spend with the kids.

"Making commercials is like a breath of fresh air . . . you get the boards on Tuesday, you scout on Thursday, you cast, you shoot the following Thursday and Friday, you edit the next week and you're done," he says. "And there's something really wonderful about feeling the productivity of being able to do ten, twelve, fifteen projects a year. There's nothing worse than being on a movie and realizing halfway into it that it's not what you wanted it to be, and you still have a long way to go."

What about the money? "Have you seen the parking lot here?" Schwartzman jokes. "If you're a successful commercial director, you do better than most feature film directors." One former colleague could typically make $1 million a month, he says.

And RSA is known for its treatment of artists as much as its artists. "They're listening to my ideas," Schwartzman says, "and I'm being treated with a level of maturity that would take me several years as a director in films to get."

# Matchstick Men

DANIEL ROBERT EPSTEIN / 2003

I was really nervous when interviewing Ridley Scott. I don't think I've been that nervous since the first time I met David Cronenberg. Sometimes when I meet those people who have had such on impact on my life, I get a little jumpy. Scott has created many films that were staples of my childhood such as *Blade Runner, Alien,* and *Someone to Watch Over Me.* Later he directed films I enjoyed very much like *Thelma & Louise* and *White Squall.* I haven't been as much of a fan of his latest renaissance (*Gladiator, Hannibal,* and *Black Hawk Down*), so I didn't expect too much from *Matchstick Men,* especially since it had Nicolas Cage playing another weirdo.

But *Matchstick Men* is fantastic. It moves like a jazz riff—jumpy, quick, and always surprising. It's the story of a professional "con man" [Nicolas Cage] struggling with an obsessive-compulsive disorder who meets the daughter [Alison Lohman] he never knew he had, inadvertently putting his very organized and artificially controlled life in jeopardy. Sam Rockwell plays Frank, his partner and protégé in the "con-man" business.

Scott is one of the more interesting filmmakers to come out of the music video/commercial field. Since breaking into the mainstream with *Alien,* which is basically a B-horror movie, he has become one of the most enigmatic directors in the world. Many people try to pigeonhole him as a mere visualist, but he proves them wrong when he creates compelling characters like Maximus in *Gladiator* and now Roy in *Matchstick Men.* Visually Scott has no peers, but he knows that one must rise above the image or be critically dashed. That's why he has worked

Originally posted on www.suicidegirls.com in September 2003. Reprinted by permission of the author. Additions to original text copyright 2003 Daniel Robert Epstein.

with such brilliant screenwriters as David Webb Peoples, Callie Khouri, and David Mamet.

I've heard for years that Scott could actually be quite grumpy in interviews, but I found him to be affable, charming, and willing to talk about anything. We talked con men, gladiators, and replicants.

DANIEL ROBERT EPSTEIN:    *What makes Nicolas Cage so good at playing weirdos?*

RIDLEY SCOTT:    He definitely has a chameleon quality that not many have. They try, but Nic really succeeds at extremities from shooting guns to rolling cars to playing an alcoholic in *Leaving Las Vegas* or comedy in *Adaptation*. He really is brave. Nic is very smart, very film-savvy. And he directed a pretty good movie last year [*Sonny*]. He just tackles everything.

DRE:    *How did you and Nic develop his character's obsessive-compulsiveness?*

RS:    Nic has some personal experience with it through friends, and I'm a neatnik. I find neatness comes out of being lazy. It's actually much easier to be neat than a slob. With a slob eventually you're going to be walking all over everything. I'm obsessive because it's easier. I just do it at the moment and get it done.

DRE:    *If there is a spot of dust on your desk, do you go nuts?*

RS:    There is nothing on my desk because I deal with it. It's a table I sit at. Nic and I connected on that. We had a big laugh comparing notes on obsessive-compulsive behavior.

DRE:    Matchstick Men *was definitely a smaller movie for you, harking back to* Someone to Watch Over Me. *What was it like working with a relatively smaller budget again?*

RS:    Refreshing and easy. No one likes to go away for a year. When I'm doing a big movie, I'm away for ten months to a year. So I'm always try-ing to find something to keep me at home. This to me was more like doing *Thelma & Louise*. During *Thelma & Louise* I only left L.A. for three weeks when we went to Moab, Utah; the rest of the time we were in Bakersfield. I loved the script for *Matchstick Men* and asked [co-screenwriter/producer] Ted Griffin if he had any objections to moving the locations from Philadelphia to the Valley in California.

Doing what you haven't done is the key. Shifting gears. Some people always like to do a study of the same thing. John Ford tended to do a career of westerns. My career seems to be one of nonspecific subjects which are all over the place.

DRE:    *What was the main reason for doing* Matchstick Men?
RS:    I was engaged by the writers. I get so used to working with writers because my prime occupation is development. I know exactly what I'm doing in 2006. I'm doing *The Crusades* in January then maybe *Gladiator 2* in 2005. I'm not going to mention what I'm doing in 2006 because I don't want everyone else doing it. But when you hear what it is it will be obvious. It's historical. I find that history tends to be more exotic than fiction.

DRE:    *How important was it getting the right cast for the other main roles?*
RS:    Casting is everything. Some journalist once asked me if I had any-thing to do with the casting. I replied, "What does that mean?" and asked him how long he had been doing this. He said a long time and I responded with, "You usually ask questions like that?"

Alison Lohman and Sam Rockwell were the best candidates for the roles. It's a visceral choice. I know if an actor is right for the role from the second they walk through the door. You can expect blond and tall, but what walks through the door is dark and short. Then dark and short suddenly fits the part. It's all about how good they are. It's very compet-itive. When I read the script, I was thinking of Nicolas Cage mainly because of the peculiar aspects of the character. Then I was thinking who should play opposite Nic. I knew Sam's work from *Confessions of a Dangerous Mind.* Neither character is a straight man. Then again, who was the straight man between Oscar and Felix in *The Odd Couple*? Sam seems to be cool but he's as neurotic as they come. Twenty-four years ago I would have agonized over the casting, but now I just pick it. It's better that way. The hard one after that was the girl. My casting director came up with Alison. I met with her, and she's so charming.

DRE:    *I remember back in film school our teacher froze a frame of* Blade Runner *and made us re-create the scene where Harrison Ford gets hit with*

*light through horizontal blinds. What is your obsession with putting light*
*through horizontal blinds as you've done with many of your movies?*
RS:   Did that happen in this one?

DRE:   *Sure did.*
RS:   Oh Christ [laughs]. For this movie I was looking for kind of a
John Doe '50s look, nonspecific and unnoticeable. If you are a good con
man you don't want to be noticed. I remembered talking to a guy who
works in customs. He told me that he looks for someone whose button
is undone and just picks them out. When you get good FBI officers, they
are unnoticeable. I figured that Roy must never draw your attention,
and he wants that. Then I imagined what kinds of things he would
like—probably Bobby Darin, a bit retro of a house—and it starts to
build from there.

DRE:   *You're producing* Alexander the Great. *How did that happen?*
RS:   I started that off with Dino De Laurentiis, who produced
*Hannibal.* Then I dropped out of it because *Gladiator 2* would be com-
ing, and I didn't want to do two projects that might have similarities.

DRE:   *This year is the twenty-fifth anniversary of* Alien, *and they're releas-*
*ing it back into the theatres with more footage. What did you add into it?*
RS:   The nest scene, which runs about five minutes. It explains what
happened to Dallas and the others.

DRE:   *Was that something that you wanted to get in originally?*
RS:   No, I never have a problem with making cuts. It seemed to slow
down the dynamic at the time but looking at it now, it doesn't. I think
we didn't give it a fair shot then.

DRE:   *How will* Gladiator 2 *work?*
RS:   We won't be bringing Maximus back from the dead. It will be the
next generation. Roman history is so colorful and dramatic. When you
look at that period in detail and what they did, that's far more exotic than
what's coming next in the future. The only fiction in [the first] *Gladiator*
was Maximus. Everything else was on target. There was something

about the Roman Empire that was fascistic and Teutonic in its elegance and majesty.

DRE: *Do you find that historical epics have to more authentic because the audience is more sophisticated?*
RS: I think we kicked off a genre again in Hollywood with *Gladiator* while everyone was snickering about it. There hadn't been an epic like that for forty years or more. For 1925 *Ben-Hur* was fantastic.

DRE: *You've done something that many directors have not. You were really popular at one point then had a long period of commercial failures, and now you're back bigger than ever. It's very unusual.*
RS: The key is not caring. You can only do what you do. A hit for me is if I enjoy the movie. I watched *Someone to Watch Over Me* the other night, and I thought it was a really good movie. When I ran the film for [Columbia Pictures studio head at the time] David Putnam, he then told me he was leaving the studio. So all the marketing for the film got removed immediately.

DRE: *Will you be involved if they do a fifth* Alien?
RS: No, I don't think so. If I'm going to do a science-fiction movie, I want to go down a new path. It will probably involve social disorder and be fifteen years in the future.

DRE: *What is your favorite Tony Scott movie?*
RS: *True Romance.* I think it's his most private film. I know what he should do next, but he won't pay any attention to me because he never does.

DRE: *You have a major Goth following because of movies like* Alien *and* Blade Runner. *Have you ever met any of those fans?*
RS: No, fortunately not.

DRE: *How do you look back on* Blade Runner *now?*
RS: Pretty good. I like both versions of the film as well. At the time neither Harrison nor I liked the voiceover very much. At that moment there was a very successful voiceover in *Apocalypse Now* that gave full

depth to Martin Sheen's character and made him nihilistic. *Apocalypse Now Redux*, that extended version, shouldn't have been released.

DRE:    *Do you think you will ever do a film as personal as* Blade Runner *again?*
RS:    Yes, I think *The Crusades* [*Kingdom of Heaven*] will be. It's not the sword-waving thing you think.

# INDEX

107–8; financing and preproduction, 104–5; futuristic mise-en-
scene, 49; issues of alienation and
corporate control, 49–50; location
scouting, 93, 108–9; Los Angeles as
urban setting, 51; MTV, 192; narrative role of dove, 102–3; narrative
role of eye motif, 98–100; narrative
role of glowing eyes, 49, 100, 112;
narrative role of photographs, 91;
1993 Director's Cut, 87, 90–92, 115;
origin of title, 35–36, 94–95; principal photography, 102; production
design, 36–37, 61, 96, 129; prospect of
sequel, 113–14; punk aesthetic, 38–39;
question of Deckard's humanity,
52–55, 90–91, 95, 111–14; replicant
morphology and psychology, 37–38,
53–54, 96–97, 100; retrofitting and
additive architecture, 39, 50–51;
Scott's conflicts with producers,
103–5, 190–91; Scott's creative differences with Harrison Ford, 106–7;
Scott's relationship with film crew,
105–6; script development (as
*Dangerous Days*), 94–95, 104; set
design, 50–51; special effects, 39–40;
tacked-on happy ending, 92, 108–9;
test previews, 93, 108–11; transition
from novel to screenplay, 36; violence against women and male
chauvinism, 100–1; voiceover narration, 101, 107–8, 115, 227; Voight-
Kampff machine, 99–100; Warner
Bros. backlot, 93–94
*Boy and Bicycle*, x, 134
*Duellists, The*, vii, xi, xiv, 3–10, 28,
32–33, 35, 40, 42, 56–57, 59–60, 66,
70, 83, 89, 103, 110, 123, 132, 138–39,
144, 187, 190, 192, 220; budget and
financing, 7; casting and performances, 7–9; cinematography, 8, 117,
139, 179; editing, 9–10; preproduction, 6–7; script development, 6–7;
storyboarding, 8
*G.I. Jane*, xi–xiii, 89; actor training,
148, 151–53; alternate ending, 161–63;
alternate opening sequence, 142; box
office, 166; casting, 141, 147, 151–52;
cinematography, 137–38, 162–63, 164;
cut scenes, 155; depiction of SEAL
training, 148–50; editing, 164;

feminist subtext, 157, 167; forma-
tion of characters, 142–44, 146–47;
haircutting scene, 153–55, 164;
Department of Defense, 144–45, 146;
interrogation scene, 155–58; location
shooting, 143, 145, 156, 161; opening title sequence, 159; political
subtext, 157; postproduction, 164;
preproduction, 135; production
design, 140–41, 143, 150, 161; score,
164–65; screenplay, 136–37, 159;
soundtrack, 164–65; strong female
characters, 114; stunts, 153; supporting characters, 151–52; use of poetry,
147–48
*Gladiator*, vii, xi, xiii–xiv, 132, 171,
187, 188, 198, 202–4, 223, 225, 227;
Academy Award nomination, 193,
206; art department, 213; battle
sequences, 181, 185; CGI, 185; cinematography, 180, 183–84; influences,
182; location shooting, 184–85, 210;
preproduction, 180; production
design, 182–83; screenplay rewrites,
168; special effects, 185; success, 193;
technical experimentation, 193; test
screening, 186
*Hannibal*, xi–xii, xiv, 187, 189, 223,
226; adjustments from the book,
189; animal coordination, 202–3;
animatronics, 203; casting, 199,
200–1; cinematography, 203; end
credits, 202; intro title sequence,
204; legal rights to characters, 200;
make-up, 202; Scott's acceptance of
the role of director, 198; screenwrit-
ing, 186, 199; secrecy, 189; sound
design, 196
*Kingdom of Heaven*, vii, 130
*Legend*, viii, xii–xiii, xv, 40, 56–63, 70,
89–90, 190, 192; archetypal sources,
57–59; Cannes, 191; casting, 58; cinematography, 117, 179; production
design, 61–63; script development,
57–59
*Matchstick Men*, xi–xiii, 223; budget,
224; casting, 225; character development, 224; lighting, 225; location
shooting, 224; motivation, 225
*1492: The Conquest of Paradise*, vii, xii,
xiv, 74, 79–89, 117–18, 138, 187, 193;
casting, 85; cinematography, 179;

CONVERSATIONS WITH FILMMAKERS SERIES
PETER BRUNETTE, GENERAL EDITOR

*The collected interviews with notable modern directors, including*

Robert Aldrich • Pedro Almodóvar • Robert Altman • Theo Angelopolous •
Bernardo Bertolucci • Tim Burton • Jane Campion • Frank Capra •
Charlie Chaplin • Francis Ford Coppola • George Cukor • Brian De Palma •
Clint Eastwood • John Ford • Terry Gilliam • Jean-Luc Godard •
Peter Greenaway • Alfred Hitchcock • John Huston • Jim Jarmusch •
Elia Kazan • Stanley Kubrick • Fritz Lang • Spike Lee • Mike Leigh •
George Lucas • Michael Powell • Jean Renoir • Martin Ritt • Carlos Saura •
John Sayles • Martin Scorsese • Steven Soderbergh • Steven Spielberg •
George Stevens • Oliver Stone • Quentin Tarantino • Lars von Trier •
Orson Welles • Billy Wilder • Zhang Yimou • Fred Zinnemann